IARIA



# ALLSENSORS 2018

The Third International Conference on Advances in Sensors, Actuators, Metering and Sensing

March 25 – 29, 2018

Rome, Italy

**ALLSENSORS 2018 Editors**


Paulo E. Cruvinel, Embrapa Instrumentation, Brazil

Takeshi Onodera, Kyushu University, Japan

Sandrine Bernardini, Aix Marseille University, France

Jaime Lloret Mauri, Polytechnic University of Valencia, Spain

Almudena Rivadeneyra-Torres, Technical University of Munich, Germany

**Printed from e-media with permission by:**

Curran Associates, Inc.
57 Morehouse Lane
Red Hook, NY 12571

**Some format issues inherent in the e-media version may also appear in this print version.**



Printed by Curran Associates, Inc. (2018)

International Academy, Research, and Industry Association (IARIA)
412 Derby Way
Wilmington, DE 19810

Phone: (408) 893-6407
Fax: (408) 527-6351

petre@iaria.org

**Additional copies of this publication are available from:**

Curran Associates, Inc.
57 Morehouse Lane
Red Hook, NY 12571 USA
Phone: 845-758-0400
Fax: 845-758-2633
Email: curran@proceedings.com
Web: www.proceedings.com

# ALLSENSORS 2018

## Forward

The Third International Conference on Advances in Sensors, Actuators, Metering and Sensing (ALLSENSORS 2018), held in Rome, Italy, March 25 - 29, 2018, follows the inaugural event covering related topics on theory practice and applications of sensor devices, techniques, data acquisition and processing, and on wired and wireless sensors and sensor networks.

Sensor networks and sensor-based systems support many applications today above ground. Underwater operations and applications are quite limited by comparison. Most applications refer to remotely controlled submersibles and wide-area data collection systems at a coarse granularity. Other remote sensing domains and applications are using special sensing devices and services. Transducers and actuators complement the monitoring and control and constitute an area of interest related to sensors. They make use of specific sensor-based measurements and convey appropriate control actions.

ALLSENSORS 2018 was intended to serve as a forum for researchers from the academia and the industry, professionals, standard developers, policy makers, investors and practitioners to present their recent results, to exchange ideas, and to establish new partnerships and collaborations.

The accepted papers covered a large spectrum of topics on techniques and applications, best practices, awareness and experiences as well as future trends and needs (both in research and practice) related to all aspects of sensor-based applications and services.

We take here the opportunity to warmly thank all the members of the ALLSENSORS 2018 technical program committee as well as the numerous reviewers. The creation of such a broad and high quality conference program would not have been possible without their involvement. We also kindly thank all the authors that dedicated much of their time and efforts to contribute to the ALLSENSORS 2018. We truly believe that thanks to all these efforts, the final conference program consists of top quality contributions.

This event could also not have been a reality without the support of many individuals, organizations and sponsors. In addition, we also gratefully thank the members of the ALLSENSORS 2018 organizing committee for their help in handling the logistics and for their work that is making this professional meeting a success.

We hope the ALLSENSORS 2018 was a successful international forum for the exchange of ideas and results between academia and industry and to promote further progress on the topics of sensors.

We also hope that Rome provided a pleasant environment during the conference and everyone saved some time for exploring this beautiful city.

**ALLSENSORS 2018 Chairs**

**ALLSENSORS Steering Committee**
Sergey Yurish, Excelera, S. L. | IFSA, Spain
Michael Niedermayer, Beuth University of Applied Sciences - Berlin, Germany
Jagannathan Sarangapani, Missouri University of Science and Technology, USA
Qingsong Xu, University of Macau, Macau, China
Càndid Reig, University of Valencia, Spain
Sandrine Bernardini, Aix Marseille University, France
Gholamreza Alirezaei, Institute for Theoretical Information Technology | RWTH Aachen University, Germany
Tamer Nadeem, Old Dominion University, USA

**ALLSENSORS Industry/Research Advisory Committee**
Paulo E. Cruvinel, Embrapa Instrumentation, Brazil
Yuriy S. Shmaliy, Universidad de Guanajuato, Mexico
Suzanne Lesecq, LIALP - Commissariat à l'énergie atomique et aux énergies alternatives MINATEC Campus, France
Xin Wang, Qualcomm, Inc., USA
Matteo Tonezzer, Italian National Research Council - Institute of Materials for Electronics and Magnetism (CNR - IMEM), Italy

# ALLSENSORS 2018

# COMMITTEE

**ALLSENSORS Steering Committee**

Sergey Yurish, Excelera, S. L. | IFSA, Spain
Michael Niedermayer, Beuth University of Applied Sciences - Berlin, Germany
Jagannathan Sarangapani, Missouri University of Science and Technology, USA
Qingsong Xu, University of Macau, Macau, China
Càndid Reig, University of Valencia, Spain
Sandrine Bernardini, Aix Marseille University, France
Gholamreza Alirezaei, Institute for Theoretical Information Technology | RWTH Aachen University, Germany
Tamer Nadeem, Old Dominion University, USA

**ALLSENSORS Industry/Research Advisory Committee**

Paulo E. Cruvinel, Embrapa Instrumentation, Brazil
Yuriy S. Shmaliy, Universidad de Guanajuato, Mexico
Suzanne Lesecq, LIALP - Commissariat à l'énergie atomique et aux énergies alternatives MINATEC Campus, France
Xin Wang, Qualcomm, Inc., USA
Matteo Tonezzer, Italian National Research Council - Institute of Materials for Electronics and Magnetism (CNR - IMEM), Italy

**ALLSENSORS 2018 Technical Program Committee**

Amin Al-Habaibeh, Nottingham Trent University, UK
Giovanni Albani, Istituto Auxologico Italiano - IRCCS, Italy
Falah H. Ali, University of Sussex, UK
Parastoo Alinia, Washington State University, USA
Gholamreza Alirezaei, Institute for Theoretical Information Technology | RWTH Aachen University, Germany
Anett Bailleu, Hochschule für Technik und Wirtschaft Berlin, Germany
Roberto Beghi, Università degli Studi di Milano, Italy
Roc Berenguer, Tecnun - University of Navarra, Spain
Sandrine Bernardini, Aix Marseille University, France
Ismail Butun, Abdullah Gul University, Kayseri, Turkey
Mauro Callejas Cuervo, Universidad Pedagógica y Tecnológica de Colombia, Colombia
Hung Cao, University of Washington, USA
Juan-Vicente Capella-Hernández, Universitat Politècnica de València, Spain
Paula María Castro Castro, Universidade da Coruña, Spain
Nunzio Cennamo, University of Campania Luigi Vanvitelli, Italy
Omar Cheikhrouhou, Taif University, KSA
Nan-Fu Chiu, National Taiwan Normal University, Taiwan
Sung Ho Cho, Hanyang University, Korea
Adriano Cola, CNR- IMM (National Council of Research - Institute of Microelectronics and Microsystems), Italy

## Copyright Information

**Table of Contents**

# A Contribution to the Measurement of Skin to Textile Friction

Lukas Pfarr, Bernhard G. Zagar

Institute for Measurement Technology
Johannes Kepler University
Linz, Austria
Email: lukas.pfarr@jku.at, bernhard.zagar@jku.at

*Abstract*—**In this work, we detail the problems encountered and recommended associated solutions in determinig the tribological properties of fabric frictioning vis-à-vis human skin under various conditions like dry skin, conditioned skin, and sweaty skin, to name just a few. Furthermore, we report on the necessary measurement setup to reliably determine the non-linear frictional behaviour of different fabric being the friction partner to like and other types of fabric, which are either stretched and thus mechanically loaded or otherwise untensioned and possibly hanging loose. Those cases are encountered in textiles worn under different physical activities like various sport activities or might play an important role in textile-based medical devices like surgical stockings, band–aids, etc. By analyzing various influences it can be shown that Coulomb's law for rigid body friction must be extended to also include the dependency on parameters such as yarn orientation, skin hydration, contact force and fabric pre–stretch. The developed system is easy to use and measures reliably and reproducibly both dynamic and static friction for most typically encountered friction partners.**

***Keywords–non-coulomb friction; coefficient of friction; in–vivo human skin friction; tribological behaviour of human skin; friction measurement.***

## I. INTRODUCTION

Lately, there has been a dramatic increase in interest in rapid prototyping in the textile industry, which is relying on high performance garment simulations with the overall goal to increase wear comfort in particular in sportswear. Clearly, meaningful simulations heavily depend on reliable textile parameters and associated friction models and result in design advantages that can be named as:

- faster progress from idea to final product,
- greater flexibility by instantaneous feedback,
- fitting in motion (results see Figure 1 for a tennis player's action as input for a garment simulation software),
- and comparison of fabric materials.

The exactness of garment simulations is dependent on the knowledge of the textile's stress-strain profile (tensile & shear), its bending stiffness, its coefficient of friction and specimen surface weight [1] [2]. A universal measuring machine to address and measure all those parameters (except surface weight) was developed and tested successfully [3] for a colleague (mentioned in the acknowledgement) who also provided the garment simulation results from previous work of her which is which is depicted in Figure 1.

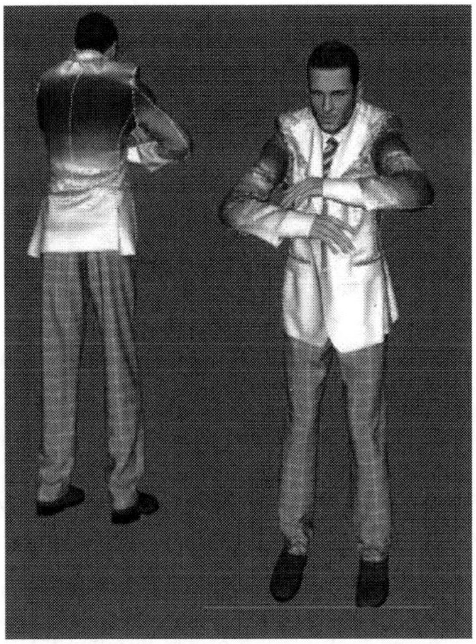

Figure 1. Garment simulation to result in strain values (colorcoded) with permission from [1].

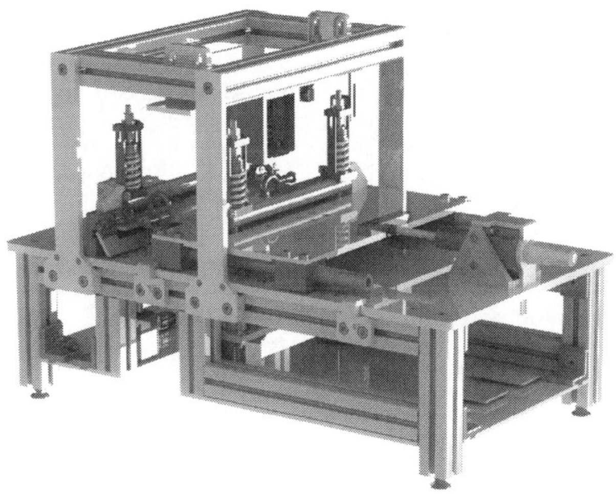

Figure 2. Photo of a textile characterization system [3].

The paper is structured as follows, in Section II the peculiarities of textile friction partners are stressed over those showing solid body friction, Section III details the chosen sensors and their arrangement to allow even human skin as friction partner in dynamic friction tests, Section IV describes experiments to characterize textiles on their friction behaviour for both skin and other textiles as friction partners and discusses the measurement results obtained, and Section V concludes the paper.

## II. TRIBOLOGICAL DESCRIPTION OF TEXTILES

In the regime of Coulomb type friction between two dry solid bodies the maximum tangential force can be defined as $F_t = \mu F_N$, where $F_N$ is the normal force acting on the interface perpendicularly to two parallel flat surfaces of the friction partners and $F_t$ is the maximum sustainable friction force. The coefficient of friction $\mu$ is a dimensionless, in this particular case, scalar constant that describes the maximum friction force below which static friction occurs. Exceeding that tangential force will lead to kinetic friction and the partners will slide against each other effectively generating heat. The coefficient of friction is dependent on the materials of the frictioning partners, the possible deformation of one or both partners, and surface roughness, both seen at the microscopic level and is conveyed by the chemical bonding between atoms in the bulk materials. For static friction of solid bodies, the following equation is to hold: $-\mu F_N < F_R < +\mu F_N$. For textiles that can presumably be stretched, however, and thus do not act as solid bodies this friction model seems to be oversimplified. For resilient materials, areas of the friction partners might experience higher than average normal forces whereas other areas might in turn see even bulging of the textile, specifically where compressive tangential forces might act upon the textile resulting in local wrinkling. Clearly, this bulging might be located at areas where the textile formed into a garment experiences belt-type friction at wrapped around locations, particularly at the knees or elbow areas.

Moreover, if these textiles are to absorb sweat during sports activities the model of dry-friction might not be able to describe properly the friction behaviour under these conditions. Slightly damp garments might on the other hand be only described by a deficient fluid-type friction, since in true fluid friction a fluid film effectively separates the two — most of the time — solid surfaces thus decreasing the friction forces. As it is common knowledge damp or almost wet garments tend to even stick better to the skin (and can be taken off harder) than still dry garments. To complicate things even further skin of different body parts also tend to behave differently friction–wise and need to be studied case by case using an easy to use equipment.

From the above presented facts, it seems clear that the measurement of tribological parameters of skin to textile friction is an involved problem and requires a careful planning of the experiments and also a very flexible kind of measurement equipment to cover the wide variety of friction partners under different pre–loading conditions and also allows for skin at different body parts to be used as friction partner. In this contribution, we present a system that is able to allow the analysis and measurement of tribological parameters using even human skin as friction partner.

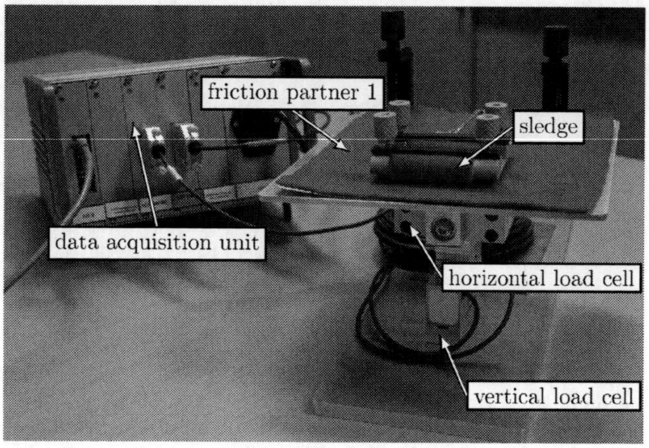


Figure 3. View of the measurement system exhibiting the cross–mounted load cells ($F_{\max} = 100$ N for the vertically oriented and $F_{\max} = 50$ N for the horizontally oriented cell).

While analyzing results obtained for the coefficient of friction from the universal textile measurement machine, which still assumed that a single figure of merit might characterize all of the tribological behaviour of such complex friction partners like garment and dry, or conditioned or hydrated skin it became apparent that a more detailed study has to be undertaken. This contribution extends considerably to and concentrates only on the single parameter coefficient of friction but as such it is covered in greater detail as given in [2]. The tribological parameter(s) of textiles from our experience and underpinned by practical experiments turned out to be the most demanding mechanical property. The difference between static and dynamic friction is as equally crucial in the slipping of objects (garment vs. skin) as is the consideration of the compliance of textile under mechanical load in the direction of the yarn if stretched under sports action and also if the more complicated belt–friction case is considered if the friction partner is wrapped around a knee or an elbow for example. In clothing simulation software for example, it is typical to have only a single value to cover both the static and dynamic effects due to friction [4]. So, the results can not cover the known tendency, caused by larger differences between static and dynamic friction, of clothes to stick to the body for a flexing action and loosen for a stretching action, which is often perceived as rather uncomfortable.

In Figure 2 a textile testing maschine developed in a former project by the authors is depicted. It is able to measure in a single unit stress–strain behaviour, bending stiffness, and coefficient of friction (here still assuming the simple Coulomb's model). While analyzing all the problems encountered operating this machine it was decided to single out the friction measuremen part of the fabric characerization and devise a novel set–up, which is depicted in Figure 3.

## III. OPTIMIZED ARRANGEMENT OF THE FRICTION UNIT

This optimized set up of the friction-only unit is shown in Figure 3. It mainly consists of two orthogonally mounted load cells (products of HBM GmbH, Germany) and a specimen receptacle to fix to friction partner 1.

The horizontally oriented load cell (measuring range 50 N)

measures the resulting friction force $F_R$ and the vertically oriented one (measuring range 100 N) the normal force $F_N$ applied to by friction partner 2. From the highly time resolved aquired data (sampling time 2 ms) the ratio of $F_R(t)$ to $F_N(t)$, the friction coefficient $\mu(t)$ can be calculated.

The value of this ratio clearly is only representative for the friction coefficient if the two related forces are measured at the same instant in time $t$. Therefore they are measured simultaneously by two separate 24 bit analog to digital converters with associated analog front ends (Analog Devices' AD7194). Their master clocks are synchronized via SPI communication after powering up the friction unit's electronic. The sampling rate is 500 Hz and the result consists of measurands stable to approximately 21 bits (according to the data sheet). This fast sampling in combination with the accurate electronics enables a high quality analysis of friction properties.

The working principle of this set up makes it also possible to determine the breakaway force (needed to determine static friction's $\mu_S$) as well as the acting friction force after the breakaway (needed to determine dynamic friction's $\mu_D$) in a single experiment. It is easy to handle and delivers results very fast and accurately, because the only necessary operation is to pull friction partner 2 over the held fixed friction partner 1. All kinds of influences (relative velocity, contact force, direction of movement, skin hydration, etc.) can be varied by the user.

The most outstanding feature of this friction unit, however, is the possibility to use arbitrary materials for friction partner 2. This mighty tool for textile development allows to quantify the wearing comfort of garments by not only assessing the textile to textile friction but to an even greater extend, the friction between skin and, e.g., the inner layer of any garment.

A novel version that incorporates three orthogonally acting load cells is currently under construction and should then be able to determine the coefficient of friction for the dynamic case as a tensor. The idea of which is commonly seen if two textiles are rubbed against each other using thumb and forefinger on a circular motion *trajectory* and experiencing a preferential direction leading to a non–circular reaction. Furthermore, the next version of the system will be so compact in design as to also allow for the second partner (the fabric) to be fixed to a (then non–planar) template mimicking the counterpart of a knee or an elbow with the actual like human part's skin as friction partner for the test. Thus, the results obtained from such a unit will be very close to the true tribologic behaviour of garment.

To demonstrate the versatility of the current system the experimental results presented in this paper are divided in the two main groups *textile to textile friction* and *textile to skin friction*.

## IV. Experiments and Results

A selection of textiles (44 in all) were tested to get a feeling in the development phase about the necessary ranges of the forces involved. As was expected, the friction forces covered a very wide range from very little friction of a thin barely loaded silk scarf vis-à-vis silk, to structured wool vis-à-vis almost pressed against fatty skin. A subset of the materials are presented in Table 1, to get a feeling about the variety. The tested specimen were material compositions of cotton, elastane, polyamide, polyester, virgin wool; smooth and bulky surfaces; striking and poor texturization; ones with predominant direction and ones without. While testing it turned out that the high frequency oscillations initially seen in a dramatic way in all the time domain signals acquired ($F_N$ and $F_R$) largely were due to the dynamic behavior of the measurement system itself, which exhibits sufficient stiffness to be excited to oscillations beyond approximately 70 Hz for the horizontal and approximately 50 Hz for the vertical load cell. A striking example of these deteriorating oscillations is given in Figure 5, so appropriate measures were needed to suppress, thus a moving average filter of appropriate bandwidth (< 30 Hz) has been used to do so to only record the dynamic forces induced by the interaction of the friction partners.

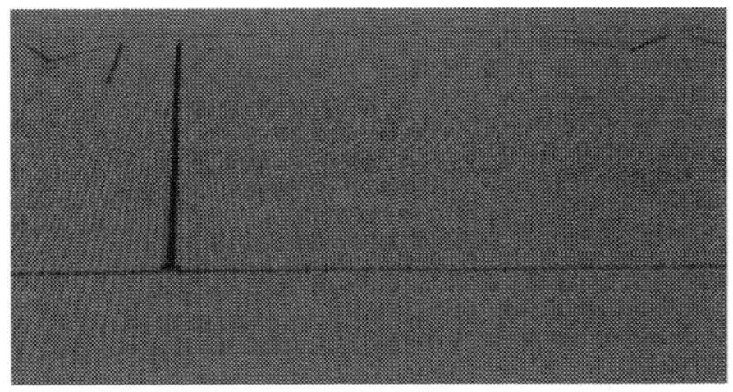

Figure 4. Zoomed in view of the structure of a textile. The width is approximately 100 mm.

TABLE I. DESCRIPTION OF THE MATERIALS UNDER TEST

| Nr. | Surface density | Composition | Surface condition |
|---|---|---|---|
| 1 | 165 $g\,m^{-2}$ | 55 % polyester, % 45 % virgin wool | bulky, strong texturization |
| 2 | 120 $g\,m^{-2}$ | 100 % polyester | smooth, poor texturization |
| 3 | 165 $g\,m^{-2}$ | 100 % polyester | bulky fleece, no texturization |
| 4 | 200 $g\,m^{-2}$ | 93 % polyester, 7 % elastane | smooth, usual texturization |

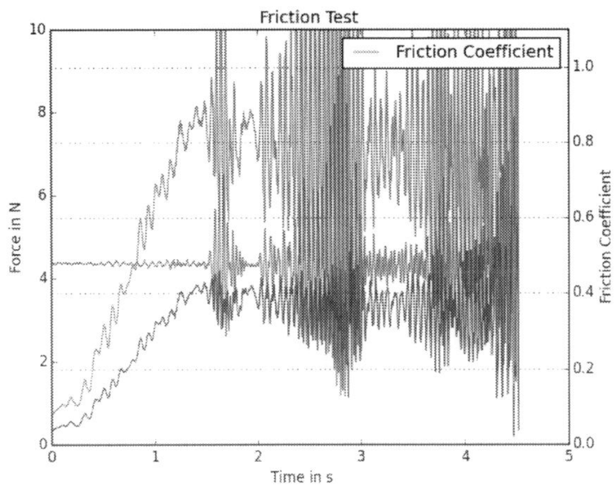


Figure 5. Initial test results exhibiting significant parasitic oscillations.

### A. Analysis of the textile to textile friction

This loading case is especially important in garments for sportswear that is subject to periodic repeated movements, e.g., in running, when the two pant legs rub against each other during each stroke. Mainly the outer layers of the garments are affected in this process. The following properties were expected to seriously influence the friction coefficient in this experiment.

- orientation of yarns (warp vs. weft) of the frictioning partners
- texturizing of garments outer layer
- relative velocity of the friction partners
- contact force between them
- possible predominant orientation of textile fibres

*B. Results of textile to textile test case*

A first conclusion drawn from the experiments is that rarely a noteworthy difference between static and dynamic friction can be observed. In almost all cases both are almost equal as long as the experimental parameters (magnitude and orientation of the acting contact force) remains constant. Only bulky materials, such as textile 3, exhibit an exception. They tend to have a significant friction force overshoot preceeding the point of breakaway from friction partner 2, which can be seen in Figure 6. For all following diagrams, the green graph

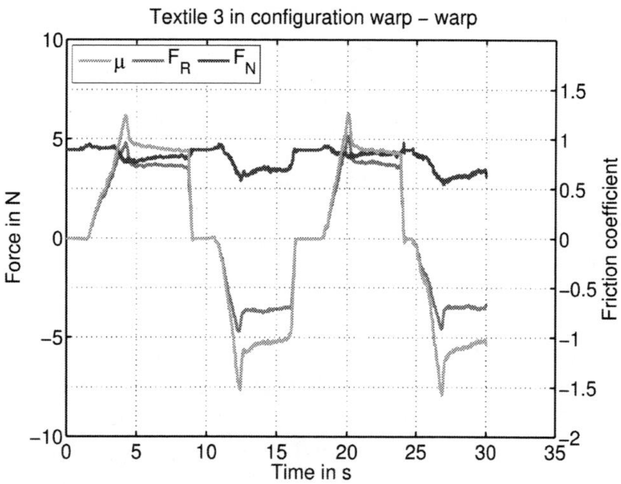


Figure 6. Significant overshoot of friction force preceeding the point in time when the kinetic friction sets in (at appox. 4 s, 12 s, 20 s, and 27 s in time).

stands for the friction coefficient, the blue one for the measured normal force and the red one for the measured friction force (always opposing the possible motion). Figure 6 shows the highly time resolved value (1000 samples recorded per second) of the friction force opposing the motion, dependent on the textile's orientation. Just this high resolution in time enables the detection of breakaway peaks, which define according to Coulomb's law the static coefficient of friction $\mu_S$.

In this experiment, friction partner 2 slides against friction partner 1 two times back and forth in warp direction while $F_N$ remains almost constant (note: $F_R$ and so mathematically also $\mu$ changed sign on the backward stroke. This sign was only kept for clarity of presentation.). While the peaks of the forward direction reach just about $\mu_S \approx 1.25$ the ones of the backward direction go up to $\mu_S \approx 1.5$. As already mentioned, this bulky material shows variations of the static and dynamic

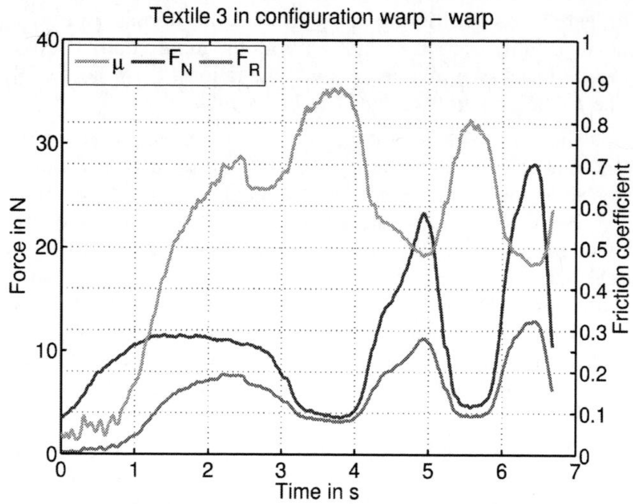


Figure 7. An unexpected dependency on the normal force can be seen in structured materials exhibiting significant texturization. This behaviour might hint on mechanical interlocking of structures.

friction. In the forth direction the dynamic friction $\mu_D$ reaches a value slightly lower than 1.0 and in backward direction slightly higher than 1.0. These results clearly exhibit the presence of a predominant direction for this material.

Textiles with a significant texturization of the surface (see magnified image of the yarns of a textile in Figure 4), exhibit a rather pronounced impact on the orientation of the yarns with respect to the intended motion. This empirical observation confirms once more the assumption of a possible mechanical interlocking. Thus, especially knitted and woven materials have to be characterized separately in warp and weft direction.

Contrary to expectations there is hardly seen any influence on the relative velocity between the friction partners. It is negligible and thus not necessary to be analysed in a Stribeck-type curve [5].

The most important influence comes with the contact force, which is equal to the normal force $F_N$. It has comparably small consequences ($\approx$ 10 % of $\mu$) for materials with smooth surface conditions, such as textile 2. But especially for bulky materials (e.g., textile 1 and 3), it is crucial as Figure 7 emphasizes. Variations of $F_N$ lead to variations of the friction coefficient. While low forces lead to high friction ($\mu_{\max} \approx 0.9$), do high forces lead to low friction ($\mu_{\min} \approx 0.5$).

*C. Analysis of the textile to skin friction*

This loading case is important for each garment's inner layer that directly gets in contact to the user's skin. All dependencies of the textile to textile case have to be considered here as well. Additionally the factors *skin hydration* as well as *body region* were expected to seriously influence the friction coefficient in these experiments. These attributes have been examined in [4] as well, where the goal was a generalized examination of human skin friction. The conclusion of [4] resulted in the opinion, that the friction behaviour of in-vivo human skin is too complex to be replaced by any representative material in the research of textile to skin friction. Nonetheless

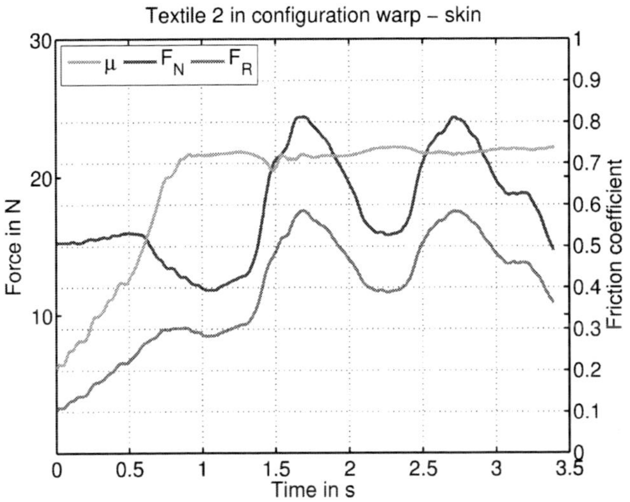


Figure 8. A textile to skin friction experiment (with constant, though undetermined skin hydration) exhibited very little dependency on the applied normal, contact force.

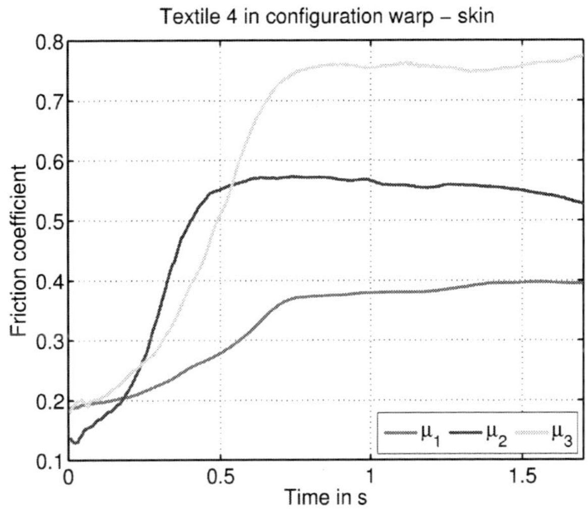


Figure 9. Tribologic significance of textile to skin friction dependent on skin hydration. (Red) skin of upper arm, hydration 27 %, (Blue) palmar side of hand, hydration 45 %, (Green) palm of (sweating) hand, hydration 99 %.

it should be mentioned, that the synthetic skin substitute HUMSkin [6] achieves great results in the field of cosmetic development and should be considered for future friction tests.

*D. Results of textile to skin test case*

The main dependencies in these experiments turned out again to be the contact force and additionally, the skin hydration. The consequences are also limited for smooth surfaces but turned out to be significant for bulky ones. In analyzing textile 2 the results showed the friction coefficient remains largely constant even if the variation of the normal force is significant (see Figure 8). Skin hydration and its location on the body also have a major influence on the apparent friction between the garment and the user's skin. Figure 9 shows the variation of the friction coefficient dependent on the skin hydration. The skin hydration was determined with a device used by beauticians and those results can not be really be considered measured quantities, although the results in Figure 9 seem to indicate some effects with the correct trend.

The red curve $\mu_1$ was recorded at the dorsal upper arm with 27 % hydration, the blue one $\mu_2$ was recorded with the palmar side of the hand with 45 % hydration and the green one $\mu_3$ was recorded also with the palm of the hand though sweating with 99 % skin hydration. The skin hydration level was determined as indicated above using a device called *Ckeyin SK-IV*, which uses the so-called bioelectric impedance analysis to indicate skin hydration.

## V. Conclusion

The assumption that the tribology of textiles in both textile to textile or textile to skin friction cases can be described accurately by a single parameter $\mu_R$ was shown to be clearly wrong. There are types of fabric that show a significant dependency on the acting normal force and other types seem to show no dependency at all. The most interesting fact exhibited for the cases of skin to fabric friction is the clearly shown dependency on skin conditions like hydration and location on the body of the considered skin as friction partner. These facts lead to the conclusion that garment simulation software will have to incorpoate a much more involved tribological model for any pairing of friction partners relevant to the garment industry.

## Acknowledgment

We are indebted to Prof. Dr. Christiane Luible of "kunstuniversität linz" for bringing up the measurement problem, for discussions on fabric properties and their influences on wearing comfort, and further for providing us with the wide variety of textiles to be tested in the presented system. Furthermore for allowing us to include the simulation data presented in Figure 1.

## References

[1] C. Luible, "Study of mechanical properties in the simulation of 3D garments", Ph.D. Univ. Geneve, 2008

[2] L. Pfarr, and B. Zagar, "Measuring Machine for Mechanical Properties of Garments", Proc. 2nd Intl Conference on Sensors and Electronic Instrumentation Advances, pp. 79–81, International Frequency Sensor Association (IFSA) Publishing, S. L., Castelldefels, Spain, Sept. 2016

[3] L. Pfarr, and B. Zagar, "In-Vivo Human Skin to Textiles Friction Measurements", Proc. 17th World Textile Conference AUTEX 2017, Corfu, Greece, May 2017, IOP Conference Series-Materials Science and Engineering, Vol. 254, Article Number UNSP 142017

[4] N. K. Veijgen, "Skin Friction — a novel approach to measuring in vivo human skin", Ph.D. Univ. of Twente, 2013

[5] V. L. Popov, "Contact Mechanics and Friction: Physical Principles and Applications", 2nd ed., Springer, Berlin, 2017

[6] Q. Li et al., "Friction Between a Viscoelastic Body and a Rigid Surface with Random Self-Affine Roughness", Physical Review Letters, Vol. 111, Issue 3, Article number 034301, pp. 034301-1 - 034301-5, Jul. 2013

[7] B. Gortan, "HUM-skin — artificial skin replacement material", www.hohenstein.de [retrieved 01, 2018]

# Ultra-Wide-Band SAW Sensors Based on Hyperbolically Frequency Modulated Signals

Victor Plessky
GVR Trade SA
Gorgier, Switzerland
Email: victor.plessky@gvrtrade.com

Aleksey Shimko, You Jen Cho
Tai-Saw Technology Co. Ltd.
Taiwan
Email: aleksey.shimko@mail.taisaw.com, larrycho@mail.taisaw.com

***Abstract*— A SAW (Surface Acoustic Wave) sensor including grooved-grating chirp reflectors is designed, manufactured and measured/probed on wafer. The device includes two wide-band SAW interdigital transducers (IDTs) on a YZ-cut $LiNbO_3$ substrate, operating in the frequency range of 2000MHz-2500MHz (B=500MHz), situated in parallel acoustic tracks having two dispersive reflectors operating at the same frequencies. The reflector period increases linearly with distance from the IDTs and, correspondingly, the frequency of the impulse response of the reflectors is *hyperbolically* dependent on time. The duration of the impulse response is 1000ns, so that the signal base is B*T= 500. In remote measurements, such a sensor transforms interrogation signals received from the reader in its specific way and the reflected signals can be compressed such that the processing gain is greater than 20dB compared to other parasitic reflections. In contrast to classic Linear Frequency Modulated (LFM) signals, for the proposed signal, the compression process remains invariant with respect to the thermal expansion of the sensor, which significantly simplifies the "reading" algorithms. For the measurement of temperature, the device uses two offset reflectors, with the delay between the reflection peaks being dependent on temperature. At the moment of writing this paper, the different designs of the device were probed on wafer. Compressed signals are obtained with an expected duration of about 2 ns. We plan to package the sample devices and subsequently measure them remotely using a "reader" for measuring the S11(f) on the defined frequency grid.**

***Keywords – SAW sensors; hyperbolic frequency modulation; signal compression; reflecting grating; processing gain.***

## I. INTRODUCTION

There are a few reasons why using Ultra-Wide-Band (UWB) signals in passive, remotely-controlled, sensors and SAW-tags can be interesting [1]. Such a sensor including chirp Interdigital Transducer (IDT) or chirp reflector, reflects interrogation signals sent by the "reader" thereby significantly transforming it. Knowing how the sensor is coding the signals allows to decipher the code (for signal compression) using the "matched to signal" filtering [2]. Such a procedure results in the processing gain of B*T times because the signal of duration T is compressed into a short pulse of duration ~ 1/B. In SAW devices, we have typical delays comparable to a few microseconds. Therefore, if we can use short compressed pulses, we can read simultaneously numerous sensors by the same reader, distinguishing them by delays of the peaks. Finally, the processing gain allows increasing the reading distance, or higher accuracy of measurements, or reducing the size of a sensor.

While using LFM chirps [3], or "orthogonal frequency coding" [4], the unknown change in temperature of the sensor results in an unknown extension or compression of the impulse response of the sensor. Consequently, the reader must find the matched filter to a signal which is not exactly known, which creates additional complications to the reader algorithms. It was recently proposed [5] to use the "Hyperbolically Frequency Modulated" (HFM) signals in SAW sensors for which the period, and not frequency, of the signal linearly varies with time. The advantage of such signals is that the extension or compression of the signal is equivalent to a small shift of it in time. Therefore, for "matched to signal" compression the reader can always use the same algorithm, independent of the sensor temperature.

In this paper, the following aspects are discussed. In Section II, design of the devices along with some key parameters are presented. Experimental results of manufacturing and measurements of the devices made in frames of Swiss-Lithuanian research project [7], along with prospective application in temperature sensing after post signal processing of the measured HFM signals, is presented in Section III. The paper is concluded by presenting the advantages of using these devices for remote temperature sensing with future work in Section IV.

## II. DEVICE DESIGN

The device is designed to operate at 2000-2500MHz (B=500MHz) frequency range with dispersive reflectors providing chirp reflected signal 1000ns (T=1 μs) long, with the product B*T equal to 500. The device includes two parallel connected IDTs (9 fingers in each), and 2 reflectors, with either a uniform or weighted aperture, as shown in Figure 1.

Figure 1. Sensor with aperture-weighted reflectors.

The following numbers and dimensions were used in the design: SAW velocity inside the IDTs $V_T$= 3290 m/s for YZ-LN with about 70nm thick Al electrodes, the pitch in the IDTs $p_T$ =0.73μm. For the shallow grooved reflectors on YZ-LN, the equivalent SAW velocity $V_G$ = 3488 m/s with pitches at the beginning and at the end of reflectors $p_0$= 0.6976μm and $p_N$= 0.872μm respectively and total length of the reflectors L= 1744μm. Therefore, the number of grooves in each reflector grating is $N_G$= 2231. The initial delay between the IDTs and close-in reflector in different sensors were designed to be 500ns, 550 ns and 600ns, and the off-set between reflectors was always the same – equal to 500ns. The initial delay can be reduced (discussed in Section IV).

Metal (***Al***) thickness of electrodes was close to 72 nm, metallization coefficient was 0.5 on the mask, but looked higher on the wafer. The targeted nominal depth of grooves was h= 15 - 40 nm; this has not been measured yet.

## III. PROBE RESULTS AND SIGNAL PROCESSING

### *A. Probes on the wafer*

The manufactured devices were probed on wafer. We had a few wafers with evidently different quality of devices and the depth of etched grooves in reflectors seems not to be very uniform. S11(f) of the devices were measured using a Network Analyzer (NWA) from 1500-3100MHz (B=1600MHz) with a uniform grid of step 0.2MHz (8001 frequency points), providing visible delay of 5 μs.

On the Smith chart, shown in Figure 2, one can see a small loop due to impedance of the IDT in the capacitive zone, in the bottom-right quadrant of the chart. It can be matched with a series inductance of 5.5 nH reasonably close to the center of the Smith chart, with real part of admittance Re(adm) ~ 1/50 1/Ω as shown in Figure 3.

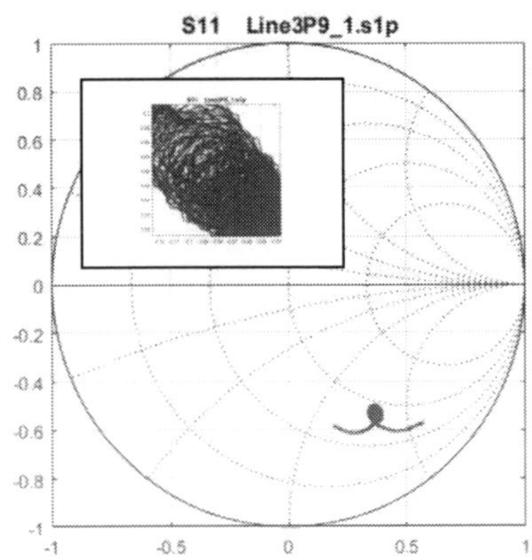


Figure 2. S11 on the Smith's chart, as measured. The insert shows the part of the curve corresponding to the reflections.

The reflected waves from the gratings arrive to the IDTs with phases fast varying with frequency and appearing as chaotic oscillations on the Smith chart as seen in the insert of Figure 2 and on the real and imaginary part of admittance, shown in Figure 3. It is also noted that the reflections are much stronger at high frequencies, close to 2.5 GHz, which run a shorter distance and hence, their propagation loss is about 6 dB lower than that of lower frequency (2.0 GHz) components. The device under test (P9) had uniform aperture and the SAW with shorter wavelength are also more strongly reflected.

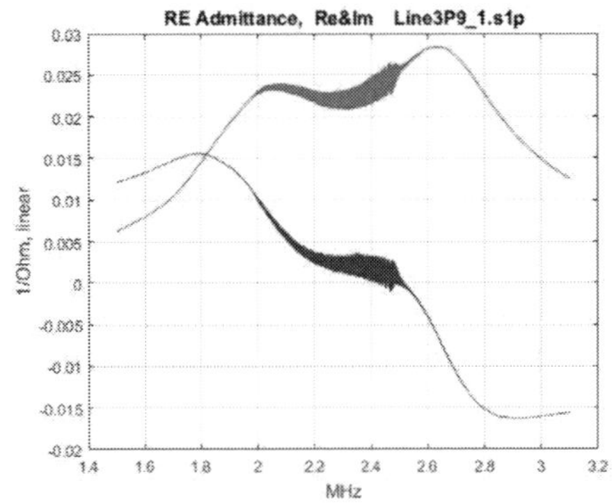


Figure 3. ReAdm(red) and ImAdm(blue).

### *B. Signal processing*

After deleting the slowly varying part of S11, corresponding to the signal reflection from the IDT itself, we can see only the remaining contribution of the signals arriving from the reflectors, as seen in Figure 4.

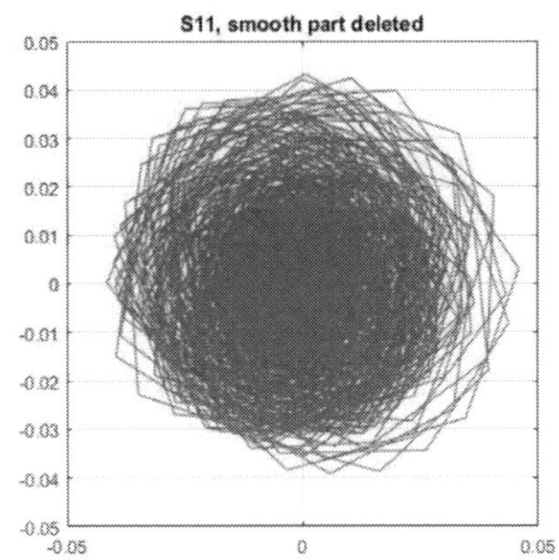


Figure 4. Fast rotating part of S11(f) – reflections from the chirp reflectors.

From Figure 4, we can estimate that the reflected signals have the level below $20*\log_{10}(0.04)$ = - 28 dB or so, at all frequencies of the reflector. The main part of the signals have losses close to -34dB.

Transforming the response from Figure 4 to the time domain, we can see the reflected pulses (impulse response of the device), as depicted in Figure 5. As expected, the reflections from the first reflector begin at a delay of 500ns and continue until 1000ns, overlapping with identical reflections from the second reflector beginning at t=1.0 μs.

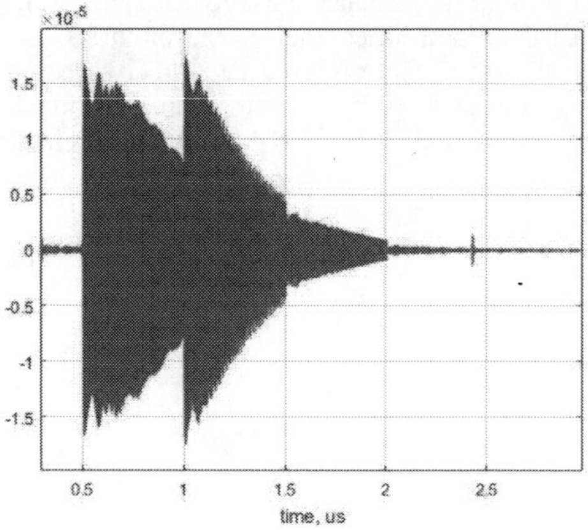


Figure 5. Reflections in time domain.

Between t= 1.0 μs and t=1.5μs both signals overlap creating beating due to the frequency change in the chirp signals, as seen in Figure 6. In order to make all periods of the signal visible, we used a so-called "zero-padding" technique, extending the frequency range to 40 GHz by filling the missing S11(f) points (outside of the actual measured frequency range) with zeros. The strong amplitude of the beats confirms that the reflected signals coming from the same distance from two reflectors have about equal amplitude, as expected.

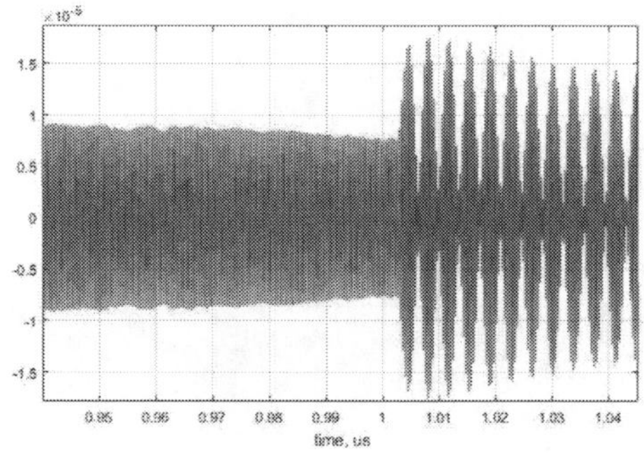


Figure 6. Overlapping of the chirp signals.

Calculating the periods of the reflected signals between the time delays 0.5μs – 1.0μs (where they do not overlap) we can see in Figure 7 that the period of this chirp signal is a linear function of time. To compress the signals, we used an ideal theoretical signal inverted in time and generated according the formulas [5]:

$$\theta_2 = -2\pi \frac{T}{B}\left(f_0^2 - \frac{B^2}{4}\right)\log\left(1 - \frac{Bt}{(f_0 + B/2)T}\right) \quad (1)$$

$$A_2 = \exp(i\theta_2) \quad (2)$$

where T=1 μs is the duration of the signal, B=500MHz - its frequency band, $f_0$=2250 MHz – center frequency, and $t$ – is current time.

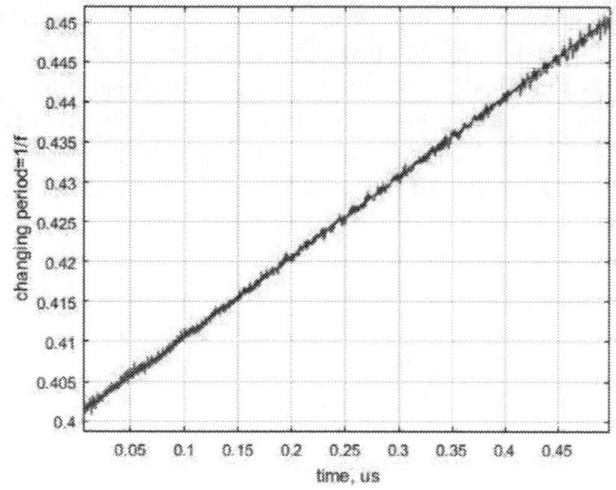


Figure 7. Periods in the signal linearly depend on time; red streight line is drawn for comparison.

This theoretical unit amplitude signal was convolved with the device response in the time domain, shown in Figure 8. The compressed pulses show -3dB duration of about 2 ns, as expected, and their amplitude is of the order of -10.5 dB (first blue peak in Figure 8), which corresponds to about 20dB of the processing gain. The brown peaks in Figure 8 correspond to the following numeric experiment. We have increased the duration of the used theoretical pulse T => 1.01 T, that is by 1%, and decreased its frequency band correspondingly (B/1.01). This would correspond to a +120°C change in temperature of "matched to signal" YZ-LiNbO3 based physical filter (if used). The experiment shows that the compression remains practically unchanged, only the compressed pulses are shifted. But the distance between the pulses is unchanged.

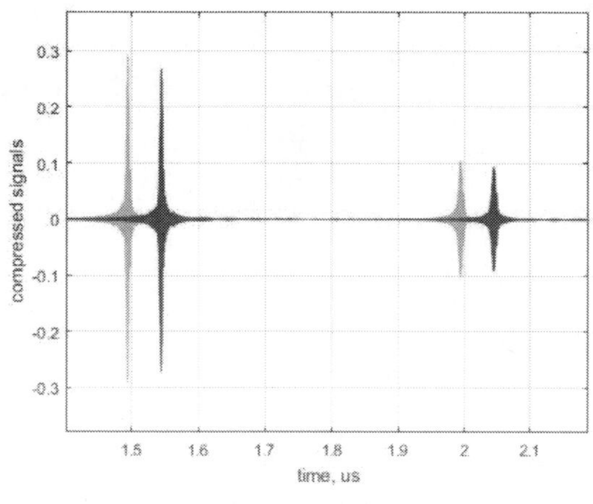


Figure 8. Compressed pulses (blue);the theoretical pulse used for colvolution extended by 1% (brownline).

Figure 9 illustrates compressed pulses for 6 probed devices. The devices consist of two sets of three designs with different initial delays. Reasonable reproducibility of results has been obtained.

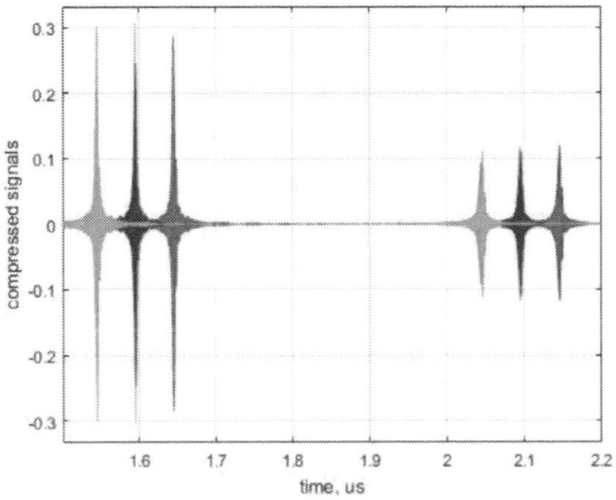


Figure 9. 6 sensors, 12 peaks.

At this scale, the compressed peaks with the same delay completely overlap.

## IV. Discussion and Conclusions

The numeric experiment, illustrated by Figure 8, shows that for compression of the UWB pulses we do not need to care much about exact inversion in the time of the measured pulse. Moreover, that would be impossible without additional experimental devices, because in the present samples the reflected pulses do overlap. The compression is invariant for small changes of the reference signal as it results in a simultaneous shift of the two compressed peaks. However, the distance between said peaks remains unchanged. On the other hand, if there was a significant change in temperature of the measured sensor itself, the compression process will remain invariant, but the distance between compressed peaks is temperature dependent. Namely, this allows measurement of temperature by accurate measurement of the said time delay between the compressed peaks. The described procedure makes multiple trials of matched to signal filter parameters and, in this way, essentially simplifies reader software and accelerates extraction of the measured physical value (in this case, temperature).

Figure 9 allows us to estimate the number of sensors that can be interrogated simultaneously by one reader. The identification of the individual sensor can be done by the position of the compressed peak pairs. The distance between the reader and the sensors is of the order of a few meters and can introduce the uncertainty of the initial delay of around 10 ns. A change in temperature of 100°C introduces a variation of the 2nd peak position of the order of 20ns. Therefore, we must allocate a time slot about 30 ns long for each 2nd peak. Otherwise, the peak from a "cold" sensor might be confused with the peak of "hot" sensor separated at larger distance. In this design, we have about 500ns for all "2nd" peaks, which means that we can have 500/30 ~16 sensors interrogated simultaneously. Potentially, we could increase the off-set between the reflectors to about 1 μs, and thus, increase the possible number of interrogated sensors to about 30. On contrary, the initial delay of 500ns, serves no purpose since the compressed pulse appears after the end of the impulse response of the 1st reflector, that is after 1 μs delay in our case. Therefore, the empty space between the IDTs and the 1st reflector can be significantly reduced. The above estimations show that the maximal number of sensors interrogated by one reader is also dependent on the expected operation temperature range of the sensor system.

### A. *Futher work*

After packaging a sufficient number of sensors, we plan to measure them remotely using the interrogation device ("the reader") developed earlier by T. Ostertag, RSSI GmbH, Germany [6]. The reader device measures distantly the reflected sensor signals S11(f) in a predetermined set of frequency points. According to our previous experience [1], the expected precision of the measurements must be better than 0.1°C. We plan direct experiments by varying sensor temperature. The software being developed now will fully profit from the above discussed invariance of the compression pulse procedure with respect to the sensor temperature.

Our other goal is the accurate measurement of power levels (instant and average) of the electromagnetic radiation of the reader in different measurement regimes and comparisons with existing UWB regulations.

## Acknowledgment

This work was done within the frame of the Swiss-Lithuanian Eurostars Project No. E!10640 UWB_SENS and was co-funded by the State Secretariat for Education, Research and Innovation. This support is welcomed by authors with gratitude. V.P. is grateful to Lithuanian colleagues, R. Miskinis, S. Ragaisis and A. Mitasiunas for the discussions and to R. Hammond of Resonant Inc. for showing interest in the sensor research area. Many thanks to S. Yandrapalli, P. Turner and to J. Koskela for reading the text.

## References

[1] M. Lamothe, V. Plessky, J.-M. Friedt, T. Ostertag, and S. Ballandras, "Ultra-wideband SAW sensors and tags," Electronics Letters, Volume 49, pp. 1576 – 1577, Issue 24, 21 November 2013, doi:10.1049/el.2013.3333.

[2] D. Morgan, "Surfave acoustic wave filters", Amsterdam, Elsevier, 2007.

[3] S. Harma, V. Plessky, Xianyi Li, and P. Hartogh, "Feasibility of ultra-wideband SAW RFID tags meeting FCC rules", IEEE Transactions on Ultrasonics, Ferroelectrics, and Frequency Control, vol. 56, no. 4, pp. 812-820, April 2009, doi: 10.1109/TUFFC.2009.1104.

[4] D. C. Malocha, D. Puccio, and D. Gallagher, "Orthogonal frequency coding for SAW device applications," IEEE Ultrasonics Symposium, 2004, pp. 1082-1085 Vol.2. doi: 10.1109/ULTSYM.2004.1417965.

[5] V. Plessky and M. Lamothe, "Hyperbolically frequency modulated transducer in SAW sensors and tags", Electronics Letters, Volume 49, Issue 24, p. 1503 – 1504, 21 November 2013, doi: 10.1049/el.2013.2815.

[6] T. Ostertag, RSSI GmbH - Contact. Retrieved January, 2018, from http://www.rssi-gmbh.de/kontakt.html

[7] UWB_SENS | EUROSTARS. Retrieved January, 2018, from https://www.eurostars-eureka.eu/project/id/10640

# Temperature Dependence of Sensing Properties of GaAs-Based Transistors with Metal-Semiconductor-Metal Hydrogen-Sensitive Sensors

Hao Lo, Chieh Lo
Graduate Institute of Electronics Engineering
National Taiwan University
Taipei, Taiwan
e-mail: hao291475@gmail.com
e-mail: a0937869023@gmail.com

Tzung-Min Tsai, Wen-Shiung Lour
Department of Electrical Engineering
National Taiwan Ocean University
Keelung, Taiwan
e-mail: tmtsai@gmail.com
e-mail: wslo@mail.ntou.edu.tw

***Abstract*—In this paper, we address the temperature dependences of sensing properties of a GaAs-based bipolar transistor with a metal-semiconductor-metal hydrogen-sensitive sensor. Experimental results reveal that (1) response times obtained from the sensing base and collector currents in 0.01% $H_2/N_2$ are 350 s and 400 s at 50°C; (2) Only a power consumption of 0.25 to 1.25 μW is required in a standby mode; and (3) the sensing collector current gain in 1% $H_2/N_2$ is increased from 900 at 25°C to 1910 at 50°C, then to 2010 at 80°C and finally to 2890 at 110°C.**

***Keywords-hydrogen; transistor; Schottky; sensor.***

## I. INTRODUCTION

Hydrogen has been widely used as an energy carrier, while its flammable and explosive properties make the safety an important issue. After the report on detection of hydrogen using a Si-based metal oxide semiconductor (MOS) structure [1], metal-semiconductor (MS) diodes and field-effect transistors (FETs) [2][4] combined with catalytic metals were employed as hydrogen-sensitive sensors. Commonly accepted sensing sequences for the MS-type sensors are as follows: the hydrogen molecules are adsorbed and dissociated at the metal surface, followed by forming a dipole layer at the MS interface. Therefore, a lowering of Schottky barrier height due to the dipole layer brings about an increased current [4]. However, these forward-biased MS-type sensors in a standby mode generally produce quite large power consumption. In this work, GaAs-based bipolar transistors were fabricated with MSM hydrogen-sensitive sensors to evaluate temperature dependence of sensing properties. Experiments and measurements about the proposed hydrogen sensor are described in Section II. In Section III, experimental results including key merits, such as sensitivity and response time, are addressed. Finally, conclusions are drawn in Section IV.

## II. EXPERIMENTS

A GaAs-based transistor together with a MSM hydrogen-sensitive sensor was proposed in this work. Figure 1(a) shows cross sectional view of the proposed sensor. Structured parameters can be found in [5]. Fabrication of the GaAs-based transistor started with performing the emitter and the base mesas in the transistor region. The emitter, the collector, and the base Ohmic contacts were formed by depositing AuGeNi and AuZn upon the cap, the sub-collector and the base layers, respectively. The base-emitter and the base-collector junction areas are $A_E = 2.56\times10^{-4}$ cm$^2$ and $A_C = 1.76\times10^{-3}$ cm$^2$, respectively. The MSM hydrogen-sensitive sensor is fabricated with two Schottky electrodes formed by depositing a 30 nm Pd mixture on the collector layer. The sensing area of each multiple-finger electrode is $8\times10^{-4}$ cm$^2$, resulting in a MSM structure with a diode current smaller than $5\times10^{-8}$ A. Common-emitter current gains of our GaAs-based bipolar transistor are generally smaller than unity when the base current is smaller than $10^{-7}$ A. Thus, such small diode current will not be amplified by the GaAs-based bipolar transistor and low power consumption is expected for our sensor in a standby mode.

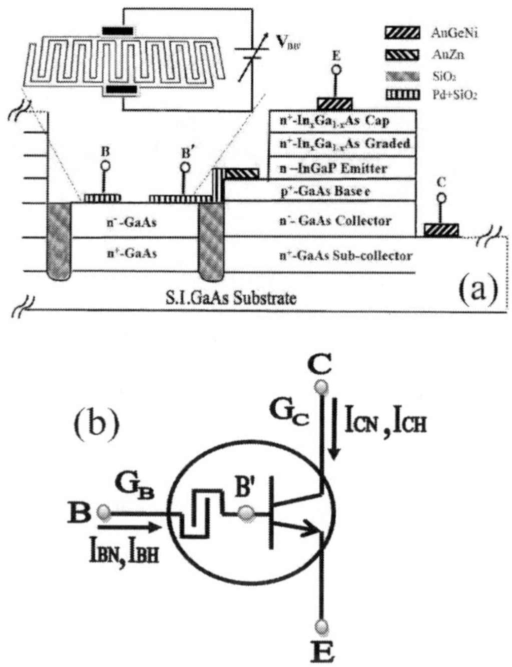


Figure 1. (a) Schematic cross-sectional view and (b) equivalent circuit symbol of the proposed hydrogen sensor.

Figure 1(b) shows an equivalent circuit symbol of the proposed sensor. In order to carry out our hydrogen detection, a custom-made, 235 ml flow-through test chamber was used. The test temperatures were at 25°C, 50°C, 80°C, and 110°C. Various hydrogen-containing gases with specific gas concentrations of 0.01% to 1% $H_2/N_2$ were employed at a flow rate of 500 sccm (Standard Cubic Centimeter per Minute). Static and dynamic sensing currents were measured using a HP semiconductor parameter analyzer.

## III. Results and Discussion

Response time is an important feature for a gas sensor. Figure 2 shows the transient current response of the proposed sensor, called hydrogen sensing transistor, to the introduction and removal of various hydrogen-containing gases at 50°C. The hydrogen sensing transistor is biased at $V_{BE}$=2 V and $V_{CE}$=5 V. Notice that $I_{BN}$ ($I_{CN}$) and $I_{BH}$ ($I_{CH}$) are the base (collector) currents in $N_2$ and hydrogen-containing ambiences, respectively. Due to limited measurements, the two transient currents were not recorded during the same run. The measured $I_{BH}$ starts to increase at the time when a 1% $H_2/N_2$ gas is introduced. After saturation in the $I_{BH}$, air gas is used to completely remove the 1% $H_2/N_2$ and the $I_{BH}$ returns to its baseline. Measurements were repeatedly performed in ambiences cycled from air/$N_2$ to other hydrogen-containing gases and then back to air/$N_2$. It is found that $I_{BH}$ saturates at $2.84\times10^{-6}$ A in 1% $H_2/N_2$ while $I_{CH}$ is much larger ($1.4\times10^{-4}$ A). This is reasonable since $I_{BH}$ is amplified by the GaAs-based transistor. We also find that $t_a$s obtained from $I_{BH}$ and $I_{CH}$ depend on both hydrogen concentration and ambient temperature. The response times defined in [4] in 0.01% $H_2/N_2$ are 350 s and 400 s from $I_{BH}$ and $I_{CH}$ at 50°C. Obviously, the proposed sensor produces good repeatability since $I_{BH}$ and ICH were not recorded at the same run while they respond well to various hydrogen-containing gases.

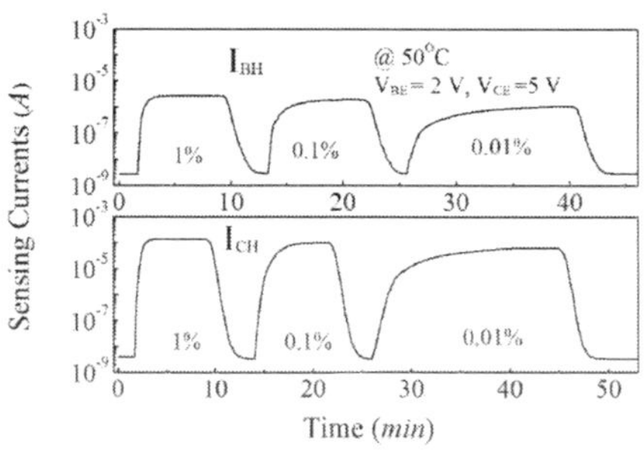


Figure 2. Transient current response of the hydrogen sensing transistorpure.

Figure 3 shows temperature dependences of sensing properties of the GaAs-based hydrogen sensing transistor. Basically, our hydrogen sensing transistor is formed by connecting the base electrode of the GaAs-based transistor with the MSM hydrogen-sensitive sensor. Eventually, the base current is mainly dominated by the MSM diode which has its current independent of biased voltage. Thus, a constant $V_{BE}$ = 3.0 V is now employed to bias the hydrogen sensing transistor. Instead of a conventional base current, $N_2$ and various hydrogen-containing gases are now used as input signals while sensing collector currents ($I_{CN}$ and $I_{CH}$) are employed as output signals. When the hydrogen sensing transistor is subjected into a $N_2$ ambience, it is in a standby mode. Figure 3(a) is indicative of $I_{CN}$ = 0.05, 0.1, 0.15, and 0.25 μA at 25°C, 50°C, 80°C, and 110°C, respectively. Only a power consumption of 0.25 to 1.25 μW is required for our hydrogen sensing transistor. When the hydrogen sensing transistor is in a hydrogen-containing ambience, a dipole-induced current occurring in the MSM hydrogen-sensitive sensor will act as the base current ($I_{BH}$) that is then amplified by the GaAs-based transistor to $I_{CH}$. As a result, relative high static sensing collector currents are expected. Figures 3(b) to 3(d) show $I_{CH}$ versus $V_{CE}$ characteristics of the hydrogen sensing transistor subjected into various hydrogen-containing ambiences for 5-fold $t_a$. Experimental results reveal that $I_{CH}$ in 1% $H_2/N_2$ at $V_{CE}$ = 3.0 V is increased from 45 μA at 25°C to 191 μA at 50°C, then to 301 μA at 80°C and finally to 723 μA at 110°C. Estimated sensing collector current gains ($G_C$) are as high as 900, 1910, 2010, and 2890 for the hydrogen sensing transistor in 1% $H_2/N_2$ at 25°C, 50°C, 80°C, and 110°C, respectively. Even if the proposed sensor is in a 0.01% $H_2/N_2$ ambience, $G_C$ = 360 (850) is still obtained at 25°C (110°C).

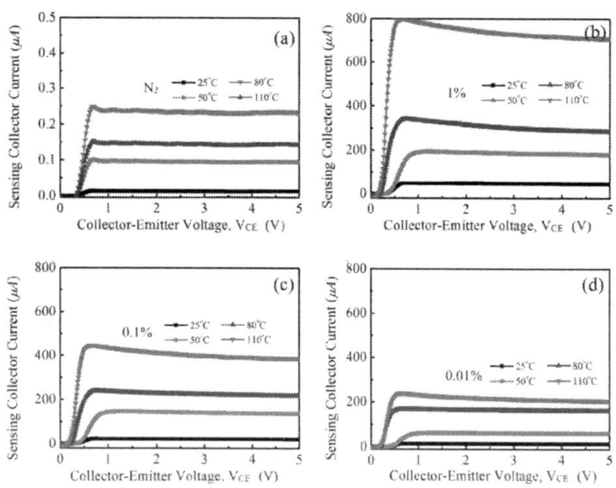


Figure 3. Sensing properties of the GaAs-based hydrogen sensing transistor at (a) 25°C, (b) 50°C, (c) 80°C, and (d) 110°C, respectively.

## IV. Conclusions

Hydrogen sensing properties of a GaAs-based hydrogen sensing transistors in the common-emitter mode were studied. Hydrogen-containing gases, instead of the base currents were employed as input signals. Common-emitter characteristics ($I_{CH}$ vs. $V_{CE}$) show sensing current gains of 900 and 2890 in 1% $H_2/N_2$ at 25°C and 110°C. Besides, a low detection limit of 100 ppm of the proposed sensor was also presented.

## ACKNOWLEDGMENT

This work was financially supported by the Ministry of Science and Technology under contract no. MOST 106-2221-E-019-068-MY2.

## REFERENCES

[1] L. Lundstrom, S. Shivaraman, C. Svensson, and L. Lundkvist, "A Hydrogen Sensitive MOS Field-effect Transistor," Appl. Phys. Lett., vol. 26, pp. 55-57, 1975.

[2] K. W. Lin et al. "Characteristics of Pd/InGaP Schottky diodes hydrogen sensors," IEEE Sens. J., vol. 4, pp. 72-79, 2004.

[3] A. Salchi, A. Nikfarjam, and D. J. Kalantari, "Pd/porous-GaAs Schottky Contact for Hydrogen Sensing Application," Sens. Actuators B, vol. 113, pp. 419-427, 2006.

[4] S. Y. Chiu et al. "High-Sensitivity Metal-Semiconductor-Metal Hydrogen Sensors with a Mixture of Pd and $SiO_2$ Forming Three-Dimensional Dipoles," IEEE Electron Device Lett., vol. 29, pp. 1328-1331, 2008.

[5] S. Y. Chiu et al. "Integrated Hydrogen Sensing Amplifier with GaAs Schottky-type Diode and InGap-GaAs Heterojunction Bipolar Transistor," IEEE Electron Device Lett., vol. 30, pp. 898-900, 2009.

# Ionic Liquid Based Coulometric Trace Humidity Sensors

Marc Detjens, Carlo Tiebe, and Ulrich Banach
8.1 Sensors, Measurement and Testing Methods
Federal Institute for Materials Research and Testing
Berlin, Germany
email: marc.detjens@bam.de, carlo.tiebe@bam.de, ulrich.banach@bam.de

Uwe Ritter
Institute of Chemistry and Biotechnology
Technical University Ilmenau
Ilmenau, Germany
email: uwe.ritter@tu-ilmenau.de

*Abstract*—**This work presents a first attempt to use ionic liquids as a new coating for planar coulometric sensors. These sensors are used for the measurement of trace humidity in various gases. Usually, the coating of the sensors is tetraphosphorus decaoxide and its hydrolysis products. Instead, a hygroscopic ionic liquid was used as sensor coating in this work. Generated frost point temperatures $t_f$ in the gas ranged from -80 °C to -30 °C, which is equivalent to vapour mole fractions $x_v$ from 0.5 µmol·mol$^{-1}$ to 376 µmol·mol$^{-1}$. In addition to the coulometric sensors, the generated humidity is determined by a precision dew point hygrometer as reference. First results show that it is possible to measure humidity with ionic liquid based coulometric sensors.**

***Keywords-Coulometric sensors; Sensor coating; Trace humidity measurement; Ionic liquids.***

## I. INTRODUCTION

The accurate value of humidity in gases, which are used in technical and chemical processes, is an important quality factor. Therefore, it is necessary to measure it accurately and continuously. Even trace amounts of water vapour can influence a process negatively and thus its resulting products. Trace humidity of gases is defined by water vapour mole fraction $x_v$ smaller than 2,000 µmol·mol$^{-1}$, which is equivalent to a frost point temperature $t_f$ below -13 °C. Frost point temperature is the temperature at which the prevailing water vapour pressure is equal to the saturation vapour pressure and at which ice begins to form (constant pressure $p$) [1].

Coulometric sensors are an effective tool for trace humidity measurement in various technical gases, such as air, helium, argon, chlorine, hydrogen, nitrogen, and nitrous oxide [2][3]. In general, coulometric sensors are coated with tetraphosphorus decaoxide ($P_4O_{10}$) due to its hygroscopic property. One limitation of coulometric sensors is the measurement in gases which contain ammonia or amines. These substances can react with the $P_4O_{10}$ and thus influence the reaction mechanism of the $P_4O_{10}$-$H_2O$-system [4].

In this work, a first attempt is presented to use a hygroscopic ionic liquid as coating for coulometric sensors. Section 2 briefly explains coulometric sensors, ionic liquids, trace humidity generation, and sensor integration. In Section 3, the obtained measurement results are shown and Section 4 presents the conclusion.

## II. EXPERIMENTAL SETUP

### A. Coulometric Sensors

Coulometric sensors were described first by Keidel as a method to determine water content of gases in 1959 [2][4][5].

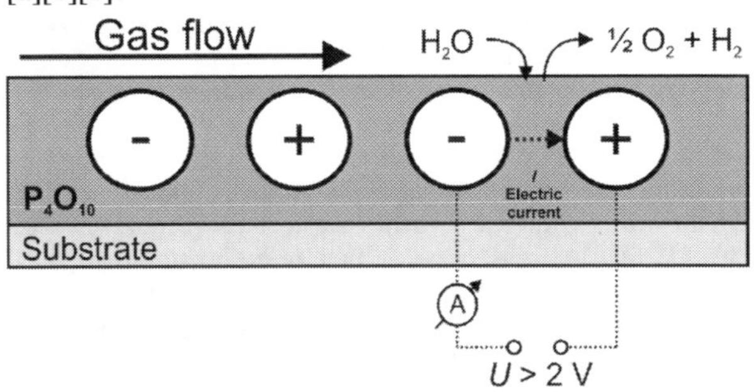


Figure 1. Sensor principle of a coulometric sensor; $U$: voltage, $P_4O_{10}$: tetraphosphorus decaoxide, $H_2O$: water, $O_2$: oxygen and $H_2$: hydrogen.

The sensing principle depicted in Figure 1 is based on the electrolysis of absorbed water in which it is decomposed to hydrogen and oxygen at a voltage of at least 2 V. Electrolysis of water can be described by means of Faraday's law, see (1), which states a correlation between the amount of electrical charge $Q$ in C and water substance $n_{\text{Water}}$ in mol:

$$Q = n_{\text{Water}} \cdot F \cdot z \quad (1)$$

where $F$ is FARADAY'S constant ($F$ = 96485.3 C·mol$^{-1}$) and $z$ is the number of transferred electrons per converted molecule of $H_2O$ ($z$ = 2). In equilibrium state, the measured electrical current $I$ is proportional to the mass of water $m_{\text{Water}}$ in the gas flow as shown in (2).

$$I \propto m_{\text{Water}} \quad (2)$$

Resulting electrical current is influenced by incomplete water absorption, dependence on the gas flow, given voltage, gas pressure, temperature, and coating thickness.

### B. *Ionic Liquids*

Ionic liquids have a huge potential for nanoparticle synthesis, electrochemistry, batteries, fuel cells, and for sensor applications [6]. In general, ionic liquid is a salt in the liquid state at room temperature and consists usually of an organic cation and an inorganic anion. Further interesting properties are electrochemical stability against oxidation and reduction, electrical conductivity, and non-acid character.

### C. *Trace Humidity Generation*

Trace humidity generation consists of a gas supply, dryer, humidifier, pressure controllers, mass flow controllers and a reference hygrometer. Test gas is generated by mixing two gas flows: a dry and a wet one. One flow is dried with a molecular sieve and the other flow is humidified by passing it through a bubbler filled with pure water. After this, the rate of both flows is controlled by mass flow controllers and mixed together resulting in a test gas. Next the generated test gas is split into four single gas flows: whereby three flows pass over coulometric sensors and one passes a calibrated dew point hygrometer (S4000 TRS, Michell Instruments).

### D. *Sensor Integration*

During the measurements, the coated planar sensor elements (dr. Wernecke Feuchtemesstechnik GmbH) were protected by a porous polymer membrane to diminish the influence of a fluctuating gas flow rate [7]. Furthermore, the protected elements were embedded in stainless steel cells with gas inlet and outlet. A multiplexer allowed the simultaneous reading of the electrical current via a digital multimeter (3458A, Agilent) and provided the connection to the voltage supply, which was modified by adding a polarity reversal [8].

## III. Results

Figure 2 shows the results of a performed measurement with three coulometric sensors that are dip-coated with an ionic liquid. The generated humidity in the gas expressed as frost point temperature ranged from -80 °C to -30 °C.

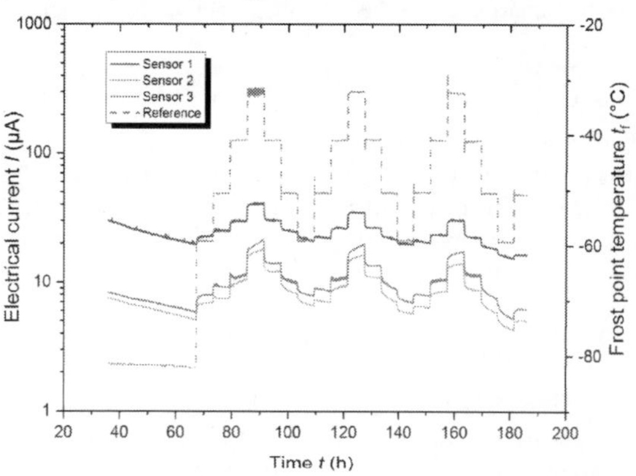


Figure 2. Electrical current $I$ in µA of six coulometric sensors (left y-axis) and the reference humidity $t_f$ in °C (right y-axis) over measuring time $t$ in h.

Electrical current $I$ (sensor signal) of the sensors (one to three) and reference value of humidity $t_f$ (red-dotted line) are represented on the left and right y-axis, respectively. It is proved that electrical currents increase with a raise of humidity in the gas. Converse behavior is shown by a reduction of the humidity in the gas. However, the results show obvious deviations of the sensor signals. In total, sensor one measures higher signals in comparison to sensors two and three. A feasible explanation for the different signal intensity could be the unknown thickness of the sensor coating. Additionally, a distinct drift was observed for all three sensors.

## IV. Conclusion

In this work, a first attempt is presented to use ionic liquids as coating for coulometric trace humidity sensors. First results show that sensors coated with ionic liquids response to humidity changes in the gas. However, the sensor intensities were different and an obvious sensor drift was observed. Further measurements are required to understand the reaction mechanism of water vapour and ionic liquid.

## Acknowledgment

The authors thank Thomas Bernstein, Sylvia Filarski, and Jörg Schlischka for technical assistance. This work has been financially supported by the Federal Ministry for Economic Affairs and Energy (BMWi)–ZIM-project No. 2201085KM4.

In memoriam of Dr. Thomas Hübert.

## References

[1] VDI/VDE 3514-1:2016-11, Measurement of gas humidity – Characteristics and symbols, 2016.

[2] R. Wernecke and J. Wernecke, Industrial Moisture and Humidity Measurement: A Practical Guide. Wiley, 2014.

[3] VDI/VDE 3514-1:2013-03, Measurement of gas humidity - Methods of measurement, 2013.

[4] J. Mitchell and D. M. Smith, Aquametry: a treatise on methods for the determination of water. Wiley, 1984.

[5] F. A. Keidel, "Determination of water by direct amperometric measurement," Analytical Chemistry, vol. 31, no. 12, pp. 2043-2048, 1959.

[6] P. Wasserscheid and T. Welton, Ionic Liquids in Synthesis. Wiley, 2006.

[7] A. Lorek, A. Koncz, and R. Wernecke, "Development of a gas flow independent coulometric trace humidity sensor for aerospace and industry," in First European Conference on Moisture Measurement, Aquametry 2010, 2010, pp. 289-296: MFPA Weimar.

[8] A. Koncz, A. Lorek, R. Wernecke, and V. Schwanke, "Coulometric humidity sensor and corresponding method", Patent EP 2264445 B1, 2017.

# Design and Optimization of Gas Sensor Testing Chamber

Fatima Ezahra Annanouch[1], Nicolas Morati[1], Virginie Martini-Laithier[1], Tomas Fiorido[1], Khalifa Aguir[1] and Marc Bendahan[1]
[1]Aix Marseille Univ, Université de Toulon, CNRS, IM2NP, Marseille, France
e-mail: {fatima.annanouch, nicolas.morati, virginie.laithier, tomas.fiorido, khalifa.aguir, marc.bendahan}@im2np.fr

Gilles Bouchet[2], Pierre Perrier[2]
[2]Aix Marseille Univ, CNRS, IUSTI, Marseille, France
e-mail: {gilles.bouchet, pierre.perrier}@univ-amu.fr

*Abstract*—**It is important to size and optimize the chamber in which gas sensors are tested. Indeed, the amplitude, as well as the response and recovery times are very dependent on the testing chamber. In this study, we show that by optimizing the design and reducing the volume of the testing chamber, the responses of metal oxide microsensors are highly enhanced and faster, and therefore closer to the real answers of the sensor.**

***Keywords-gas sensor; gas testing chamber; metal oxides; tin oxide; mathematical modeling; simulation.***

## I. Introduction

Metal oxide gas sensors have become one of the most active research areas, owing to their low cost and flexibility in production, simplicity of their use and their large number of detectable gases. They are employed in a wide spectrum of applications, such as environmental monitoring, domestic safety, disease detection and many more [1].

So far, many works have been reported on the enhancement of gas sensing performances, either with catalysts nanoparticles modification, or by the nano-structuring of metal oxide sensitive material [2]. However, few works have studied the influence of the gas testing system on the sensors performances. Achieving a reliable and highly sensitive sensor, with fast response and recovery times, cannot be done without an optimized gas testing chamber design. Such a design needs to be modeled and simulated in terms of chamber volume, placement of sensor and gas flow direction.

In this work we study and compare the influence of gas testing chamber design on the sensor performances, namely Cross chamber (old one) and Boat chamber (new optimized testing chamber). The paper is structured as follows. Section II describes the gas microsensor platform and the testing chamber design. Section III presents and discusses the obtained results (simulation results and experimental validation of the optimized chamber). We conclude the work in Section IV.

## II. Gas Sensors and Testing Chambers

### A. Gas sensors

The microelectromechanical systems (MEMS) based microsensor platform was patented by our laboratory and fabricated using clean room facilities and various micro-fabrication steps including photolithography, metallization and backside etching (DRIE) of the substrate to define the membrane as the transducer [3]. This latter has a size of 400μm × 400 μm. It carries three transducers S1, S2, S3 and two heaters (Fig. 1). The gap between the electrodes is 4 μm, the resistance of each heater is 100 Ω and the temperature coefficient is 3 10-3/°C. An $SnO_2$ sensing layer (50 nm) was directly deposited over the microsensor platform, by reactive radio frequency magnetron sputtering technique [4][5].

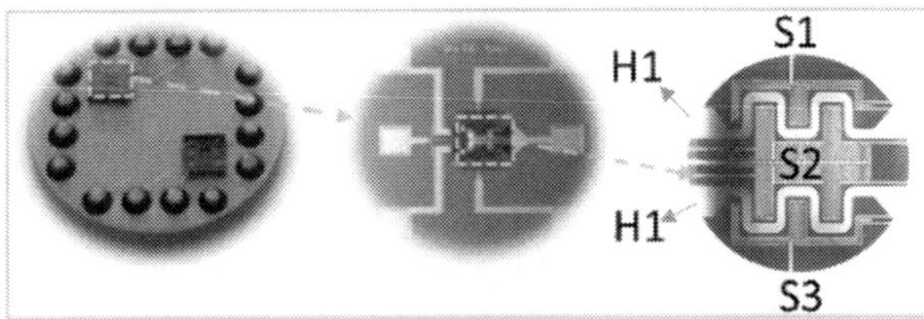


Figure 1. MEMS-based microsensor platform [3].

It is worth noting that before depositions, the microsensor platform was cleaned with acetone and then with ethanol, dried with air, and then placed inside the shadow mask.

### B. Testing chambers

Gas-sensing tests were carried out in two different chambers (Fig. 2).

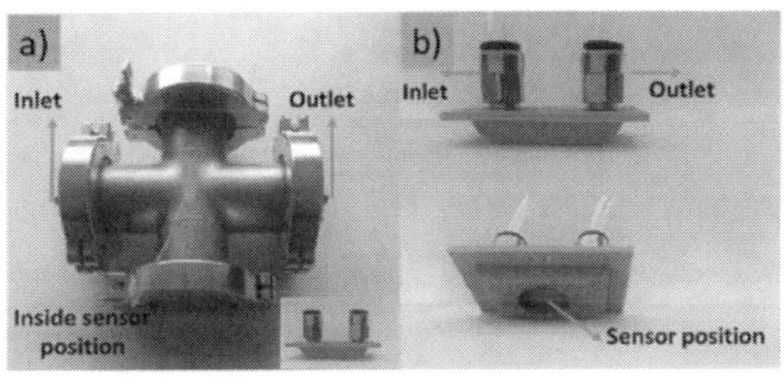


Figure 2. Photographs of: (a) cross and (b) boat chamber

The first one (Fig. 2.a) was made from stainless steel with total volume of 0.3 L and gas flow range between 0.1L/min and 1.5L/min. Besides, it has an inlet, an outlet, and the sensor optimal position is at the center, in front of the gas flow direction. The second chamber (the new one) is illustrated by Figure 2.b. It was made from polylactic acid (PLA) with a small volume of 2.35 $10^{-3}$L and gas flow range between 0.01 L/min and 0.5 L/min. It has a boat shape with a planar inlet and outlet. Additionally, the optimal sensor position is at the center of the boat back-side, in the same plan as the gas flow direction. In both chambers, the gas flow was maintained at 0.1 L/min, the sensor response was defined as $R=R_a/R_g$, where $R_a$ and $R_g$ are the sensor resistances at the stationary state in air and after 1 min of exposure to the target gas, respectively.

## III. RESULTS AND DISCUSIION

### A. Mathematical modelling and simulation results

The flow is modeled by a finite volume method solving the Navier-Stokes and the energy equations in the two 3D geometries, with no-slip and adiabatic boundary conditions everywhere, except on the inlet and outlet boundaries and on the sensor. Velocity fields are presented in Figure 3.

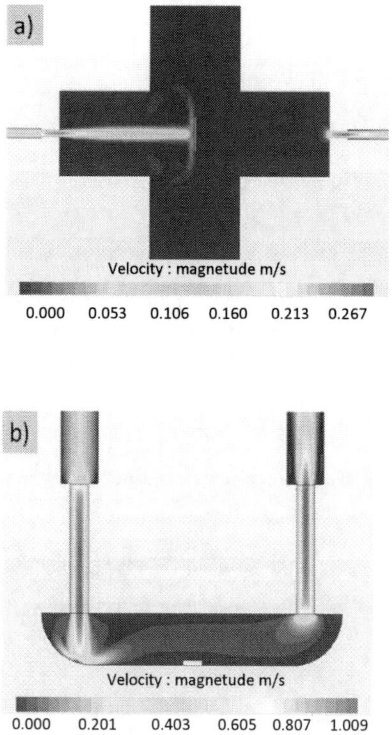


Figure 3. Velocity field of the converged flow in the Cross Chamber (a) and in the Boat chamber (b)

As we can see, in the cross chamber, at the sensor surface, the gas flow velocity is very important (0.1 m/s), which leads to the creation of many turbulences and negatively affects the sensor detection. However, in the boat chamber, it is almost zero and the gas flow direction is linear with the sensor position, which eliminates the creation of gas turbulences.

The target gas is injected at the inlet (0.1 L/min during 1 min, 50 ppm ethanol in air) and the ethanol concentration is measured on the sensor position. The gas testing transport is modeled by a convection-diffusion equation applied to a passive scalar. In Figure 4, we can observe that the gas concentration in the optimized testing chamber is very similar to the setpoint (50 ppm).

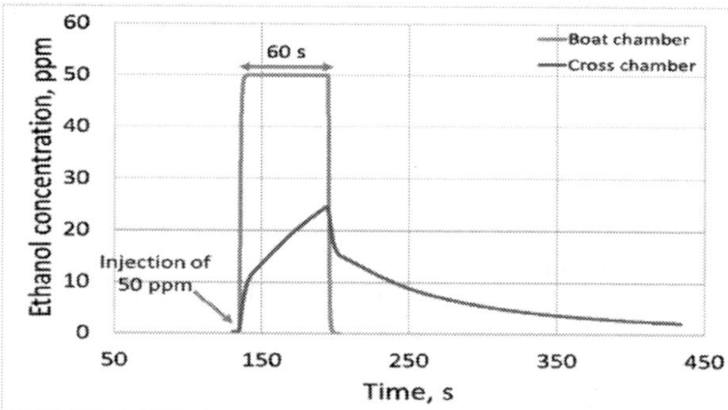


Figure 4. Ethanol concentration simulation in both chambers; injection at t=134s during 1 min

In addition, the speed of the filling and emptying in boat chamber is much faster compared to the cross one. In contrast, the ethanol concentration simulated for the cross-chamber does not reach 50 ppm with a flow rate of 0.1 L/min during 60 seconds, due to the greater volume of the cross-chamber and the presence of turbulences. The simulations show that an injection lasting 10 minutes is necessary to reach 50 ppm with such flow rate; at the same time, an injection with a flow rate of 0.5 L/min for 120 seconds allows us to reach the same level of ethanol concentration (50 ppm).

These results will be experimentally validated in the next paragraph by measuring the electrical sensor response towards 50 ppm of ethanol for an exposer of 1 minute, in both chambers.

### B. Validation of the optimized gas testing chamber

In order to validate the simulation results, we have exposed $SnO_2$ sensor (S2) to 50 ppm of ethanol, using the same measurements parameters, in both testing chambers (Fig. 5).

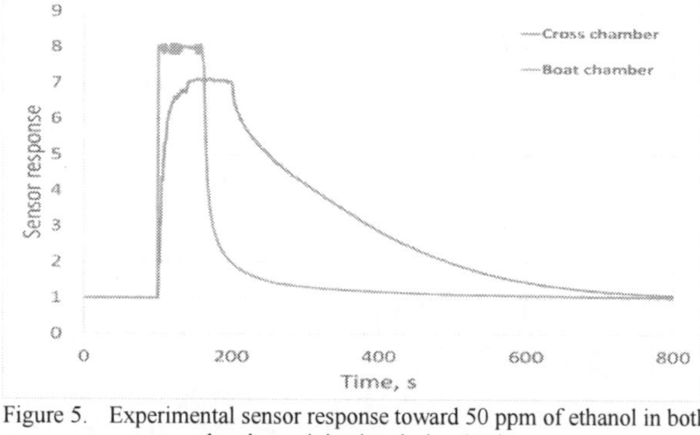


Figure 5. Experimental sensor response toward 50 ppm of ethanol in both chambers - injection during 1 min

The results show that the sensor performances are highly enhanced using the optimized chamber. For instance, the response and recovery times in the boat chamber are 4 s and 89 s, respectively. However, they are five times higher when using the cross chamber.

## IV. CONCLUSION

In this study, we have highlighted the strong influence of the test chamber design with respect to the electrical response of the sensor towards ethanol. To achieve our goals, we have reduced the dimensions of the test chamber while adapting the geometry. Besides, we have eliminated dead volumes, obtained a homogeneous gas concentration, and reduced the gas flow velocity at the sensor surface. The experimental results are in agreement with the mathematical modelling and simulation results.

## ACKNOWLEDGMENT

The authors would like to acknowledge NANOZ, a company specialized in gas sensors; SATT Sud-Est, "Accelerator of Technology Transfer", which is a key player in regional economic development associated with innovation and Mr. A. Combes for his technical support.

## REFERENCES

[1] G. F. Fine, L.M. Cavanagh, A. Afonja, R. Binions, "Metal oxide semi-conductor gas sensors in environmental monitoring", Sensors, vol. 10, pp. 5469–5502, June 2010.

[2] F. Annanouch et al., "Aerosol-Assisted CVD-Grown PdO Nanoparticle-Decorated Tungsten Oxide Nanoneedles Extremely Sensitive and Selective to Hydrogen", ACS Appl. Mater. Interfaces, vol. 8, pp. 10413–10421, April 2016.

[3] K. Aguir, M. Bendahan, V. Laithier, "Gas sensor based on heated sensitive layer", patent N° FR 13 59494, 2013, international extension 2016.

[4] M. Kaur et al., "RF sputtered $SnO_2$: NiO thin films as sub-ppm $H_2S$ sensor operable at room temperature", Sens. Actuators B-Chem, vol. 242, pp. 389–403, April 2017.

[5] G. Sberveglieri, S. Groppelli, G. Coccoli, "Radio frequency magnetron sputtering growth and characterization of indium-tin oxide (ITO) thin films for $NO_2$ gas sensors", Sens. Actuators, vol. 15, pp. 235–242, November 1988.

# Cyclical Heating to Reduce Consumption of $SnO_2$ Sensors for Alcohol Monitoring

Bruno Lawson, Virginie Martini-Laithier, Tomas Fiorido, Marc Bendahan, Rachid Bouchakour, Khalifa Aguir
Aix Marseille Univ, Université de Toulon, CNRS, IM2NP,
Marseille, France
E-mail: {bruno.lawson, virginie.laithier, tomas.fiorido, marc.bendahan, rachid.bouchakour, khalifa.aguir}@im2np.fr

*Abstract*— **In this work, we study the response of a Tin Dioxide ($SnO_2$) sensor under ethanol exposure to enable alcohol monitoring under a number of different power conditions (continuous and cyclical heating) in order to investigate the impact of reduced system level power consumption on sensor sensitivity. The sensitive thin layer of $SnO_2$ with a thickness of 50nm was deposited by a magnetron reactive sputtering technique. The power consumption of the $SnO_2$ sensor when continuously heated was 53mW (280°C). In the case of a cyclical heating operating mode, power consumption was 13mW when a frequency of 16mHz was used. The division of power consumption by four results in a slight decrease in the sensitivity of the sensor of about 25%.**

***Keywords-ethanol monitoring; cyclical heating; low power consumption; $SnO_2$ gas sensor.***

## I. INTRODUCTION

Research in the field of metal oxide chemo-resistive gas sensors (MOX Sensors) has been a growing area of interest for biomedical applications, such as the detection of Volatile Organic Compounds (VOC) released by the human body. For the monitoring of alcohol vapor emitted by transdermal perspiration after alcohol consumption [1], $SnO_2$ metal oxide sensors are often used. Tin dioxide is one of the most sensitive layers which can be used for gas detection due to its high sensitivity and stability [2]. Thus, in the case of transdermal alcohol monitoring, the main criterion to be considered when developing a mobile/battery-operated sensor is the greatest sensitivity attainable with the minimum heater power consumption conditions which allow it to be incorporated into the power-constrained mobile component.

A MOX sensor requires two voltage inputs, the heater voltage and the sensor bias voltage. The heater voltage allows the semiconductor to be maintained at a specific temperature in order to enable gas detection. A sensor bias voltage is applied to allow the measurement of the sensor response to gas exposure. One critical aspect to be considered when working with a metal oxide semiconductor gas sensor is the power consumption required for the heating element, which is in the order of 70mW or more on average. In the case of continuous monitoring using power-constrained sensors, it is important to decrease heater consumption so that they can be incorporated in microsystems such as a wristband, patch and armband, or watch (this requires a power consumption in the order of 5mW). One possible solution is to use cyclical heating, which means switching the heater on and off, thus minimizing the active period of energy consumption so as to save power [3]. Given the high value of sensitive layer resistance, the power of the sensitive layer is negligible compared with that of the heater. In order to monitor the transdermal ethanol emission of the skin, we compare the responses of the sensor in both cases, i.e. continuous heating and cyclical heating. The $SnO_2$ sensors were exposed to ethanol vapor with various concentrations ranging from 1ppm to 100ppm.

The rest of the paper is structured as follows.

In Section 2, we describe the MOX sensor device, the measuring bench and the parameters of cyclical heating. In Section 3, we present the sensor responses in each case of heating conditions and we offer a brief discussion. The paper concludes with Section IV.

## II. EXPERIMENTAL

### A. Gas sensor

Tin dioxide is an n-type wide-band-gap (3.6eV) metal oxide semiconductor, with a wide range of applications for various types of oxidizing or reductive gas/vapor detection. Figure 1 shows the sensitive thin layers of $SnO_2$ with a thickness of 50nm which were deposited by reactive radio frequency (RF) magnetron sputtering on transducers patented by the AMU-IM2NP laboratory [4]. The transducers are designed to have three sensors and two heaters. In this study we will present only the response of the central sensor.

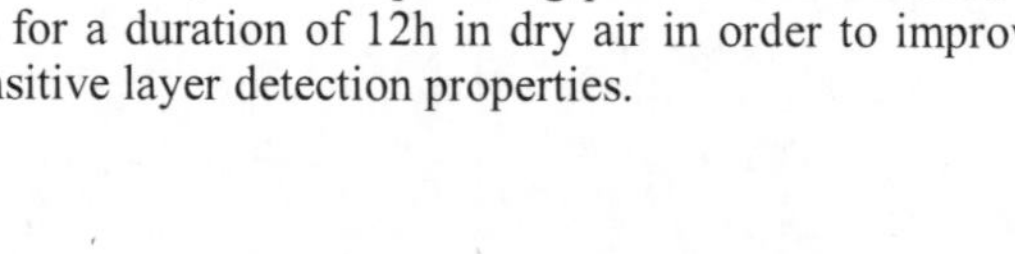


Figure 1. AMU-IM2NP ethanol sensor based on $SnO_2$

The films were deposited at a pressure of 22µbar with a mixture of $Ar/O_2$ for the sputtering process and annealed at 500°C for a duration of 12h in dry air in order to improve the sensitive layer detection properties.

*B. Measuring bench*

An innovative sensor system calibration was developed in collaboration with the OMICRON Company (http://www.omicron-technologies.com). This platform for sensor characterization generates ethanol and acetone vapor (acetone is one of the most important interference VOCs for the detection of alcohol in perspiration). Ethanol vapor is generated by heating tubes with concentrations ranging from 20ppb to 150ppm for a flow rate of 250ml/min with dry air as the gas vector. Ethanol vapor is carried in a test chamber with a volume of 1.86ml, where the sensor is polarized by means of a Keithley source meter for data acquisition and the heater power is modulated to provide the operating temperature. The sensor response is defined as Ra/Rg, where Ra is the sensor resistance measured in air and Rg is the sensor resistance measured under ethanol exposure.

When the concentration of alcohol in the blood after alcohol consumption reaches 0.5g/l (2 standard glasses of alcoholic beverage), its equivalent in the breath is 139ppm and lower concentrations varying between 1 and 100ppm may be expected on the surface of the skin. We therefore varied the ethanol concentration from 1ppm to 100ppm every 2 minutes of exposure in our application.

*C. Cyclical heating*

MOX sensors involve high working temperatures (220°C-300°C) in order to detect gaseous species. This is because temperature provides the sensitive layer with the activation energy required for adsorption between the gaseous species and the surface of the oxide. Temperature also influences the gas desorption. Figure 2 illustrates the sensor response as a function of the heater voltage supply for 50ppm of ethanol. 2V is the heater polarization which corresponds to the optimal heating temperature for the best response. Below this value, the response decreases.

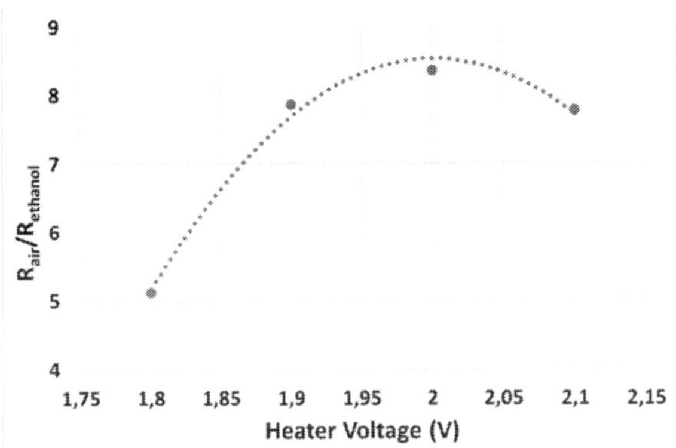


Figure 2. Ethanol sensor response according to the heater voltage

A frequency of cyclical heating was studied previously to determine the optimum active time of a heating element. Figure 3 illustrates an example of a sensor response according to different heater activation times (6s, 10s, 15s, and 20s) under different ethanol concentrations.

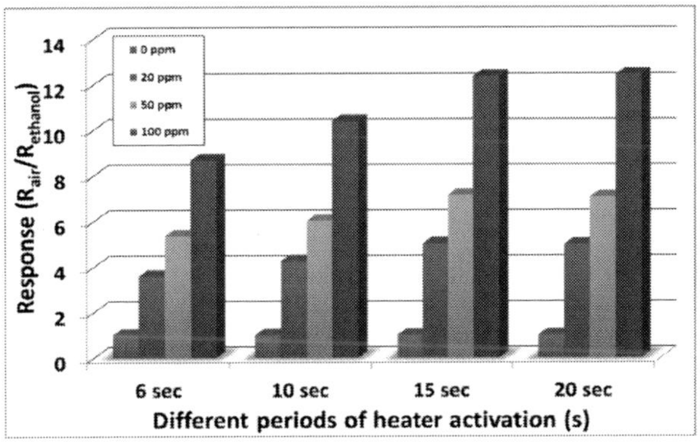


Figure 3. Cyclical frequency study

Figure 3 shows that, for a heater activation of 15s, the response of the sensor stabilizes and the sensitive layer almost reaches the optimal temperature for the detection process.

Before applying the voltage for the cyclical temperature, we used an oscilloscope to visualize the output voltage modulation. Figure 4 shows an example of cyclical heating which was considered.

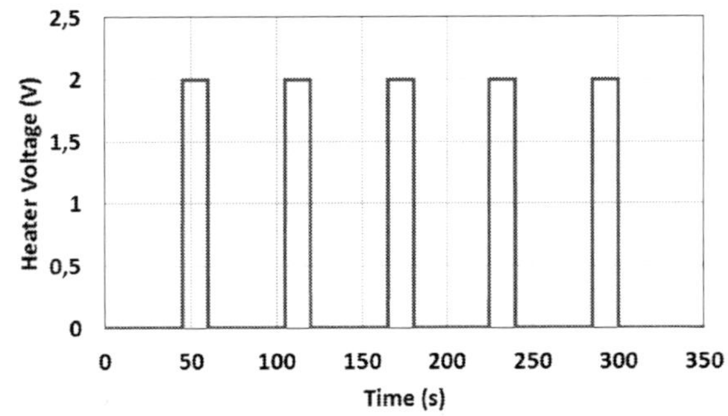


Figure 4. Cyclical heating applied to $SnO_2$ sensor (2V~53mW/280°C)

During a period of 60s (1min), the heater is switched off for 45s, and on for 15s. This is repeated throughout the measurement. The period of this cyclical heating is 60s, its frequency is 16mHz and the cyclical ratio is 0.25.

## III. RESULTS AND DISCUSSION

The $SnO_2$ sensor shows a good sensitivity to ethanol, mainly for low concentrations and a slight saturation of around 70ppm. This slight saturation occurs when the coverage rate of the adsorption sites decreases. Figure 5 shows the variation of sensor resistance in the case of continuous heating (53mW).

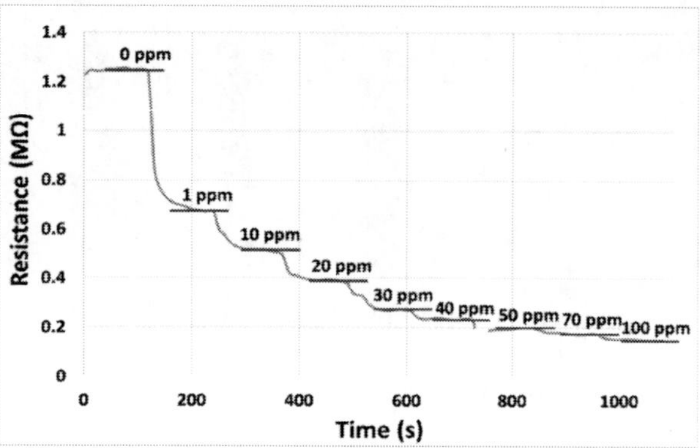


Figure 5. $SnO_2$ sensor reponse under different ethanol concentrations: continuous heating

Figure 6 shows the variation of sensor resistance in the cyclical heating mode (13mW). The power reduction (by a factor of 4) causes a slight decrease in sensor responses, as shown in Figure 7. In fact, in the case of continuous heating the sensor operates at 280°C and 53mW. With cyclical heating, the heating time is decreased and thus power consumption too, without any reduction of the operating temperature (280°C) during the detection process.

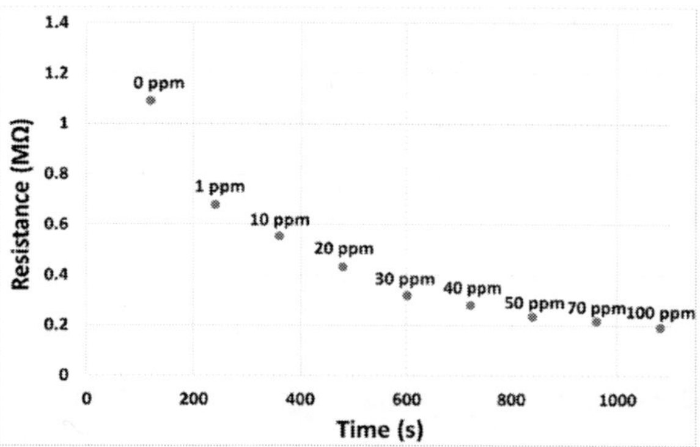


Figure 6. $SnO_2$ sensor reponse under different ethanol concentrations: cyclical heating

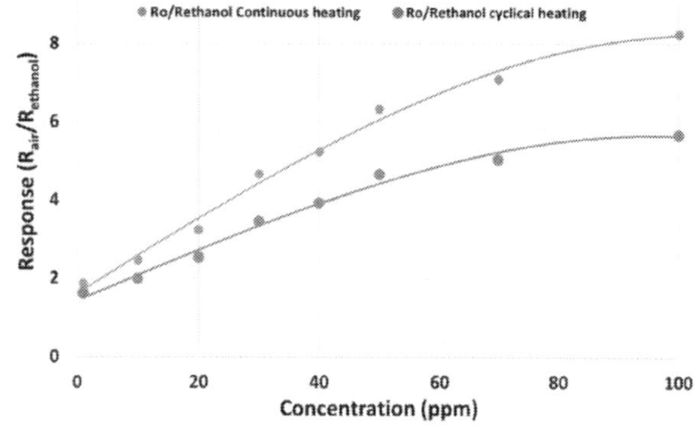


Figure 7. Comparison of $SnO_2$ responses with continuous heating (53mW) and cyclical heating (13mW)

However, even if cyclical heating allows a reduction of power consuption of 75%, it is important to note that pulse mode heating can also reduce slightly the sensor response.

## IV. CONCLUSION

This paper describes the efficiency of cyclical heating in the gas/vapor detection process. This method allows a reduction of power consumption in the integrated gas detection microsystems. Thanks to this heating modulation and to the short response time of the microsensors, energy consumption can be further reduced with only a slight decrease in the response.

## V. REFERENCES

[1] J. S. Hawthorne, and M. H. Wojcik, "Transdermal alcohol measurement: a review of the literature," Canadian Society of Forensic Science, vol. 39, No 2, pp. 65–71, 2012.

[2] L. K. Bagal, J. Y. Patil, M. V. Vaishampayan, I. S. Mulla, and S. S. Suryavanski, "Effect of Pd and Ce on the enhancement of ethanol vapor response of $SnO_2$ thick films," Sensors and Actuators B Chemical, vol. 207, pp. 383-390, 2015.

[3] D. Spirjakin, A. M. Baranov, A. SomoV, and V. Sleptsov, "Investigation of heating profiles and optimization of power consumption of gas sensors for wireless sensor networks," Sensors and Actuators A Physical, vol. 247, pp. 247-253, 2016.

[4] K. Aguir, M. Bendahan, and V. Martini-Laithier, "Gas sensor based on heated sensitive layer," patent N° FR 13 59494, 2013, international extension 2016.

# Sub-ppm Nitrogen Dioxide ($NO_2$) Sensor Based on Inkjet Printed CuO on Microhotplate with a Pulsed Temperature Modulation

Aymen Sendi, Grérory Besnard, Philippe Menini, Chaabane Talhi, Frédéric Blanc, and Bernard Franc
Laboratoire d'Analyse et d'Architecture des Systèmes
LAAS-CNRS, University of Toulouse
7 Avenue du Colonel Roche
Toulouse, France
E-mail: {aymen.sendi, gbesnard, menini, talhi, blanc, bfranc}@laas.fr

Myrtil Kahn, Katia Fajerwerg, and Pierre Fau
Laboratoire de Chimie de Coordination
LCC-CNRS, University of Toulouse
205 Route de Narbonne
Toulouse, France
E-mail: {myrtil.kahn, katia.fajerwerg, pierre.fau}@lcc-toulouse.fr

***Abstract*— Nitrogen dioxide ($NO_2$), a toxic oxidizing gas, is considered among the main pollutants found in atmosphere and indoor air as well. Since long-term or short-term exposure to this gas is deleterious for human health, its detection is an urgent need that requires the development of efficient and cost effective methods and techniques. In this context, copper oxide (CuO) is a good candidate that is sensitive and selective for $NO_2$ at sub-ppm concentrations. In this work, CuO nanoparticles have been deposited by inkjet printing technology on a micro hotplate that can be operated up to 500°C at low power consumption (55 mW). The optimum detection capacity is obtained thanks to a temperature modulation (two -consecutive temperature steps from 100°C to 500°C), where the sensing resistance is measured. Thanks to this operating mode, we report in this study a very simple method for data processing and exploitation in order to obtain a good selectivity for the nitrogen dioxide over few interferent gases. Only four parameters from the sensor response allow us to make an efficient discrimination between individual or mixed gases in humid atmosphere.**

***Keywords- $NO_2$; CuO nanoparticles; temperature modulation; gas sensor; selectivity.***

## I. INTRODUCTION

Humans spend more than 90% of their time in closed environments, even though this indoor environment offers a wide variety of pollutants [1][2].

Indoor air pollution is a real health threat, so measuring indoor air quality is important for protecting the health from chemical and gaseous contaminants. Nitrogen dioxide ($NO_2$) is a dangerous pulmonary irritant [1]. $NO_2$ is generated by multiple sources of combustion in indoor air, such as smoking and heaters, but it also comes from outside air (industrial sources, road traffic) [3]. $NO_2$ may have adverse effects of shortness of breath, asthma attacks and bronchial obstructions [4]. It is also classified as toxic by the "International Agency for Research on Cancer (IARC)" [5], hence the necessity for sensor development for accurate $NO_2$ detection is an acute need. Among sensors techniques, the metal oxide gas (MOX) sensors are promising candidates because of their high performance in terms of sensitivity on top of their low production cost. The copper oxide (CuO) material is highly studied because of its high sensitivity and its ability to detect oxidant gaseous compounds, but also for other indoor air pollutants, such as acetaldehyde ($C_2H_4O$), formaldehyde ($CH_2O$), $NO_2$, CO, etc. However, CuO suffers from a major disadvantage which is the lack of selectivity with respect to targeted gas.

In this study, our main objective is to develop an innovative and simple pulsed- temperature operating mode associated with an efficient data processing technique, which enables good selectivity toward $NO_2$ in gas mixtures. This technique is based on few parameters extracted from the dynamic response of sensor versus temperature changes in a gaseous environment. These parameters are: the normalized sensing resistance, the values of the slope at the origin, the intermediate slope and the final slope of the response of $NO_2$ against different reference gases, such as $C_2H_4O$, $CH_2O$ and moist air. The selectivity of $NO_2$ was examined in relation to air moisture with 30% humidity, $C_2H_4O$ at 0.5-ppm, $CH_2O$ at a concentration of 0.5-ppm and the binary mixture of these gases with 0.3-ppm of each.

In Section II of the paper, we describe the materials and methods used in our work. Section III presents our results and the discussion. We conclude this work in Section IV.

## II. MATERIALS AND METHODS

The sensitive layer made of CuO nanoparticles is deposited by inkjet printing on a silicon microhotplate [6]. The ink is prepared with 5% CuO weight, which was dispersed in ethylene glycol by an ultrasonic bath for about one hour. The dispersions obtained were allowed to settle for 24 hours. The final ink was collected and then used for printing using Altadrop equipment control, where the numbers of the deposited drops of ink were controlled [6]. This technique is simple and allowed us to obtain reproducible layers thicknesses of a few micrometers depending on the number of deposited drops. In addition, this technique permits to have a precisely localized deposit without need of additional complex photolithographic steps [7]. The CuO layer is finally annealed in ambient air from room temperature to 500°C (rate 1°C/min) followed by a plateau at 500°C for 1 hour before cooling to room temperature (1°C/min). This initial temperature treatment is necessary because CuO requires operating temperatures between 100°C<T<500°C. The thermal pretreatment is necessary to generate ionized oxygen species in atomic or molecular form at the oxide surface and therefore to improve the reactivity between the reacting gas and the sensor surface [6].

In this study, we have used a pulsed temperature profile, presented in a previously published work, which showed that optimized sensitivity can be achieved with the use of two different temperature stages at 100°C and 500°C respectively. This dual temperature protocol also reduces the total power consumption of the device (see Figure 1).

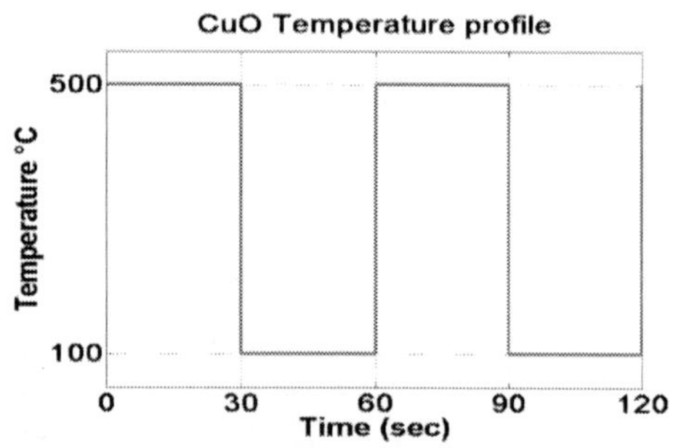


Figure 1. CuO temperature profile.

The CuO sensor was placed in a 250 ml test chamber and the test conditions were as follow:

- A flow rate of 200 ml/min, controlled by a digital flowmeter.
- A relative humidity (RH) level of 30% is obtained by bubbling synthetic air flow controlled by a mass flow controller.
- The measuring chamber is at ambient temperature, controlled by a temperature sensor placed inside the vessel.
- A bias current is applied to the sensitive layer, controlled by a Source Measure Unit (SMU).

We started a test with single gas injections after a phase of two-hours stabilization in humid air, then with injections of binary mixtures for 16-min. During 32-min, moist air is injected between two successive gas injections. This time is enough to clean the chamber and stabilize the sensor to its baseline.

The gas injections concentrations are summarized in Table 1. A schematic representation of these injections is presented in Figure 2.

TABLE 1. INJECTED GASES CONCENTRATIONS

| Gas | Concentration |
|---|---|
| Acetaldehyde ($C_2H_4O$) | 0.5-ppm |
| Formaldehyde ($CH_2O$) | 0.5-ppm |
| Nitrogen dioxide ($NO_2$) | 0.5-ppm |
| Acetaldehyde and Formaldehyde ($C_2H_4O$/ $CH_2O$) | 0.3-ppm/0.3-ppm |
| Acetaldehyde and Nitrogen dioxide ($C_2H_2O$/ $NO_2$) | 0.3-ppm/0.3-ppm |
| Formaldehyde and Nitrogen dioxide ($CH_2O$/ $NO_2$) | 0.3-ppm/0.3-ppm |

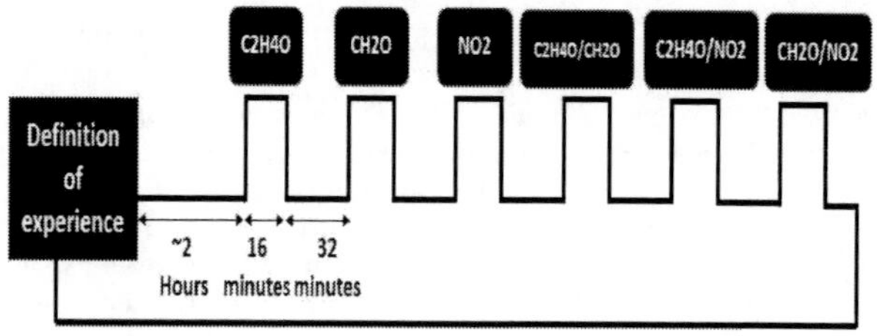


Figure 2. Synoptic representative of a sequence of gas injections.

During all the experience (stabilization phase, gases injections and stage between two successive gases) , the sensor is powered by a square signal voltage applied on the heater in order to obtain two temperature steps as shown in Figure 1. To ensure a constant overall flow, we adapted the gas injection sequences duration in correlation with the heating signal period (see Figure 3).

The resistance variation of CuO is measured under a fixed supply current of 100 nA in order to obtain voltage measurements in the range of few volts, far from compliance limit of the measuring device (20V). We also verified that this procedure (temperature cycling) doesn't affect the sensor reproducibility in terms of baseline or the sensor sensitivity.

Under such test conditions, we achieved a continuous 6.5 hours testing period without observing any drift on the raw sensor response. The sampling period is 500 ms, which gives us 60 points on a 30-second response step, this acquisition rate being enough for accurate data processing.

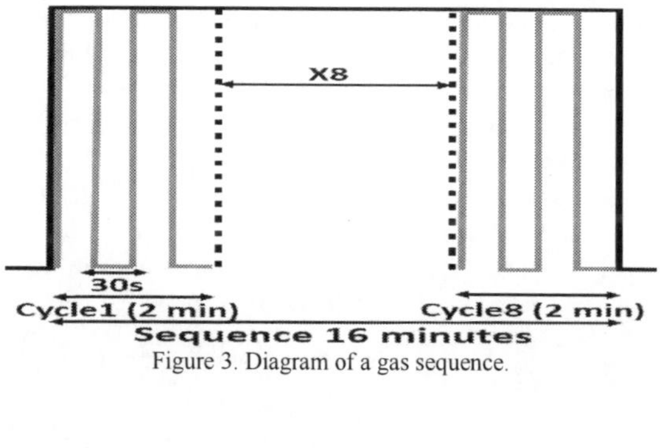


Figure 3. Diagram of a gas sequence.

Finally, we analyzed the sensor responses at each steps, according to the different gas injections, using a simple method of data processing in order to have the better selectivity of $NO_2$.

## III. RESULTS AND DISCUSSION

### *A. Method of analysis*

During each gas injection, 16 periods of temperature modulation are applied. After verifying the reproducibility of sensor responses along these cycles, we only present here the responses of the last cycle, which is stabilized and reproducible from one cycle to another. As mentioned previously, we used new simple data treatment methods to obtain the better selectivity toward $NO_2$ with respect to several interferent gases. Among the multiple possible criteria, we chose representative variables that take into account the dynamic sensor behavior during a change of gaseous conditions and during a pulsed temperature; these criteria are obtained from the sensor resistance slopes during the gas response on each 30-second-steps. The data acquisition relies on the decomposition of the response into three distinct domains (see Figure 4):

- Starting Slope: from the 1st point to the 10th point (in yellow),
- Intermediate slope: from the 10th point to the 30th point (in red),
- Final slope: from the 30th point to the 60th point (in black).

The normalized resistance is measured from the last point on each step: this is the absolute difference between the resistance of the sensor under a reference gas (like moist air) and the resistance of the sensor under targeted gas(es), at the final cycle of each injection:

$$R_n = ((R_{gas} - R_{air}) / R_{air}) * 100 \quad (1)$$

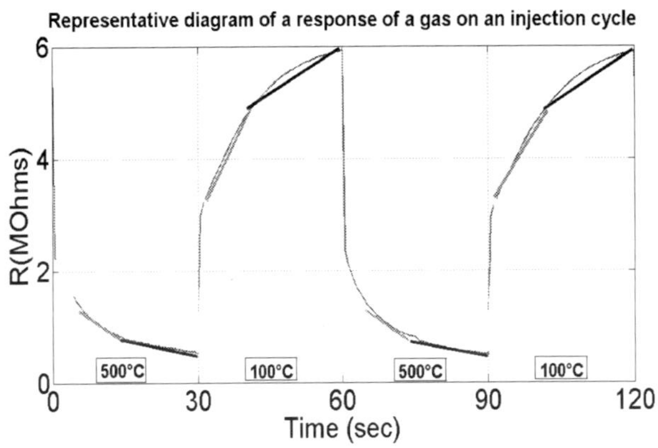


Figure 4. Representative diagram of a response of a gas sensor during an injection cycle and showing the 3 domain slopes.

By treating these four parameters, a good selectivity of $NO_2$ can be obtained with respect to moist air, $C_2H_4O$ and $CH_2O$.

### *B. Slope at the origin*

The slope at the origin is calculated on the first 10 points of each temperature step of the 8th cycle of each injection. Regarding the reference gas (moist air); we took the response of the 8th cycle of the last sequence under humid air before the injection of gases. The values of these slopes (in Ohms/ms) are shown in Figure 5; each bar represents the value of the slope at the origin of each gas at 500 and 100°C.

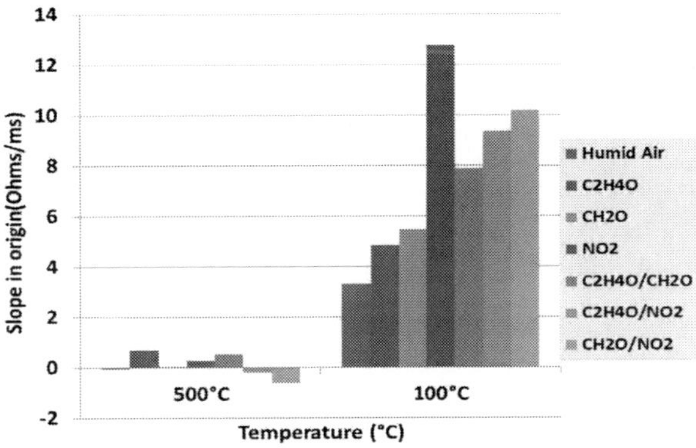


Figure 5. Representation of the slopes at the origin under different gases of the 8th cycle in "Ohms/ms" according to the temperature of the sensors.

Figure 5 clearly shows that the calculations of this parameter enable us to differentiate $NO_2$ from the other reference gases by measures on the plateau at 100°C. Regarding the other step at 500°C we note that the response is almost zero, because the transition from a cold to a hot state decreases the detection sensitivity and therefore reduces the sensors resistance variations under gas. We also note that with this criterion we evidence a significant difference between the value of the starting slope under $NO_2$ compare to others under other gases and mixtures without $NO_2$.

### *C. Intermediate slope*

The intermediate slope is calculated from the 10th point to the 30th point of each temperature step of the last cycle during each gas injection and compared with the value under air. The calculated values are shown in Figure 6.

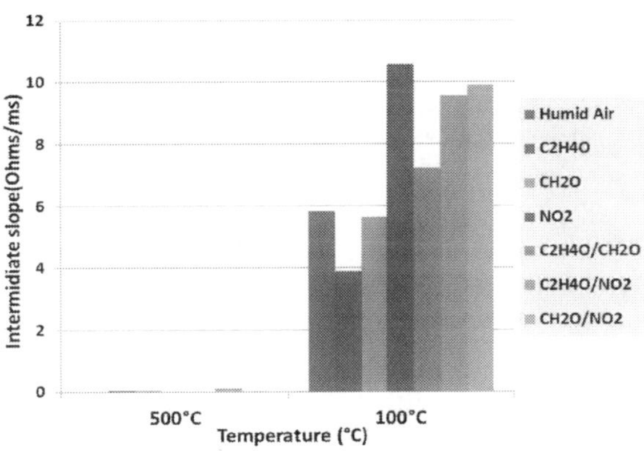


Figure 6. Representation of the intermediate slopes under different gases at the 8th cycle in "Ohms/ms" according to the temperature of the sensors.

According to Figure 6, the value of the intermediate slope of individual $NO_2$ injection or of the gas mixtures in which there is $NO_2$, is not prominent compared with the other reference gases even on the plateau at 100°C. This parameter is less effective than the previous one to detect $NO_2$ in gas mixtures.

### *D. Final slope*

The final slope is the slope of the second half of the gas response; it is calculated between the 30th point and the 60th point. The response to the different temperature steps of the last cycle during $NO_2$ injection and the reference gases is presented in Figure 7.

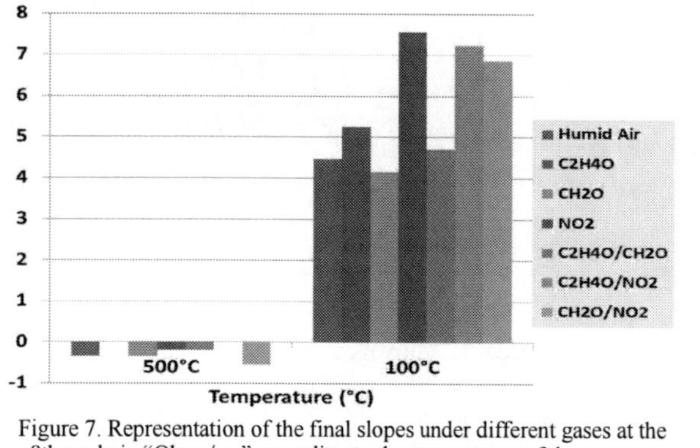


Figure 7. Representation of the final slopes under different gases at the 8th cycle in "Ohms/ms" according to the temperature of the sensors.

It is worth noting that the value of the final slopes of $NO_2$ or gaseous mixtures, which contain the $NO_2$, are very different compared to the other reference gases on the two stages at 100°C only. This parameter allows us to select $NO_2$ with respect to other interfering gases.

### *E. Normalized resistance*

As previously presented, the normalized resistance is calculated with respect to humid air from each last cycle level. The reference resistance used is the resistance of each stage of the last wet air sequence before the gas injection. The results obtained from these calculations are shown in Figure 8.

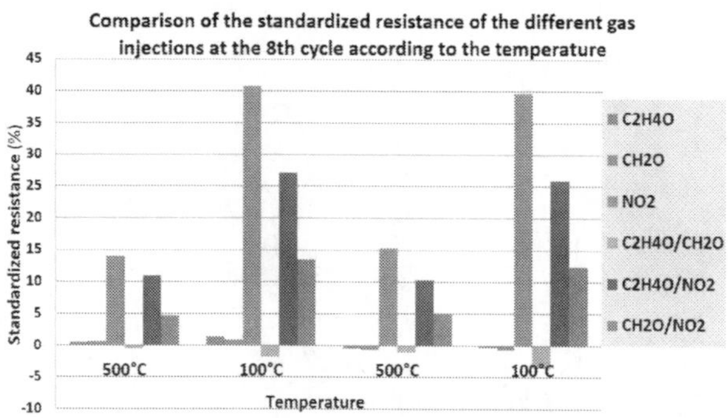


Figure 8. The normalized resistance of the different gas injections at the 8th cycle according to the temperature.

Figure 8 shows a slight variation in the values of the normalized resistance between two similar and successive temperatures for the same gases. This slight variation can be explained by data dispersion which is +/- 2%, due to the fact that the normalized resistance is calculated from the raw values during the gas injection and the raw values of resistances during the injections of humid air that may be slightly different between two similar and successive temperature stages.

The CuO sensor response to sub-ppm $NO_2$ levels when injected individually or in combination with another gas, is specific when measurements are taken on the low temperature plateau at 100°C.

## IV. Conclusion

The selectivity and sensitivity of our CuO sensor has been studied by different operating modes and simple methods of analysis. Specific temperature modulation was applied to the metal oxide with the use of temperature steps at 500 and 100°C. The response of CuO sensitive layer toward gases representatives of indoor air pollution ($C_2H_4O$, $CH_2O$, $NO_2$, humid air) has been studied. These responses were analysed with several parameters, such as the study of the slope of resistance variation at the origin, the intermediate slope, the final slope and the normalized resistance measured at each temperature steps. The study of these different parameters shows that the CuO material is able to detect sub-ppm levels of $NO_2$ with a good selectivity compared to different interfering gases. To still improve the selectivity of gas sensor device to a larger variety of polluting gases, we plan to integrate these CuO sensors in a multichip system, which will allow us to use in parallel new metal oxide layers with specific temperature profiles and data analysis criteria.

## Acknowledgment

The authors express their gratitude to neOCampus, the university project of the Paul Sabatier University of Toulouse, for the financial support and the Chemical Coordination Laboratory of Toulouse for the preparation of the CuO nanoparticle powder. This work was also partly supported by the French RENATECH network.

## References

[1] B. Lévesque et al. P-L. Auger, J Bourbeau, J-F. Duchesne, P. Lajoie, D. Menzies, "Indoor air quality," Environment and Public Health. Foundations and Practices, pp. 317-332.2003.

[2] J. Namiesnik, T. Gorecki, B. Kozdron-Zabiega, and J. Lukasiak, "Indoor air quality (IAQ),". Pollutants, their sources, and concentration levels. Build. Environ. 27. 1992. pp. 339-356.

[3] Roger Cadiergues, "Indoor air quality," Guide RefCad: nR15.a. pp. 16-17. 2017.

[4] K.Koistinen et al. D. Kotzias, S. Kephalopoulos, C. Schlitt, P. Carrer, M. Jantunen, S. Kirchner, J. McLaughlin, L. Mølhave, E. Fernandes, B. Seifert, "The INDEX project: executive

summary of a European Union project on indoor air pollutants Allergy," 63. 2008. pp. 810-819.

[5] D Loomis, W Huang, and G Chen, "The International Agency for Research on Cancer (IARC) evaluation of the carcinogenicity of outdoor air pollution: focus on China." Chin J Cancer. 2014 Apr;33(4):189-96. doi: 10.5732/cjc.014.10028.

[6] N. Dufour, A. Chapelle, F. Mesnilgrente, V. Conedera, and Ph. Menini, "Technological improvements of a metal oxide gas multi-sensor based on a micro-hotplate structure and inkjet deposition for an automotive air quality sensor application," 25th Micromechanics and Microsystems Europe workshop. MME 2014. Aug-2014. Istanbul, Turkey.4p.

[7] M. Morozova et al. P. Kluson, J. Krysa, P. Dzik, M. Vesely, O. Solcova, "Thin TiO2 films prepared by inkjet printing of the reverse micelles sol–gel composition," Sensors and Actuators B 160. 2011.

# Development of Taste Sensor with High Selectivity and Sensitivity

Yusuke Tahara and Kiyoshi Toko
Research and Development Center for Taste and Odor Sensing
Kyushu University
Nishi-ku, Fukuoka 819-0395, Japan
e-mail: tahara@belab.ed.kyushu-u.ac.jp, toko@ed.kyushu-u.ac.jp

*Abstract*—**We have developed a taste sensor for objective taste evaluations of foods, beverages and pharmaceuticals. The taste sensor is based on the potentiometric measurement system and has sensor electrodes with lipid polymer membranes as working electrodes and as reference electrode. It is desirable for the sensor to be able to evaluate not only the taste, but also the aftertaste, similar to the way humans experience it. In this study, we report relationships between sensor responses, the amount of adsorbed monosodium glutamate (MSG) onto the lipid polymer membrane and human sensory score for the evaluation of the aftertaste of umami.**

***Keywords-taste sensor; lipid polymer membrane; sensory score.***

## I. INTRODUCTION

In food and beverage industries, it is very important to evaluate taste for development of new products, market research and quality control. The main method of taste evaluation is based on sensory tests that well-trained panelists actually perform by tasting and evaluating samples. The sensory tests have some problems, such as low objectivity and reproducibility, and the physical and psychological stress imposed on the panelists. To solve these problems, we have developed a taste sensor based on potentiometric measurement system [1]-[3]. The taste sensor has sensor electrodes which use lipid polymer membranes for the taste sensing part and output a change in the membrane potential caused by the interaction between the membrane and the taste substances. There are several kinds of membranes for evaluations of saltiness, sourness, umami, bitterness or sweetness. The surface charge density and the hydrophobicity of each membrane are designed by adjusting the sorts and amount of lipid and plasticizer on the sensor membrane, considering the basis of physicochemical properties of substances with each basic taste [4]. The taste sensor has been widely applied in manufacturing of foods and beverages such as green tea, milk, rice, soy sauce and pork [5]. Figure 1 shows a taste map of beer on the market, which is one of applications using the taste sensor for market survey.

It is desirable for the sensor to be able to evaluate not only the taste, but also the aftertaste, similar to the way humans experience it. Although the taste sensor has been used for evaluation of aftertaste [2], the interaction between the membrane of a sensor electrode for umami and umami substances for evaluating the aftertaste of umami was not investigated well. In this study, we report relationships between sensor responses, the amount of adsorbed monosodium glutamate (MSG) onto the membrane and human sensory score for the aftertaste of umami. The aftertaste of umami, which is called "kokumi", is recognized as a complicated taste, which is described in various ways, such as "mouthfulness", "thickness" and "continuity" [6][7].

## II. MATERIAL AND METHOD

### A. Lipid polymer membrane

The lipid polymer membrane used in the sensor electrode for umami used in this study comprises polyvinyl chloride (PVC) as the supporter constituting the membrane, trioctylmethylammonium chloride (TOMA) and phosphoric acid di(2-ethylhexyl) ester (PADE) as the lipids, and dioctyl phenylphosphonate (DOPP) as the plasticizer. Details on the preparation of the procedure can be found in a previous report [2].

### B. Measurement of CPA value using taste sensor

Measurements of sample solutions using the sensor electrode for umami utilize the taste sensor (TS-5000Z, Intelligent Sensor Technology, Inc.). Monosodium glutamate (MSG) was used as kokumi substances. MSG in a reference solution consisting of 30 mM KCl and 0.3 mM tartaric acid was used as umami solutions. The change of membrane potential caused by adsorption (CPA) [1]-[3] is used as sensor outputs of the samples. The measurement procedures were performed using the same technique, following the manual.

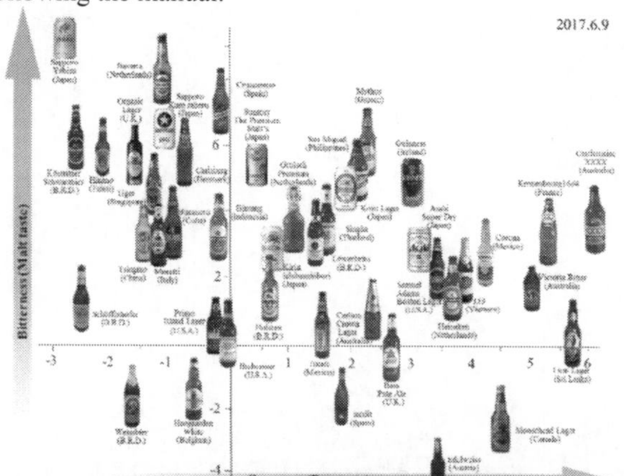


Figure 1. Taste map of beer using the taste sensor.

### *C. Measurement of the amount of adsorbed MSG*

The amount of MSG was measured by an enzymatic method (L-glutamate kit, Yamasa Co., Japan) and a spectrophotometer (UV-1800, Shimadzu Corporation). First, 5 ml of MSG solution with a known concentration was added dropwise onto a petri dish on which a lipid polymer membrane had been formed, and left to stand for 30 s to allow MSG molecules in the solution to be adsorbed onto the membrane. After 30 s, 3 ml of the MSG solution was taken from the petri dish to measure the absorbance of the solution. The concentration of MSG in the measured solution was calculated from the measured absorbance and calibration curve. The difference between the concentration of the MSG solution added dropwise and that of the MSG solution calculated from the absorbance was defined as the amount of adsorbed MSG.

### *D. Sensory test of aftertaste of umami*

Five well-trained panelists (2 male and 3 female healthy adults) evaluated the following. The panelists drank each MSG solutions. Then, they were instructed to answer questions about the taste (kokumi) at 20 s after drinking.

## III. Results and Discussion

Figure 2 shows the CPA response values to MSG solutions using the sensor electrode for umami. The CPA values increased with increasing MSG concentration from 30 to 300 mM. Figure 3 shows the amount of adsorbed MSG onto the membrane. The amount of adsorbed MSG increased with increasing MSG concentration from 30 to 300 mM. These results indicate that the CPA is generated when a taste substance adsorbs onto the surface of the lipid polymer membrane and the electrical charge density of the membrane surface changes. In order to confirm that the aftertaste of MSG shows kokumi, a sensory test was conducted. The well-trained panelists evaluated the aftertaste of the MSG solution (10, 100 and 300 mM). They all answered that MSG solution showed kokumi at 20 s after drinking the MSG solution and the intensity of kokumi increased with increasing MSG concentration.

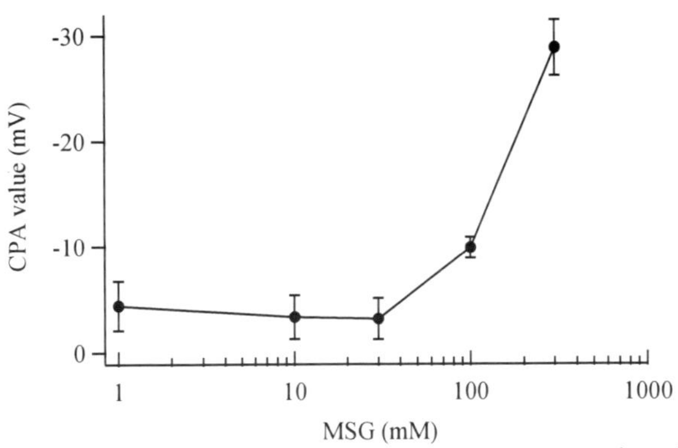


Figure 2. The CPA values response to MSG solution using sensor electrode for umami.

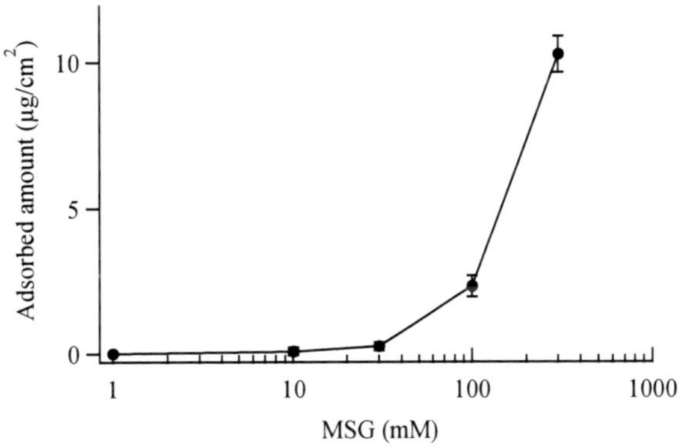


Figure 3. The amount of adsorbed MSG onto the membrane.

In conclusion, the CPA value by the sensor electrode for umami showed a good agreement with kokumi by sensory score. It was suggested that kokumi by MSG could be evaluated by the sensor electrode for umami.

## Acknowledgment

We would like to thank laboratory students Mr. C. Liu and Mr. Y. Liu, Kyushu University, Japan, for their help with some experiments.

## References

[1] K. Toko, Biomimetic Sensor Technology, Cambridge University Press, 2000.

[2] Y. Kobayashi et al., "Advanced taste sensors based on artificial lipids with global selectivity to basic taste qualities and high correlation to sensory scores," Sensors, vol.10, pp. 3411-3443, 2010.

[3] Y. Tahara and K. Toko, "Electronic tongues – a review," IEEE Sens. J., vol.13, pp. 3001-3011, 2013.

[4] Y. Kobayashi, H. Hamada, Y. Yamaguchi, H. Ikezaki, and K. Toko, "Development of an artificial lipid-based membrane sensor with high selectivity and sensitivity to the bitterness of drugs and with high correlation with sensory score," IEEJ Trensactions on Electrical and Electronic Engineering, vol. 4, pp. 710-719, 2009.

[5] K. Toko, Y. Tahara, M. Habara, Y. Kobayashi, and H. Ikezaki, "Taste sensor: electronic tongue with global selectivity," in Essentials of Machine Olfaction and Taste, T. Nakamoto, Ed, John Wiley & Sons Singapore Pte Ltd., pp. 87-174, 2016.

[6] M. Imamura and K. Matsushima, "Suppression of umami aftertaste by polysaccharides in soy sauce", J. Food Sci., vol.78, pp.1136-1142, 2013.

[7] T. Miyaki, H. Kawasaki, M. Kuroda, N. Miyamura, and T. Kouda, "Effect of a kokumi peptide, γ-glutamyl-valyl-glycine, on the sensory characteriscs of chiken consommé", Flavour, vol.4, pp.1-8, 2015.

# Array of Chemosensitive Resistors with Composites of Gas Chromatography (GC) Materials and Carbon Black for Detection and Recognition of VOCs: An Optimization Study

Bartosz Wyszynski, Rui Yatabe, Kiyoshi Toko
Research and Development Center
for Taste and Odor Sensing
Fukuoka, Japan
email: wyszynski.pawel.bartosz.939@m.kyushu-u.ac.jp
{yatabe, toko} @nbelab.ed.kyushu-u.ac.jp

Atsuo Nakao, Masaya Nakatani, Akio Oki, Hiroaki Oka
Panasonic Automotive & Industrial Systems Company
Sensing Solutions Development Center
Osaka, Japan
email: {nakao.atsuo, nakatani.masaya, oki.akio, oka.hiroaki} @jp.panasonic.com

*Abstract*—**In our previous work, we developed the concept and tested the viability of fabricating a 16-element chemosensitive resistor array for detection and recognition of volatile organic compounds. The sensing elements were fabricated using blends of Carbon Black (CB) and Gas Chromatography (GC) stationary-phase materials by coating over chemosensitive resistor devices. In this work, we extend our basic study with an ongoing attempt at optimizing the performance of our developed 16-element array versus vapors of pyrrole, benzenal, nonanal, and 2-phenethylamine. Our main concern here was studying the percolation threshold and aging of the sensing devices. The results indicate that the best performance of the fabricated sensing devices can be expected for sensing films with CB to GC-material ratio of 1.5:1 to 2:1. Sensing devices coated with blends of such composition performed in a relatively similar manner right after fabrication and after around 5-month long aging at room temperature.**

***Keywords- odor sensor; chemical sensor; artificial olfaction; chemoresistance; sensor array; GC material; carbon black.***

## I. INTRODUCTION

Biological olfaction can be regarded as a powerful tool, acquiring and analyzing airborne chemical information [1]. The sense of smell has been widely applied in numerous fields for either expert or non-expert evaluations, using techniques of sensory analysis [2]. In certain cases, the sensory analysis has been supported by instrumental analytical methods such as spectroscopy or chromatography [3]. However, the use of both sensory and instrumental analyses is seriously limited by their cost, time and lack of mobility. A still relatively novel field of instrumental analysis called artificial olfaction has emerged as a promising and attractive alternative to the above analytical techniques [4][5].

The biological sense of smell can be generally represented as consisting of two general stages: (i) receptive - olfactory receptors, and (ii) processing - olfactory bulb and the subsequent stages of olfactory cortex. Mimicking that general configuration, the electronic noses consist of a sensing stage (chemical, gas/vapor sensors) and a signal preprocessing/processing stage (various pattern recognition and classification techniques).

The gas/vapor sensors used in the artificial olfaction applications need to be non-specific, i.e., respond to groups of odorants rather than a particular one. Responses of such non-specific sensors' arrays are then processed using various pattern recognition techniques – from quite simple principal component or linear discriminant analyses to neural networks [6]-[10].

Electronic nose systems and their components are intensively studied with a number of successful attempts at their application ranging from food and beverage industries to environmental monitoring to medical diagnostics [11]-[17].

The chemical sensors used in the electronic nose systems can be classified in the following manner: Metal Oxide Semiconductor (MOS), Metal Oxide Semiconductor Field-Effect Transistor (MOSFET), calorimetric, optical, Quartz Crystal Microbalance (QCM), Surface Acoustic Wave (SAW), conducting polymer, and carbon material composites (carbon nanotubes or carbon black particles) [14][18]-[20].

The carbon material composites sensors, often called volumetric sensors, have a number of features that make them great candidates for the artificial olfaction applications. Among them, one can list a relatively simple structure, ease of fabrication and customization, as well as potential miniaturization that seems perfect for creation of large sensor arrays [21]-[24]. Such sensors are typically composed of two electrodes and an analyte-interactive film capable of changing its volume upon sorption of analytes. The film has to be electrically conductive, which is usually realized by application of either intrinsically conductive materials or composites/blends of conductive particles (e.g., carbon black or zinc oxide) with sorptive, insulating materials [25]-[28]

In our previous work, we presented our basic study on selection and application of GC stationary phase materials as the sorptive (non-conductive) part in odor-sensing composites used in chemosensitive resistor-based odor sensors [29]. An important issue concerning performance of the chemosensitive resistors is a relation between the carbon black content in carbon black–organic polymer composites and resistivity of such composite described by percolation theory [27]. Briefly, the composite is effectively an insulator at low carbon black content. Increasing the amount of carbon black results in decreasing resistivity of the composite, which is gradual until a sharp transition occurs in which the resistivity of the composite can fall dramatically (by up to 10 orders of magnitude) with a small variation in the carbon black concentration. At this transition point, designated as the percolation threshold, a connected pathway of carbon black particles is formed.

In the present work, we focused on two topics important from the standpoint of the ongoing optimization of the composites of GC-material with carbon black particles, namely: (i) evaluation of aging of the fabricated sensitive devices, and (ii) evaluation of the percolation threshold conditions for 16 composite materials described in our basic study.

## II. MATERIALS AND METHODS

The chemosensitive resistors used in this work were 16-channel microdevices fabricated on a p-type Si monocrystalline substrates (8 × 8 mm2). Two platinum electrodes were formed as concentric circles using a photo lithography process. The distance between the electrodes was 50 µm to 280 µm. Schematic representation of the 16-channel device is shown in Figure 1. All devices were fabricated by Panasonic.

The carbon black particles were mixed with the GC materials dissolved in DMSO (Dimethylsulfoxide) or DMSO/MeCN. Concentration of the GC materials in each composite was 10 mg/mL. Concentration of carbon black was 5, 10, 15, 20, 30 and 40 mg/mL.

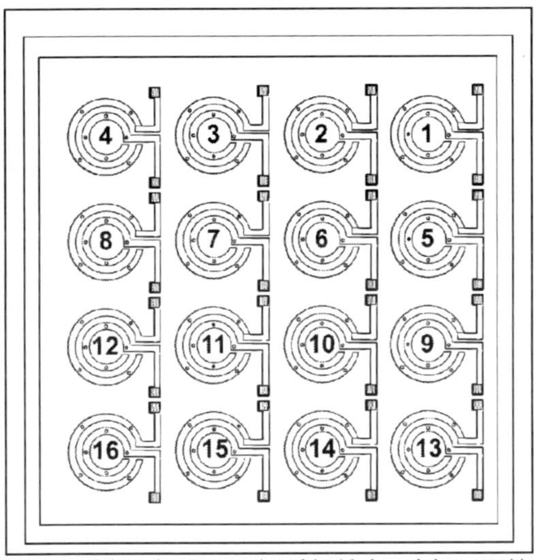


Figure 1. Schematic representation of the 16-channel chemosensitive resistor device used in this study. The numbers refer to Table I.

The GC materials used in this study are listed in Table I. Materials 1, 3 and 11 were obtained from GL Sciences Japan. Materials 2 and 10 were obtained from Tokyo Kasei. Materials 4, 5 7, 8, 9, 12 and 16 were purchased from Sigma Aldrich. Lastly, materials 6, 13, 14 and 15 were obtained from Shimadzu. All materials were used as obtained. Conductive carbon black particles (graphite carbon black) were obtained from Sigma-Aldrich.

The composites were coated as a circle mark using a customized automatic spotting machine with a microsyringe. The volume of the ejected solvents was 25 nL. The ejections were carried out 4 times for each mark. The diameter of a spotted mark was 950 µm while the thickness of the deposited film was typically 700–800 nm.

The fabricated sensors were evaluated in exposure experiments using nonanal, benzaldehyde, 2-phenethylamine, and pyrrole. The samples were purchased from Tokyo Kasei Co. and Sigma-Aldrich and were used as obtained.

The exposure experiments consisted of 60 s exposure to carrier gas, followed by alternating 60 s exposures to analyte vapor and carrier gas (recovery phase). Each sensor was exposed thrice to analytes presented at 4 concentration levels (i.e., total of 12 exposures = 4 concentration levels × 3 exposures at each level).

TABLE I. GC MATERIALS USED IN THE STUDY

| Spot number | GC material | Abbreviation |
|---|---|---|
| 1 | Tetrahydrohyethylenediamine | THEED |
| 2 | N,N-Bis(2-cyanoethyl)formamide | BCEF |
| 3 | LAC-3-R-728 (12% DEGS) | LAC-3 |
| 4 | Diethylene Glycol Succinate | DEGS |
| 5 | Poly(ethylene succinate) | PES |
| 6 | UCON 75-H-90000 | UCON |
| 7 | 1,2,3-Tris(2-cyanoethoxy)propane | TCEP |
| 8 | SP-2330 | SP-3 |
| 9 | SP-2340 | SP-4 |
| 10 | Diglycerol | DI |
| 11 | Reoplex 400 | Re-400 |
| 12 | Poly[di(ethylene glycol)adipate] | PDEGA |
| 13 | Poly(ethylene glycol) 4000 | PEG4k |
| 14 | Poly(ethylene glycol) 20000 | PEG20k |
| 15 | Poly(ethylene glycol) 20M | PEG20M |
| 16 | Free Fatty Acid Phase | FFAP |

## III. Results and Discussion

The chemosensitive resistor sensors were initially evaluated in the exposure experiments carried out within 48h after fabrication. Prior to the evaluation, each fabricated sensing device was first conditioned in the atmosphere of dry nitrogen for 24h. After that, each device was exposed to the odorant samples.

### A. *Aging Effect*

Evaluation of the aging effect was carried out on the basis of the exposure experiments using pyrrole in dry nitrogen, right after fabrication and after 5-month aging. Two characteristics of each sensing element were compared: S/N ratios and responses at 1.8 ppm. The Signal level (S) was calculated as a response to pyrrole at 1 ppm while the Noise level (N) was the response recorded for the carrier gas only. The results are shown in Figure 2.

As can be seen, responses of nearly all sensing elements decreased to some extent after 5-month aging period (exception being the PEG4k composite at channel 13). Interestingly, however, evolution of the S/N ratio values formed quite a different pattern, with a number of materials exhibiting higher values after aging – most apparent in case of UCON, PEG and FFAP materials (channels 6, 13, 14, 15 and 16, respectively).

This ostensible discrepancy is associated with a large decrease of the noise level for those sensing elements and indicates enhanced stability of the coated composite materials after aging. Obviously, such a development would be of a great benefit for the potential application of the studied sensing devices, although further work is required to accurately model the actual evolution of the evaluated characteristics.

### B. *Percolation Threshold*

Evaluation of the percolation threshold was carried out using the sensing devices with the composites composed of GC materials at a constant 10 mg/mL concentration and varying content of the carbon black particles. According to theory, increasing the content of the conducting constituent (carbon black) should result in decreasing resistivity – initially gradual, and very sharp when the percolation threshold is reached. Figure 3 shows the results of the resistance measurements for each sensing composite material with varying content of the carbon black particles. With the exception of PES, all the composites exhibited a dramatic increase of resistivity for the carbon black concentrations in the range of 15-20 mg/mL. Again, theoretically, that dramatic increase indicates formation of the connected pathway of carbon black within the GC material matrix.

In order to validate that claim we measured responses of the sensing devices with carbon black content within 5-20 mg/mL concentration range to odorant samples at ca. 1.8 ppm. The results of those experiments are shown in Figure 4. As can be seen, the highest magnitude of responses was recorded for the composite with the carbon black concentration of 15 mg/mL. That content level has been tentatively assumed as optimal and is being verified in the ongoing experiments.

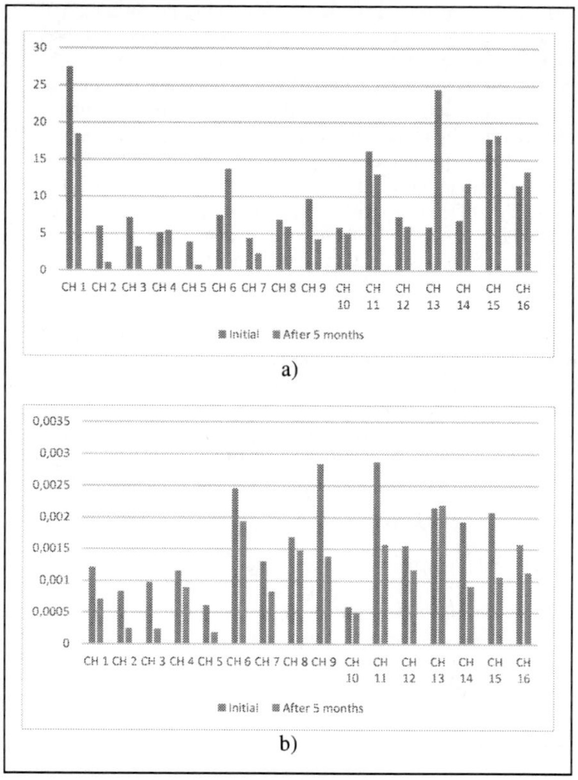


Figure 2. Sensing elements characteristics measured right after fabrication ("initial") and after 5 months of aging at room temperature: (a) S/N Ratio, (b) responses to Pyrrole at ca. 1.8 ppm.

## IV. Conclusion

The present work describes our ongoing study aiming at optimization of the 16-channel chemosensitive resistor devices with composites of GC materials and carbon black particles toward sensing of odorant vapors. We focused on two important factors pertaining to optimization – the percolation threshold and aging. The results obtained so far indicate that in case of composite materials selected in our work, the percolation threshold can be expected for the ratios of carbon black to GC material within the 1.5:1 to 2:1 range. The initial validation of those values by means of exposure to the odorant samples indicated that the best sensing characteristics can be expected for the ratio of ca. 1.5:1. The results of the exposure experiments performed within 48h and 5 months after fabrication of the sensing devices indicate that the aging effect can be of two-fold nature – the decrease of the sensor response magnitude accompanied by a slight to significant enhancement of the S/N ratio, most likely associated with the enhanced stability of the composites. The studies are being continued and their results will be presented in the future.

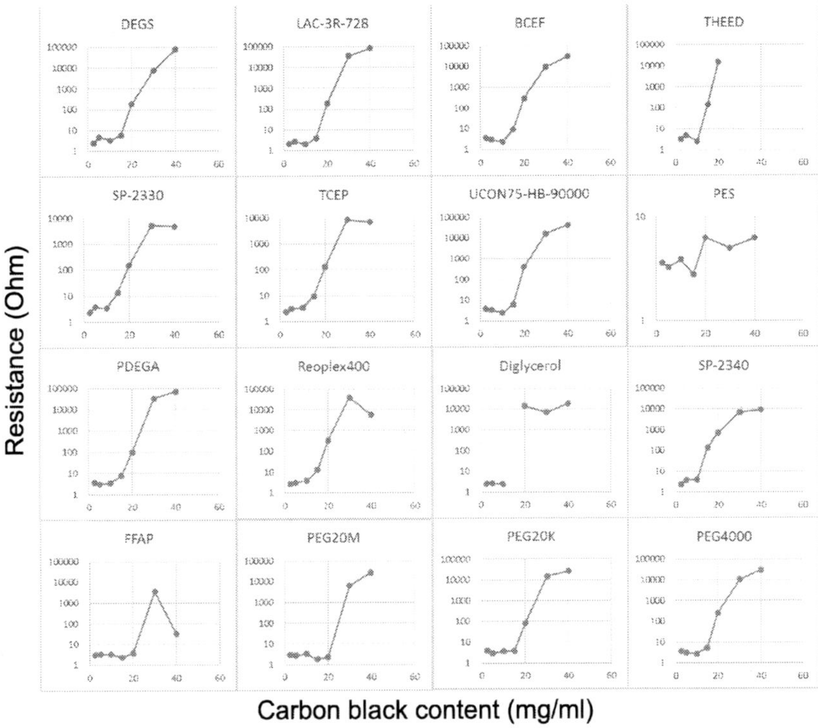


Figure 3. Resistance of the 16 composite materials versus their carbon black content. Evaluation of percolation threshold.

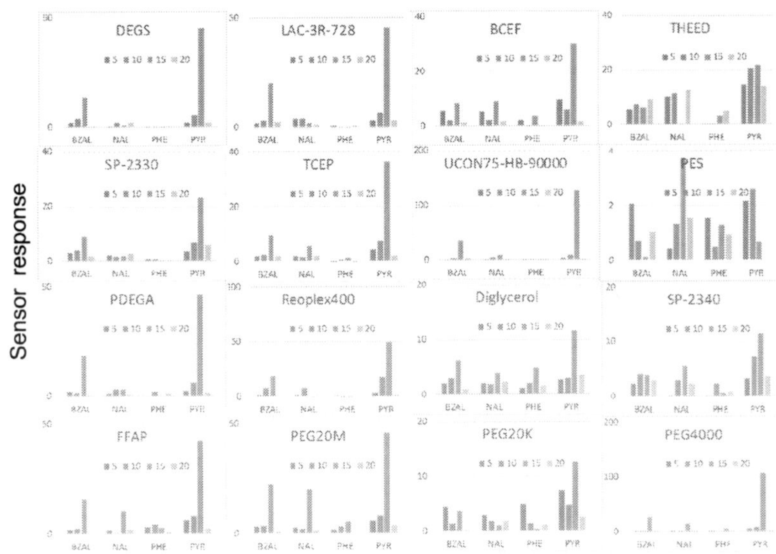


Figure 4. Responses of the sensing elements with various carbon black contents to odorant samples at ca. 1.8 ppm (carrier gas: dry nitrogen).

ACKNOWLEDGMENT

This work was funded by ImPACT Program of Council for Science, Technology and Innovation (Cabinet Office, Government of Japan).

REFERENCES

[1] S. Firestein, "How the olfactory system makes sense of smells," Nature, no. 413, pp. 211–218, 2001.

[2] H. Steinhart, A. Stephan, and M. Bücking, "Advances in flavor research," J. High Resolut. Chromatogr., no. 23, pp. 489–496, 2000.

[3] L. M. Reid, C. P. O'Donnell, and G. Downey, "Recent technological advances for the determination of food authenticity," Trends Food Sci. Technol., no. 17, pp. 344–353, 2006.

[4] K. Persaud and G. Dodd, "Analysis of discrimination mechanisms in the mammalian olfactory system using a model nose," Nature, no. 299, pp. 352–355, 1982.

[5] J. W. Gardner and P. N. Bartlet, "A brief history of electronic noses," Sens. Actuators B, no. 18, pp. 210–211, 1984.

[6] H. T. Nagle, R. Gutierrez-Osuna, and S. S. Schiffman, "The how and why of electronic noses," IEEE Spectr., no. 9, pp. 22–31, 1988.

[7] W. R. Dillon and M. Goldstein, "Multivariate Analysis," Wiley: Hoboken, NJ, USA, 1984.

[8] R. O. Duda, P. E. Hart, and D. G. Stork, "Pattern Classification," Wiley: Hoboken, NJ, USA, 2000.

[9] P. C. Jurs, G. A. Bakken, and H. E. McClelland, "Computational methods for the analysis of chemical sensor array data from volatile analytes," Chem. Rev., no. 100, pp. 2649–2678, 2000.

[10] E. L. Hines, E. Llobet, and J. W. Gardner, "Electronic noses: A review of signal processing techniques," IEEE Proc. Circ. Dev. Syst., no. 146, pp. 297–310, 1999.

[11] S. Chiu and K. Tang, "Towards a Chemiresistive Sensor-Integrated Electronic Nose: A Review," Sensors, no. 13, 14214–14247, 2013.

[12] A. Loutfia et al., "Electronic noses for food quality: A review," J. Food Eng., no. 144, pp. 103–111, 2015.

[13] T. Dymerski et al., "Application of an Electronic Nose Instrument to Fast Classification of Polish Honey Types," Sensors, no. 14, pp. 10709–10724, 2014.

[14] S. Kiani, S. Minaei, and M. Ghasemi-Varnamkhasti, "Application of electronic nose systems for assessing quality of medicinal and aromatic plant products: A review," J. Appl. Res. Med. Aromat. Plants, no. 3, pp. 1–9, 2016.

[15] S. Deshmukh et al., "Application of electronic nose for industrial odors and gaseous emissions measurement and monitoring—An overview. Talanta 2015, 144, 329–340.

[16] A. D. Wilson, "Advances in Electronic-Nose Technologies for the Detection of Volatile Biomarker Metabolites in the Human Breath," Metabolites, no. 5, pp. 140–163, 2015.

[17] Y. Adiguzel and H. Kulah, "Breath sensors for lung cancer diagnosis," Biosens. Bioelectron., no. 65, pp. 121–138, 2015.

[18] H. Nanto and J. R. Stetter, "Introduction to Chemosensors. In Handbook of Machine Olfaction," T. C. Pearce, S. S. Schiffman, H. Troy Nagle, and J. W. Gardner, Eds.; Wiley-VCH: Weinheim, Germany, pp. 79–104, 2003.

[19] A. D. Wilson and M. Baietto, "Applications and Advances in Electronic-Nose Technologies," Sensors, no. 9, pp. 5099–5148, 2009.

[20] A. D. Wilson, "Recent progress in the design and clinical development of electronic-nose technologies," Nanobiosensors Dis. Diagn., no. 5, pp. 15–27, 2016.

[21] J. W. Grate and B. M. Wise, "A method for chemometric classification of unknown vapors from the responses of an array of volume-transducing sensors," Anal. Chem., no. 73, pp. 2239–2244, 2001.

[22] F. K. Che Harun et al., "An electronic nose employing dual-channel odour separation columns with large chemosensor array for advanced odour discrimination," Sens. Actuators B, no. 141, pp. 134–140, 2009.

[23] M. Bernabei et al., "Large-Scale Chemical Sensor Array Testing Biological Olfaction Concepts," IEEE Sens. J., no. 12, pp. 3174–3183, 2012.

[24] S. Marco et al., "A biomimetic approach to machine olfaction, featuring a very large-scale chemical sensor array and embedded neuro-bio-inspired computation," Microsyst. Technol., no. 20, pp. 729–742, 2014.

[25] H. Bai and G. Shi, "Gas sensors based on conducting polymers," Sensors, no. 7, pp. 267–307, 2007.

[26] S. Unde, J. Ganu, and S. Radhakrishnan, "Conducting polymer-based chemical sensor: Characteristics and evaluation of polyaniline composite films," Adv. Mater. Opt. Electron., no. 6, pp. 151–157, 1996.

[27] E. Llobet, "Gas sensors using carbon nanomaterials: A review," Sens. Actuators B, no. 179, pp. 32–45, 2013.

[28] M. C. Lonergan et al., "Array-Based Vapor Sensing Using Chemically Sensitive, Carbon Black–Polymer Resistors," Chem. Mater., no. 8, pp. 2298–2312, 1996.

[29] B. Wyszynski et al., "Array of Chemosensitive Resistors with Composites of Gas Chromatography (GC) Materials and Carbon Black for Detection and Recognition of VOCs: A Basic Study," Sensors, no. 17, pp. 1606-1625, 2017.

# Ultra-Violet Assisted ZnO Nanocrystals for $NO_2$ Sensing at Room Temperature

Sandrine Bernardini [1], Mohamed Hameda Benchekroun [1], Khalifa Aguir [1]
Aix Marseille Univ, Univ Toulon, CNRS, IM2NP, Marseille, France
e-mail: sandrine.bernardini@im2np.fr
e-mail: hameda.benchekroun1993@gmail.com
e-mail: khalifa.aguir@im2np.fr

Meriem Gaceur [2], Olivier Margeat [2], Jörg Ackermann [2], Christine Videlot-Ackermann [2]
Aix Marseille Univ, CNRS UMR 7325, CINaM, Marseille, France
e-mail: gaceur@gmail.com
e-mail: olivier.margeat@univ-amu.fr
e-mail: ackermann@cinam.univ-mrs.fr
e-mail: videlot@cinam.univ-mrs.fr

*Abstract*—**In this paper, we focus on nitrogen dioxide detection at room temperature to avoid thermal degradation on flexible substrates. We propose nitrogen dioxide detection at room temperature by zinc oxide nanocrystals deposited on rigid substrate by spin coating from colloidal solution as sensitive layer for air quality monitoring. We investigated gas sensing properties at low post-annealed temperature and under continuous Ultra-Violet illumination for working at room temperature with a process compatible with flexible substrates.**

***Keywords-Nitrogen dioxide; Room-temperature; UV-photoactivated; ZnO nanocrystal; environment.***

## I. INTRODUCTION

Nitrogen Oxides (NO) are produced by petrol or diesel burning engines and coil/oil furnaces. NO is a poisonous, odourless, colourless gas. Once it is mixed with air, it quickly combines forming nitrogen dioxides ($NO_2$), which is highly toxic, reddish brown gas with a very pungent odour. $NO_2$ is a major component of the outdoor air pollution. The need for air quality monitoring demands the development of NOx sensitive sensors under 3 ppm [1]. The Metal OXide gas sensors (MOX) are propitious due to their high sensitivity at a low cost process. Among MOX, Zinc Oxide (ZnO) based materials have shown outstanding electrical, chemical and sensory characteristics [2]. We aimed to fabricate MOX sensors on flexible substrate to fit shapes on a smart object for $NO_2$ monitoring. However, most of flexible substrates do not resist to temperature higher than 120 °C. Previous studies have shown detection under ozone gas as low as 35 ppb [3] and depending on filter nature, $O_3$ can be totally trapped while $NO_2$ can pass over a specific concentration range [4]. In this study, our main purpose was to point out that, using continuous Ultra-Violet (UV) light on the ZnO NanoCrystals (NCs), the sensing responses at room temperature are also enhanced for $NO_2$ detection.

In Section II, the sensor fabrication will be detailed and the results will be discussed in Section III. We conclude the paper in Section IV.

## II. DECRIPTION OF APPROACH AND TECHNIQUES

This description is composed of two parts: one is the sensing film fabrication; the other is the measurement system set-up.

### *A. Gas sensors*

Our gas sensor consists of Ti/Pt interdigitated electrodes (5 and 100 nm, respectively) deposited on $Si/SiO_2$ by magnetron sputtering. Figure 1(a) shows two solutions based on ZnO NCs with a diameter of about 5 nm: one named S1 without EthanolAmine (EA) with a milky white aspect indicating the presence of agglomerates [4] and the second one named S2 with EA with a transparent aspect. These solutions (S1 and S2) were deposited by spin coating on rigid substrates during 30s at 2000 rpm/min. Figure 1(b) presents an optical images of a sensor based on ZnO NCs at 30 mg/mL with 0.2 vol.% of EA.

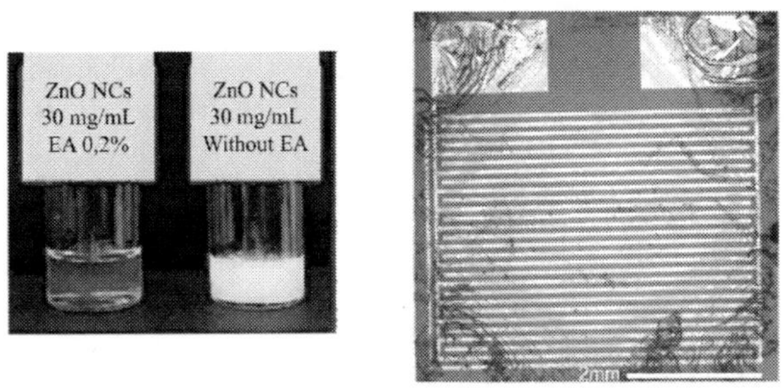


(a) (b)

Figure 1. (a) Optical images of solutions based on ZnO NCs in isopropanol at 30 mg/mL with or without 0.2 vol.% of EA. (b) Sample image with ZnO NC 30 mg/mL with EA after a post annealing at 80°C.

Previous studies have shown that 0.2% volume of EA, a short-chain surfactant, gives aggregate-free solutions [5]. After mixing ZnO NCs with 0.2 vol.% of EA in isopropanol, the EA molecules spontaneously graft on the surface of ZnO NCs and enhance the particles solubility.

The small sized nanocrystals to form sensing thin films is beneficial for the surface-area-to-volume ratio to adsorb gas molecules. To be compatible with a flexible substrate, a low post-annealing temperature (80 °C) was done for 30 min.

*B. Setup*

0.1 V DC voltage was applied to the sample while the electrical resistance was monitored using a Keithley Model 2450 SourceMeter Source Measure Unit (SMU) Instrument (Keithley, U.S.A.). Dry air was used as both the reference and the carrier gas (it means no humidity RH = 0%). A constant total flow was maintained at 500 Standard Cubic Centimeters per Minute (SCCM) via mass flow controllers. In order to find the best operating conditions, the gas detections were carried out in a closed chamber under 30 s exposures to $NO_2$ by measuring the resistance through the sensitive material in dark and temperature excitations (up to 300°C) or using UV light ($\lambda$ = 325 nm) at room temperature. We used a Light-Emitting Diode (LED) for UV illumination situated at 10 mm from the sensing material to obtain more photo generated charge carriers.

## III. RESULTS AND DISCUSSIONS

We prepared two different sensitive layers with resulting layer thicknesses measured by a contact profilometer Dektak XTS (Bruker, Germany) equipped with a stylus of 2 µm radius. The sensitive layer without EA deposited by spin coating is around 80 nm thick. The sensitive layer with EA realized by spin-coating at the same speed (2000 rpm/min during 30 s) is around 50 nm. The gas response is defined in (1) as the ratio of the resistance change on the surface of the gas sensor before and after being exposed to $NO_2$:

$$R = R_{NO2}/ R_a \quad (1)$$

where $R_a$ is the sensor resistance through dry airflow and $R_{NO2}$ the sensor resistance in presence of $NO_2$.

Figure 2 presents sensor responses of thin film obtained with solution S2 and post annealed at 300°C to test working temperatures up to 275°C. The sensors were exposed 30 s to 2 ppm of $NO_2$ in dark for four working temperatures: 25°C, 100°C, 200°C and 275°C.

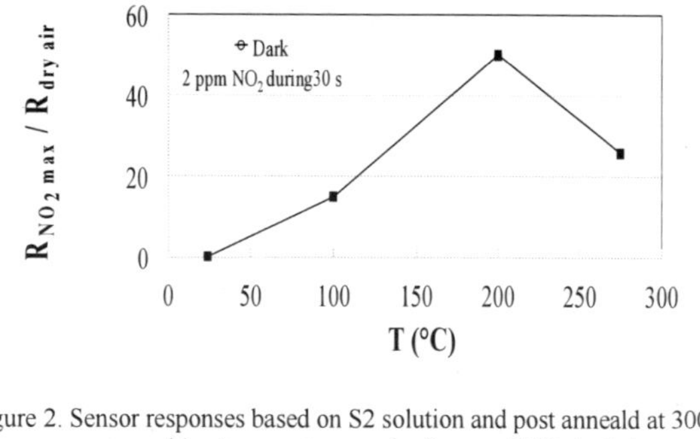


Figure 2. Sensor responses based on S2 solution and post anneald at 300°C versus working temperatures under 2 ppm of $NO_2$ in dark.

This result indicates no resistance variation at room temperature in dark and an optimum working temperature obtained at 200°C. It confirms that sensors based on ZnO NCs as most MOX sensors need a high operating temperature to enable the adsorption and desorption process. This is also in agreement with our previous studies and this optimum is lower than for ozone detection found around 300°C in dark [3][6]. To be able to work at room temperature, a continuous UV illumination is needed. Figure 3 shows the sensors responses for four concentrations under continuous UV light at 25°C.

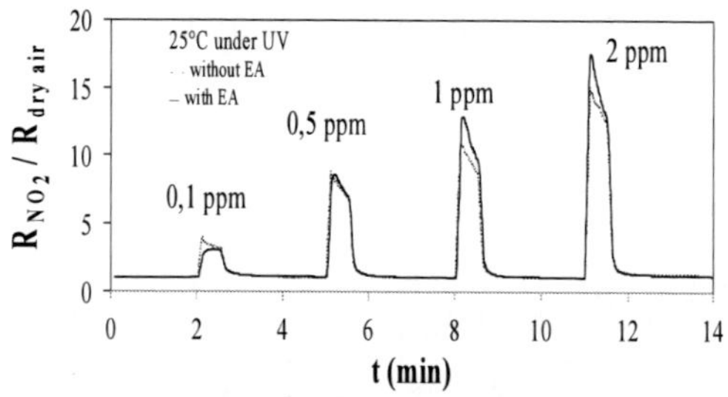


Figure 3. Sensor responses at 25°C of ZnO Ncs thin films, with or without EA, post annealed at 80°C versus $NO_2$ concentrations under UV light and dry air flow (RH = 0%).

The sensors behaviors were in the same order of magnitude.

## IV. CONCLUSION AND FUTURE WORK

This work reported an ambient temperature way to detect $NO_2$ molecules by sensors based on ZnO NCs thin films. It opens a new way to develop $NO_2$ sensors on flexible substrate. For next studies, ZnO NCs sensors will be processed on flexible substrate and tested in presence of various gases at room temperature assisted by light activation.

## ACKNOWLEDGMENT

The authors thank Mr. A. Combes for his technical support.

## REFERENCES

[1] http://www.inrs.fr/dms/ficheTox/FicheFicheTox/FICHETOX_133-4/FicheToxSynthetique_133.pdf, 2018.03.12

[2] V. A. Coleman and C. Jagadish, Chapter 1 - Basic Properties and Applications of ZnO, in: Zinc Oxide Bulk Thin Films Nanostructures, Elsevier Science Ltd, Oxford, 2006: pp. 1–20, doi:10.1016/B978-008044722-3/50001-4.

[3] S. Bernardini, et al., Ozone Sensors Working at Room Temperature Using Zinc Oxide Nanocrystals Annealed at Low Temperature, Proceeding of Eurosensors 2017, 1 , 2017, pp. 423-428. doi:10.3390/proceedings1040423.

[4] M. Othman, et al., Selective Detection of NO2 with Specific Filters for O3 Trapping, Proceeding of Eurosensors, 1 , 2017, pp. 405-409. doi:10.3390/proceedings1040405.

[5] A. K. Diallo, et al., Impact of surfactants covering ZnO nanoparticles on solution-processed field-effect transistors: From dispersion state to solid state, Colloids Surf. Physicochem. Eng. Asp. 500, 2016, pp. 214–221, doi:10.1016/j.colsurfa.2016.04.036.

[6] M. Acuautla, et al., Ozone flexible sensors fabricated by photolithography and laser ablation processes based on ZnO nanoparticles, Sens. Actuators B Chem. 203, 2014, pp. 602–611, doi:10.1016/j.snb.2014.07.010.

# Humidity Impact Reduction on $WO_3$ Gas Microsensor Response Using New Filters Based on Ionic Liquid

Alexandre Favard[1], Jean-Luc Seguin[1], Khalifa Aguir[1], Marc Bendahan[1],
[1]Aix Marseille Univ, Université de Toulon, CNRS, IM2NP, Marseille, France,
e-mail: alexandre.favard@im2np.fr
e-mail: jean-luc.seguin@im2np.fr
e-mail: khalifa.aguir@im2np.fr
e-mail: marc.bendahan@im2np.fr

Xueru Yan[2], Stéphane Anguille[2], Philippe Moulin[2],
[2]Aix Marseille Univ, CNRS, Cent Marseille, M2P2, Marseille, France, UMR 7340, Equipe Procédés Membranaires (EPM), Europôle de l'Arbois, BP80, 13545 Aix en Provence Cedex, France
e-mail: xueru.yan@centrale-marseille.fr
e-mail: stephane.anguille@univ-amu.fr
e-mail: philippe.moulin@univ-amu.fr

*Abstract*— **The detection of gaseous pollutants such as Benzene, Toluene, Ethylbenzene and Xylene (BTEX) under real conditions requires working in a humid environment. It is well known that the humidity reduces the performances of gas sensors, particularly in terms of sensitivity. Using a filter based on an ionic liquid (IL), low concentrations of BTEX can be detected with a tungsten trioxide ($WO_3$) thin film (50 nm) deposited by reactive radio frequency (RF) magnetron sputtering on a transducer which has developed in IM2NP laboratory. With this absorption upstream, we are able to detect 500 ppb of BTEX gases without a sensor sensitivity decrease with 50% relative humidity in the inlet feed.**

***Keywords - gas sensor; humidity removal; tungsten trioxide; ionic liquid based filter.***

## I. INTRODUCTION

Air quality monitoring has become an important health and societal issue. Benzene, Toluene, Ethylbenzene and Xylenes (BTEX gases) are among the targeted VOCs (Volatile Organic Compounds). It is well known that relative humidity is an important factor influencing the performance of metal oxide gas sensors, especially in terms of sensitivity [1]. In this work, we demonstrated the possibility to detect low BTEX concentration (500ppb) with 50% relative humidity in the inlet feed, without loss of the sensor sensitivity, using a $WO_3$ gas sensor with an ionic liquid (IL) based filter upstream. We also demonstrated that the ionic liquid only captures the humidity in air and does not affect the sensor response.

In Section II, we describe the $WO_3$ microsensor, the test bench and the IL filter. In Section III, we present and comment experimental results showing the effect of the IL filter on the detection of low BTEX concentration under 50% relative humidity.

## II. MATERIAL AND METHODS

### *A. Microsensor design and sensitive layer*

Our device is composed of an integrated Pt heater and Pt electrodes for the measurements, deposited by sputtering on a $Si/SiO_2$ substrate (Fig.1) [2]. The sensitive layer of tungsten trioxide (50 nm) was deposited on the top of these electrodes, by reactive RF magnetron sputtering. Then, the device was annealed at 723K during two hours in order to stabilize the crystallinity of the sensitive layer.

The tungsten trioxide ($WO_3$) is a n-type metal oxide with a large gap and oxygen vacancies. The conductivity of this oxide depends on the composition of the surrounding gas atmosphere [3].

During all our studies, we used an operating temperature of 513 K. The electrical measurements were made under a constant gas flow of 100 sccm.

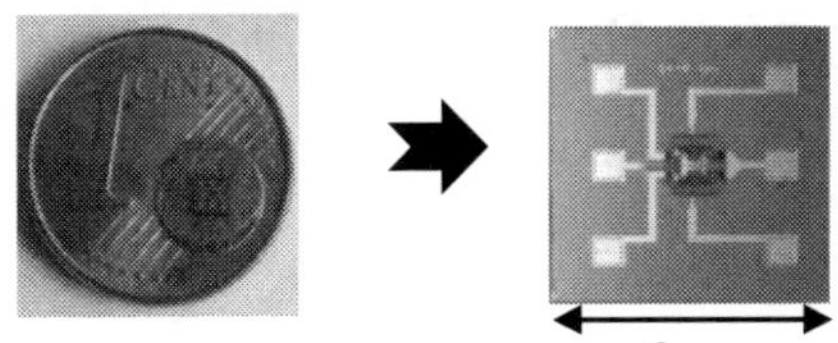


Figure 1. Design of the sensor device [2]

### *B. Test bench for electrical characterization under BTEX gases and humidity*

We used a test bench specially designed for the BTEX detection in the presence of different humidity levels. It is composed of a gas dilution and humidification system that generates an output mixture at very low concentrations (1 to 500 ppb) with a variable humidity (0 to 90%), an integrated test cell and an acquisition system to characterize the electrical responses of the gas microsensor (Fig.2).

Humidity is generated starting from pressurized liquid water, which is vaporized through a microporous membrane. The water vapor is injected into the dry gas mixture by means of a proportional valve. This valve, controlled by a humidity sensor placed at the humidifier outlet, makes it possible to keep the hygrometry of the mixture constant. The vapor pressure is kept sufficient by heating and regulating the temperature of the vaporization cell. A second humidity sensor is placed at the output of the filter.

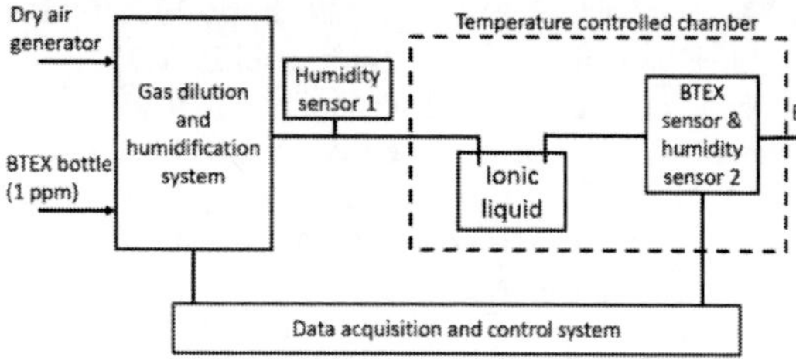


Figure 2. Diagram of the test bench.

### C. *Ionic liquid based filter*

Ionic Liquids are classified like polar solvents and they have attractive properties such as low vapor pressure, thermal stability or selective solubility [4]. The innovation of this filter is to adsorb the water molecules in the atmosphere without capturing the BTEX gas molecules [5]. The 1-Butyl-3-methylimidazolium bromide (bmimBr) has been chosen for its great hygroscopic property. In order to eliminate the influence of a solid matrix or any other form of support, the filter is made by bubbling the gas mixture into a glass container filled with the IL.

## III. RESULTS AND DISCUSION

### A. *Influence of wet air on sensor response to BTEX*

To study the humidity influence on the sensor response, we exposed our sensor to 500 ppb of BTEX for 4 minutes (Fig. 3) under dry air and wet air (50% RH). The sensor response was calculated using the relation (1):

$$Sensor\ response\ (\%) = \left(\frac{R_{air} - R_{gas}}{R_{gas}}\right) * 100 \qquad (1)$$

with $R_{air}$, the sensor resistance in air before gas exposure and $R_{gas}$, the sensor resistance in presence of BTEX.

Under dry air, the sensor response to 500 ppb of BTEX is 24%. The introduction of 50% of relative humidity in the atmosphere reduces the sensor response to 12%. The sensor response is divided by 2 under 50% of relative humidity.

This behavior is well known and has been already reported in the literature. Several hypotheses have been made about this behavior [6]. Firstly, the adsorption of the water molecules leads to a decrease in the chemical adsorption of the oxygen species on the surface of the metal oxide [7]. Secondly, The BTEX molecules compete with the water molecules to react on the same adsorption sites [8]. In both cases, the introduction of relative humidity in the atmosphere leads to a decrease of the sensor response.

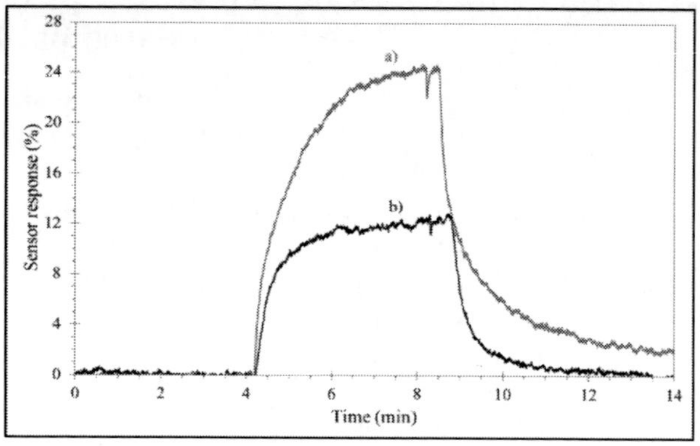


Figure 3. Sensors response under 500 ppb of BTEX, a) Dry air (0%), b) wet air (50%)

### B. *Influence of ionic liquid based filter on sensor response to BTEX under wet air*

To reduce the humidity influence on the sensor response, we placed the IL filter upstream to the sensor and we exposed the sensor to 500 ppb of BTEX for 4 minutes (Fig. 4) under wet air (50% RH). In Figure 4, we can observe that when the IL filter is placed upstream the sensor, the response to 500 ppb of BTEX remains 25%. Hence, with this filter, we keep the BTEX detection performance of our sensor, even in presence of 50% of relative humidity in the atmosphere.

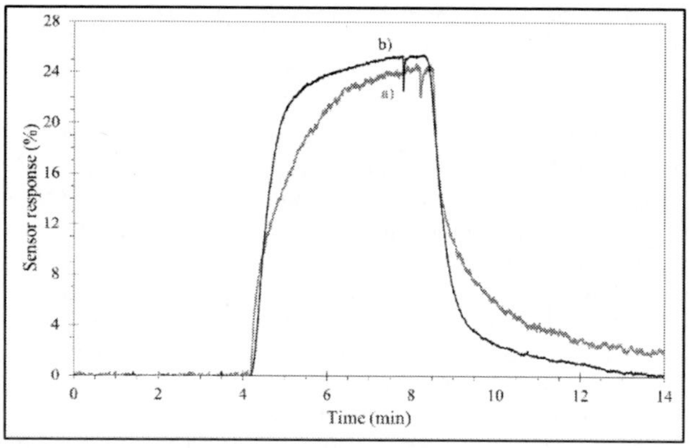


Figure 4. Sensors response under 500 ppb of BTEX, a) Dry air (0%), b) wet air (50%) with ionic liquid filter

The main objective of this work being to validate the filter ability to trap water vapor, we first chose to work with a 50% humidity rate which is considered as a good reference for gas sensors tests. Now that we have shown the performance of this type of filter, it will be interesting to study, in future experiments, the variation of operating conditions as higher humidity levels, different flow rate or BTEX concentration. This will help to understand at which humidity the sensor response significantly declines.

Furthermore, Figure 4 shows that the response of the BTEX sensor with the filter inserted into the gas flow is slightly higher and has a larger slope compared to the response under dry air. This behavior is reproducible. It may be related to the high viscosity of the ionic liquid, which causes pressure and flow rate variations at the gas sensor. Further experiments are needed to validate this hypothesis.

## IV. CONCLUSION

In this work, we proposed a new solution to protect metal oxide gas sensors from the influence of humidity. We show the possibility to detect low BTEX concentrations under wet air with a $WO_3$ gas sensor associated with a filter based on an ionic liquid. We also demonstrated that the ionic liquid did not disturb the BTEX detection.

Further work is in progress to study the behavior of the IL filter under high humidity and to insert the IL into a solid matrix to make a more convenient filter [5].

## ACKNOWLEDGMENT

The authors would like to acknowledge Mr. A. Combes for his technical support throughout this work.

## REFERENCES


[1] C. Wang, L. Yin, L. Zhang, D. Xiang, and R. Gao, "Metal Oxide Gas Sensors: Sensitivity and Influencing Factors", Sensors vol 10, 2010, pp. 2088–2106.

[2] K. Aguir, M. Bendahan, and V. Laithier, "Heated sensitive layer gas sensor", patent N° FR 13 59494, 2013, international extension in 2016.

[3] J. Guérin, K. Aguir, and M. Bendahan, "Modeling of the conduction in a $WO_3$ thin film as ozone sensor", Sensors and Actuators B 119, 2006, pp. 327–334.

[4] P. Warssercheid and T. Welton (Eds.), "Ionic Liquid in Synthesis", WILEY-VCH, 2003.

[5] S. Anguille, F. Testa, and P. Moulin, "Device for extraction of pollutants by multichannel tubular membrane", EP 14306002.8, 2016, EP2015/064462.

[6] A. Favard, T. Contaret, K. Aguir, A. Dumas, and M. Bendahan, "Highly Sensitive $WO_3$ Thin Films Integrated on Microsensor Platforms for ppb BTEX Detection in a Gas Mixture with High Rate of Humidity", Proceeding IEEE Sensor 2017, pp.1314-1316.

[7] Q. Qi, T. Zhang, X. Zheng, H. Fan, L. Liu, R. Wang, and Y. Zeng, "Electrical response of $Sm_2O_3$-doped $SnO_2$ to $C_2H_2$ and effect of humidity interference", Sensors and Actuators B 134, 2008, pp. 36–42.

[8] R. Ionescu, A. Vancu, C. Moise, and A. Tomescu, "Role of water vapour in the interaction of $SnO_2$ gas sensors with CO and $CH_4$", Sensors and Actuators B 61, 1999, pp. 39–42.

# Accuracy and Predictability Analysis of a Highly Sensitive Liquid Level Prediction Setup

Mehmet Emre Erdem
Mechanical Engineering Department
Istanbul Bilgi University
Istanbul,Turkey
e-mail: emre.erdem@bilgi.edu.tr

***Abstract*— Liquid level measurements play a major role in many industrial applications, where different physical principles have been used and tested by many researchers. Whispering Gallery Mode (WGM) theory indicates major accomplishments in a diverse area of interest where sensitivity is of utmost importance. This study is focusing on the accuracy and predictability analysis of such liquid level prediction experiments, using WGM sensor technology, indicating a dependence of WGM shifts on liquid levels, which have been assumed as perfectly linear in all the measurement ranges.**

***Keywords- accuracy; error; uncertainty; sensor; laser optics; liquid level sensor; Whispering Gallery Mode (WGM).***

## I. Introduction

Level sensors are used in automotive [8] and industrial applications [13] to gather or send valuable information to ensure that the level (of the engine oil in our case) does not become dangerously low or high without being noticed. The sensor monitors the oil level continuously during the entire engine operation. Secondary influences, such as the slope of the vehicle's lateral and longitudinal accelerations are compensated by the vehicle control unit calculating a mean value [2][8].

While searching for methods to detect the liquid levels accurately, a new laser optics sensor technology [3]-[5], based on the previously demonstrated Whispering Gallery Mode phenomenon [1] has been observed, pointing superb sensitivity over the experimental range, and finally used in our experiments for the detection of liquid levels. The experimental outcomes obtained are further processed, and the accuracy and uncertainty analysis of these liquid level prediction measurements are presented in Section 3. The results showed a linear dependence within the experimental range, and uncertainty calculations are shown in this section as well. Finally, in Section 4, general conclusions are given according to the experimental results, for the benefit of future studies.

## II. Experimental Design for the Level Measuremetns

In the Whispering Gallery Mode theory, developed by John William Strutt (Lord Rayleigh) [11], where light undergoes total internal reflection, and because it is trapped inside the sphere, WGMs are observed under certain conditions. The details of the theory, and verification of the existence of a strong relation between changes in WGM resonance shifts and force applied to a micro optical-sphere was presented by Ioppolo et al. [3]-[5]. The theory is based on a phase delay occurring during light travel inside a microsphere [11].

Figure 1 presents the experiment setup in the laboratory. The light coming from the laser goes inside the microsphere, where the measurements are exactly taken [3]-[5].

The microsphere inside the sensor, is directly in contact with the fiber optics, and works as an input and output channel for the information, while facilitating a light coupling between fiber and resonator (see Figures 2-4). This light coupling creates resonances in return signal according to the Whispering Gallery phenomenon [1]. Tracking the changes and shifts of these resonances demonstrates the basics of this new laser optics sensing technology [3]-[5] we have used in our measurements.

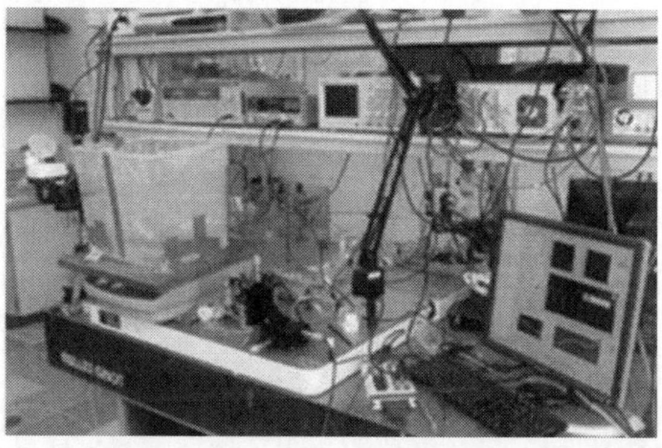

Figure 1. The experimental setup used having the sensor located inside the water container, and a pressure transducer for reference measurements [2]. WGM measurements are obtained by an inhouse software [3]-[5].

A computer controlled software both the tunes the frequency of the laser and records the shifts in the return signal resonances [3]-[5]. This technology has been used to detect the liquid levels accurately.

For the liquid level detection setup, a new sensing cell has been developed to measure the pressure changes of the medium filled with water. The initial design of the sensing cell can be seen in Figure 2, where the microsphere [6][7] sensing element is completely separated from the test medium by using an elastic membrane. The membrane is able to transfer the pressure changes precisely, while keeping the liquid outside. Actual sensing cell design used in the experiments having the micro resonator [6][7] in the form of a sphere can be seen in Figures 3 and 4.

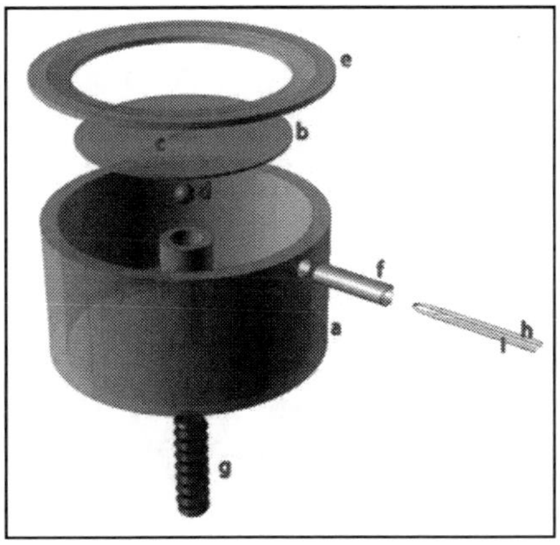


Figure 2. Initial design of the sensing cell is shown. Sensor Case(a); Latex membrane(b); Metal Boss(c); PDMS Microsphere(d); Upper cover(e); Fiber Protector(f); Screw Mechanism for leveling the microsphere(g); Optical Fiber Input(h); Optical Fiber Output(i) [2]

Figure 3. Actual Sensing cell includes: a membrane for force detection, Microsphere[3]-[5] being the sensing element inside, and Optical Fibers for data transfer[3]-[5].

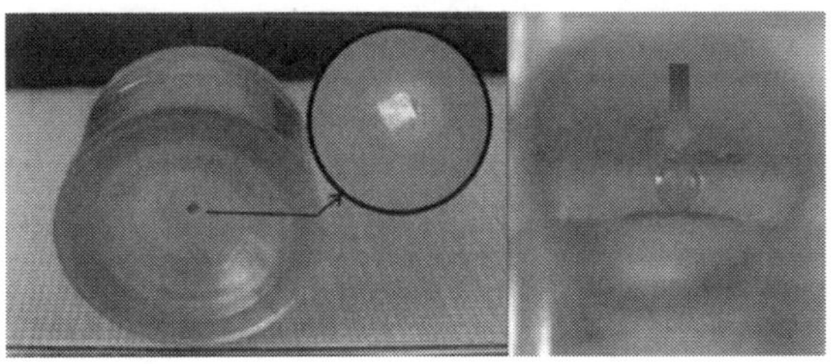

Figure 4. Metal boss added to the membrane for greater sensitivity (a) The microsphere touching metal boss (b).

As shown in Figure 3, the microsphere is in contact with the fiber outlets facilitating a light coupling, while still being able to sense the pressure changes of the medium which is being transferred by the elastic membrane. Figure 4 shows fine tuning over the actual design, where a tiny metal boss touching the microsphere, added to the membrane for greater sensitivity to transfer the pressure changes more rigidly over the microsphere.

This sensing cell is designed to be used inside liquid, therefore the experiments have been able to performed under water, shown in Figure 5. The target is to detect and track the liquid level changes, as it increases or decreases the liquid pressures according to Bernoulli's principle. A pressure transducer has also been used as the reference device, connected to the container through a U tube, tracking the changes of the pressure, in other terms the changes of the liquid levels.

## III. EXPERIMENTAL RESULTS

An experimental setup is built to measure the pressure changes of the medium, detecting the changes of the liquid height, as stated previously (see Figures 1-5) [2].

### *A. Liquid Level Measurement Results*

The liquid level measurements have been performed while filling and draining water from the container – this will be called the experiment setup from now on. The red line in Figures 6 and 8 indicates the measurements taken from a reference pressure transducer [2].

In Figure 5, the experiment setup for measuring the liquid levels can be seen in detail, where the sensing cell is located inside the bottom of the liquid container design. The sensing cell is specifically designed to have a deflectable membrane to transfer the force/pressure changes into the sensing software [3]-[5] without letting the liquid enter inside the cell (see Figures 2-4). Figure 5 shows the experiment setup for liquid level detection in greater detail.

When the liquid level increases, it also increases the pressure in the U tube connected to the pressure transducer, which results and increase in its signal. Also, when draining water, the pressure in connection tube decreases, resulting in a decrease in the Pressure Transducer signal.

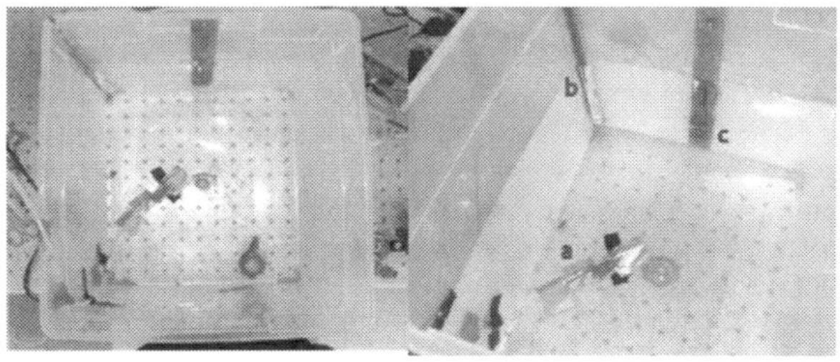


Figure 5. Water pressure change experiments (left), (a) Liquid inlet and outlet, (b) Presure Transducer connection, (c) Scaled Ruler for instant Level Readings (right).

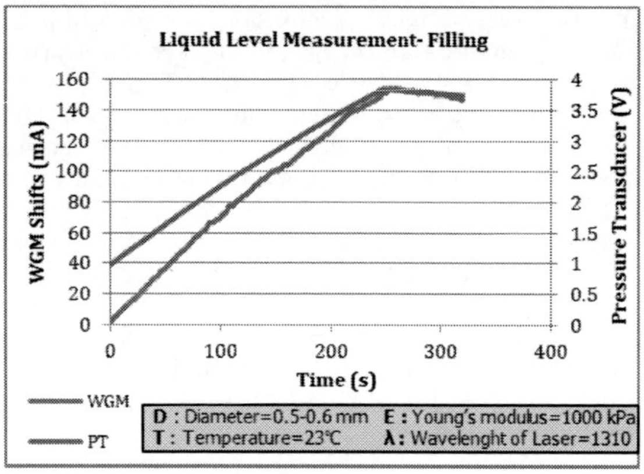


Figure 6. Liquid Level Measurements-Fillling

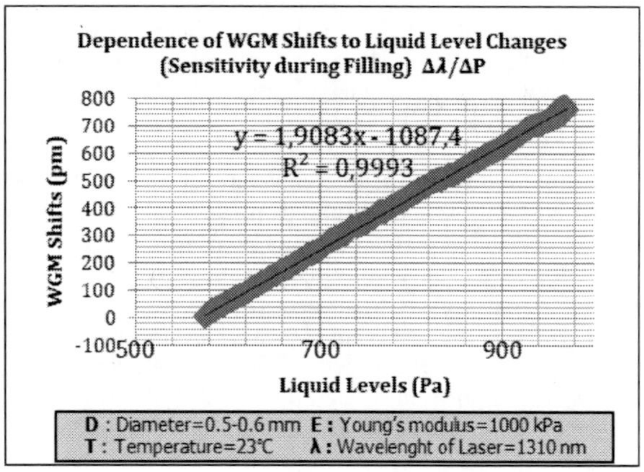


Figure 7. The Dependence of WGM shifts to Liquid Pressure changes (Pa)

The liquid levels have been converted to Pa with the basic conversion ratio of 1mm H2O=9.8065 Pa.

The WGM resonance shifts as a function of applied pressure is plotted in Figure 7, where these resonance shifts demonstrate a linear response with nearly no hysteresis in the pressure range tested, thus, providing a reliable pressure reading essential for sensor performance.

The best sensitivity dependence has been observed while draining water from the setup, as expected, due to the smoother level change characteristics of draining. Therefore, the dependence of shifts to liquid levels changes is better, in other words, higher sensitivities have been obtained while draining water from the experiment setup.

The red line in Figure 6 and Figure 8 represents the pressure transducer output, while the blue line represents the WGM resonance shifts developed in the setup [2][4].

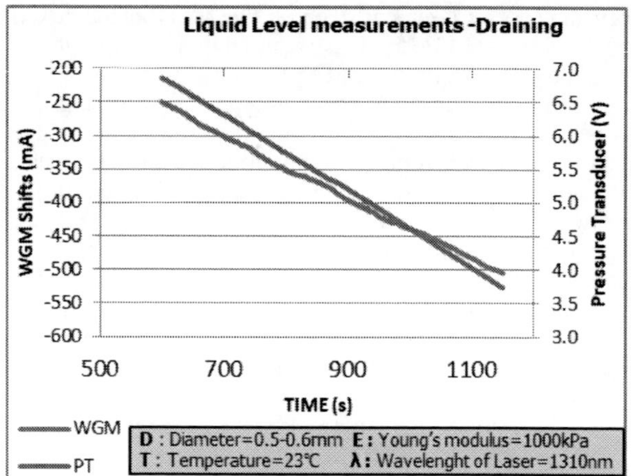


Figure 8. Liquid Level measurements while draining water from the setup

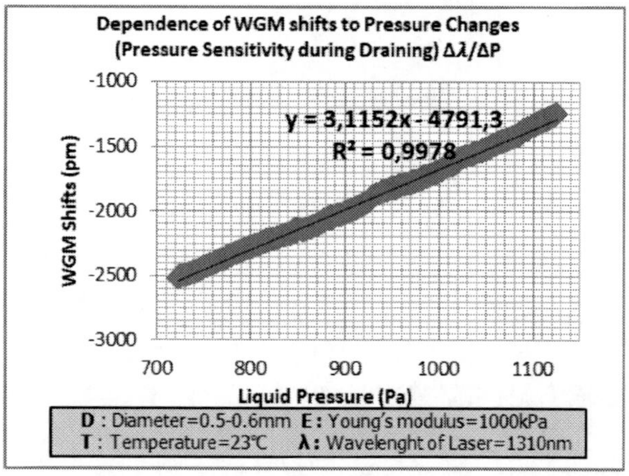


Figure 9. The Dependence of WGM shifts to Liquid Pressure changes (Pa)

In Figures 7 and 9, the Y axis represents the resonance shifts in pm scale, while the X axis represents the liquid levels in the container in mm scale [2][4]. A nearly perfect ($R^2$=0.9978 (correlation coefficient)) linear dependence of WGM shifts due to liquid levels can be observed while draining water from the experiment setup. Therefore, it can be seen that for every Pa change, experimenters observe 3.2 pm shift in resonances [2].

The pressure values seen in Figure 9, can also be converted to liquid levels (1mm $H_2O$=9.8065 Pa), whereas we are still going to use the resonance shifts over the pressure changes (pm/pa) as the sensitivity dependence definition and the formulation in our case [3]:

$$\frac{\Delta\lambda}{\Delta P} = S \quad (1)$$

Results indicate that, there is a strong correlation between WGM shifts [3]-[5] and the liquid levels. The resonance shifts appear as a function of liquid levels with a linear response with no discernible hysteresis in the pressure range tested.

*B. Accuracy and Uncertainty*

In engineering and science, the accuracy of a measurement system has been defined as the degree of closeness of measurements of a quantity to that quantity's true value [12][13].

It is considered that measurements are made by calibrated instruments for which all known systematic errors have been removed. However, even the most carefully calibrated instruments will have errors associated with the measurements [12][13].

Error is the difference between the experimentally determined value and the true value, therefore, accuracy increases as error approaches zero. In practice, the true values of measured quantities are rarely known, thus, an error should be estimated, and this estimation is called uncertainty [12][13].

$$w_R = \left[\left(\frac{\partial R}{\partial x_1} w_1\right)^2 + \left(\frac{\partial R}{\partial x_2} w_2\right)^2 + \ldots\ldots + \left(\frac{\partial R}{\partial x_n} w_n\right)^2\right]^{1/2} \quad (2)$$

According to equation (2), error in the resulting value is the result of errors in the variables. When neglecting the errors of the devices such as: laser source, laser diode controller, function generator, data acquisition card (DAQ), computer, photodiodes, and the fibers, the accuracy measurement can ben derived by using the sensitivity value obtained at the end of the experiments. The sensitivity dependence has been already defined as $\Delta\lambda/\Delta P=S$, therefore, the uncertainty error value of S becomes:

$$w_S = \left[\left(\frac{\delta S}{\delta \Delta\lambda} w_{\Delta\lambda}\right)^2 + \left(\frac{\delta S}{\delta \Delta P} w_{\Delta P}\right)^2\right]^{1/2} \quad (3)$$

The $\Delta\lambda$ term is according to the resonance shifts, while the $\Delta P$ term represents the pressure levels. By deriving each term:

$$\delta S/\delta\Delta\lambda = 1/\Delta P \text{ and } \delta S/\delta\Delta P = -(\Delta\lambda)/(\Delta P)^2 \quad (4)$$

as a result:

$$w_S = \left[\left(\frac{1}{\Delta P} w_{\Delta\lambda}\right)^2 + \left(\frac{-\Delta\lambda}{(\Delta P)^2} w_{\Delta P}\right)^2\right]^{1/2} \quad (5)$$

can be evaluated.

Thus, the uncertainty term of the resonance shifts have been obtained by 14 bit data acquisition card where the seven step software tracking algorithm takes place, resulting in a certainity of $2^{14}$ ; this means an error of [3]-[5]:

$$\sum_{n=7} \frac{1}{2^{14}} = \frac{7}{16384} = \pm 0{,}043\%, \quad (6)$$

where the uncertainty value becomes:

$$w_{\Delta\lambda\_Filling} = (761{,}85 - 0{,}228)x\frac{7}{16384} = 0{,}325\text{pm} \quad (7)$$

$$w_{\Delta\lambda\_Draning} = (2515{,}55 - 1249{,}50)x\frac{7}{16384} = 0{,}541\text{pm} \quad (8)$$

While filling water into the experiment setup, data shows $\Delta\lambda/\Delta P=1{,}9083$ pm/Pa conversion, seen in Figure 7, while draining water from the setup, the data has a $\Delta\lambda/\Delta P=3{,}115$ pm/Pa value, as shown in Figure 9.

For finding the $W_{\Delta P}$, or in other terms, the uncertainty value of the pressure component, we need the general pressure to liquid height formula $P=\rho h$, and, when we differentiate both sides, the resulting formula becomes: $\Delta P=(\rho.g).\Delta h$, where $\rho$ is the Density, and g is the Acceleration of Gravity, which are both constants.

$$\Delta P = \rho g.\ \Delta h \quad (9)$$

$$w_{\Delta P} = \left[(\rho g \cdot w_{\Delta h})^2\right]^{1/2} \quad (10)$$

The pressure value comes from the pressure transducer, and liquid level readings, thus the uncertainty calculation should include both. The reading and pressure transducer errors combined having a liquid height vs. voltage relationship seen in Figures 6 and 8. Thus, for representing the uncertainty, the conversion formula becomes:

$$\delta\Delta h = Sc\ .\ \Delta V \quad (11)$$

Therefore:

$$w_{\Delta h} = \left[(\Delta V \cdot w_{Sc})^2 + (Sc \cdot w_{\Delta V})^2\right]^{1/2} \quad (12)$$

where Sc represents the liquid height reading errors, and $\Delta V$ represents the voltage uncertainty, or accuracy of the pressure transducer.

The accuracy of the pressure transducer used during the experiments is known as ±1,0% [2], so we calculate the uncertainty value of the pressure transducer for this experiment as follows:

$$w_{PT} = w_{DV\_Filling} = 2{,}845\text{V}x0{,}01 = 0{,}0285\text{V} \quad (13)$$

and

$$w_{PT} = w_{DV\_Draining} = 3{,}079\text{V}x0{,}01 = 0{,}03079\text{V} \quad (14)$$

The uncertainty value coming from the liquid height readings consists of the scale of the ruler, and total filling or draining limits:

$$0{,}5mm/300mm = \pm 0{,}166\%, \tag{15}$$

$$w_{RulerReading} = w_{SC} = w_{SlopeOfConversion\_Filling} = 39{,}668mm \text{ x } 0{,}00166 = 0{,}065mm, \tag{16}$$

and

$$w_{RulerReading} = w_{SC} = w_{SlopeOfConversion\_Draining} = 40{,}94mm \text{ x } 0{,}00166 = 0{,}0679mm. \tag{17}$$

For finding the exact uncertainty $w_{\Delta P}$ value, errors occurred during the liquid level readings, and the pressure transducer uncertainty should be included:

$$w_{\Delta P} = \left[ (\rho g \cdot \Delta V \cdot w_{Sc})^2 + (\rho g \cdot Sc \cdot w_{\Delta V})^2 \right]^{1/2} \tag{18}$$

$$w_{\Delta P\_Filling} = \left[ (9{,}80 \cdot 2{,}845 \cdot 0{,}065)^2 + (9{,}80 \cdot 14{,}013 \cdot 0{,}0285)^2 \right]^{1/2} = 4{,}31 Pa \tag{19}$$

$$w_{\Delta P\_Draining} = \left[ (9{,}80 \cdot 3{,}079 \cdot 0{,}0679)^2 + (9{,}80 \cdot 13{,}204 \cdot 0{,}03079)^2 \right]^{1/2} = 4{,}48 Pa \tag{20}$$

In other words, we have an uncertainty level of ±1,10% for filling, and ±1,11% for draining. When these results are used in equation (8):

$$w_{S\_Filling} = \left[ \left( \frac{1}{389{,}047} \cdot 0{,}325 \right)^2 + \left( \frac{761{,}622}{(389{,}047)^2} 4{,}31 \right)^2 \right]^{1/2} = 0{,}0217 \, {}^{pm}/_{Pa} \tag{21}$$

$$w_{S\_Draining} = \left[ \left( \frac{1}{401{,}882} \cdot 0{,}541 \right)^2 + \left( \frac{-1266{,}05}{(401{,}882)^2} 4{,}48 \right)^2 \right]^{1/2} = 0{,}0351 \, {}^{pm}/_{Pa} \tag{22}$$

Therefore, the experiment performed during draining water from the setup showing $\Delta\lambda/\Delta P$ sensitivity dependence value of 3,115 pm/Pa, having a calculated uncertainty of ±1,126%.

The experiement performed during filling water to the setup showing $\Delta\lambda/\Delta P$ sensitivity dependence value of 1,9083 pm/Pa, similarly has a calculated uncertainty of ±1,137%.

## IV. CONCLUSIONS

After performing the liquid level measurement experiements, it has been observed that sensitivities of 1.9083 pm/Pa during the liquid level measurements have been reached, while having a linear dependence within the experimental range.

As the uncertainty calculations has been performed for liquid level measurements, a total uncertainty value of ±1,126% for draining, and ±1,137% for filling have been obtained. The pressure transducer, which acts as the reference device used in the experiments, has ±1,0% accuracy, which limits the total value. Any alternative device with better accuracies would definitely help future researchers to decrease the uncertainties.

## REFERENCES


[1] G. C. Righini, and S. Soria, "Biosensing by WGM Microspherical Resonators", Sensors 2016, 16(6), 905; doi:10.3390/s16060905, 2016.

[2] M. E. Erdem, and D. Gunes, "Liquid Level Sensor in Automotive Design", Proceedings of SENSORCOMM 2011: The Fifth International Conference on Sensor Technologies and Applications, Nice, France, pp. 166-171, Aug.2011.

[3] T. Ioppolo, U. K. Ayaz, and M. V. Ötugen, "High Resolution Force Sensor Based on Morphology Dependent Optical Resonators Polymeric Spheres", J. Appl. Physics, Vol. 105, 013535, 2009.

[4] T. Ioppolo, M. Kozhevnikov, V. Stepaniuk, M. V. Otugen, and V. Sheverev, "A micro-optical force sensor concept based on whispering gallery mode resonators", Applied Optics, Vol. 47, Issue 16, pp. 3009-3014, 2008.

[5] T. Ioppolo, and M. V. Otugen, "Pressure Tuning of Whispering Gallery Mode Resonators", J. Opt. Soc. Am. B, vol. 24, no. 10, 2007, pp. 2721–2726, 2007.

[6] K. J. Vahala, "Optical Microcavities", World Scientific: Singapore, 2004.

[7] K. J. Vahala, "Optical microcavities", Nature 2003, 424, pp. 839–846, 2003.

[8] W. J. Fleming, "Overview of Automotive Sensors", IEEE Sensors Journal, Vol. 1, No. 4, Dec.2001.

[9] R. K. Chang, and A. J. Campillo, "Optical Processes in Microcavities", World Scientific: Singapore, 1996.

[10] R. D. Richtmyer, "Dielectric resonators", Journal of Applied Physics, 10, pp. 391–398, 1939.

[11] L. Rayleigh, "The problem of whispering gallery". Sci. Pap., 5, pp. 617–620, 1912.

[12] O. Geceli, "Measurement Techniques, Birsen Press, ISBN 975-511-113-1, 1998.

[13] J. Fraden, "Handbook of Modern Sensors Physics, Design Applications", 4th Edition, Springer Press, ISBN 978-1-4419-6465-6, 2010.

[14] J. Heebner, R. Grover, and T. A. Ibrahim, "Optical Microresonators Theory, Fabrication, and Applications", Springer Press, ISBN 978-0-387-73067-7, 2008.

# On the Design and Construction of Dual-Probe Heat-Pulse Soil Moisture Sensor: Towards an Industrial Solution

Antonio Valente*, Arata Andrade Saraiva†, N. M. Fonseca Ferreira‡, and Salviano Soares§

*INESC TEC - INESC Technology and Science
and University of Trás-os-Montes and Alto Douro
Vila Real, Portugal
Email: avalente@utad.pt
ORCID: 0000-0002-5798-1298

†CEUMA
and State University of Piaui-Piripiri
and University of Trás-os-Montes and Alto Douro,
Vila Real, Portugal
Email: aratasaraiva@gmail.com
ORCID: 0000-0002-3960-697X

‡INESC TEC - INESC Technology and Science
and Institute of Engineering of Coimbra,
Polytechnic Institute of Coimbra,
Coimbra, Portugal
Email: nunomig@isec.pt
ORCID: 0000-0002-2204-6339

§IEETA - UA
and University of Trás-os-Montes and Alto Douro,
Vila Real, Portugal
Email: salblues@utad.pt
ORCID: 0000-0001-5862-5706

***Abstract*—There is a need for a multi-functional probe for small-scale measurements of different soil properties measured within identical soil volumes. Dual Probe Heat Pulse (DPHP) sensors are an economical solution for this since they measure simultaneously temperature, volumetric water content, and soil thermal properties: diffusivity and volumetric heat capacity. However, all DPHP sensors to date have very complex manufacturing processes. This paper aims to design and build a DPHP sensor based only on a Printed Circuit Board (PCB) board, which comprises the probes and all supporting electronics leading to a low cost and simple manufacturing process. The proposed system includes signal-processing circuits, a microcontroller, and communicates by a Serial Digital Interface at 1200 baud protocol (SDI-12). Probe spacing calibration results showed a reasonably good agreement between measured and fitted data. In conclusion, results also show that it is possible to build the multi-functional DPHP sensor in a low cost process, and this was the first time that a multi-functional probe was build using a Printed Circuit Board (PCB) as support.**

***Keywords–soil moisture sensor; soil thermal properties; dual-probe; heat-pulse sensor; thermal conductivity; thermal sensors.***

## I. INTRODUCTION

The heat pulse-based soil moisture sensors, of which stand out Dual Probe Heat Pulse (DPHP) sensors, are an economical solution for soil moisture measurements. Since Campbell [1], much research has been done and reported that the heat pulse technique is an economical technique to measure soil thermal properties and soil moisture content [1]–[19]. The DPHP-based sensor has two elements, the heat probe and the temperature sensor probe, separated by a short distance, $r$. A voltage pulse, with finite duration $t_0$, is applied to the heater element causing the heat to flow in all directions around the heater element. Heat 'traverses' the surrounding soil and the temperature rise will be measured by a sensor on the temperature probe. However, in almost all developed sensors [1]–[14], the heating probe is composed of a needle where a conductive wire (with a high resistivity, suitable for producing resistances for heating) is inserted inside. The probe with the temperature sensor is elaborated in the same way, by inserting the temperature sensor (thermocouple or thermistor) inside a needle. Both needles are then filled with an epoxy glue of high thermal conductivity and low electrical conductivity. Therefore, the use of this process is laborious and difficult, if not impossible, for industrialization. Other authors have attempted, without known success, to develop soil moisture sensors based on the heat pulse without the use of needles. In this group, there are the works of [15]–[17], [19] who developed microelectronics to try to improve the manufacturing process and in other works a button-shaped sensor was developed [14], [18]. Most of the work done with DPHP sensors uses data-loggers to acquire data from temperature probe, to control heat pulse duration and to perform calculations. A recent work [12] overcomes this problem but still uses needle type probes. In this paper, we resolve these shortcomings. In particular, we make the following contributions:

- Place all the electronics near the probes (heating and temperature probes). This contribution (Section III), although already achieved by [12], uses only a temperature probe, making the construction of the sensor simpler at the expense of measuring the flow of water in the soil.
- We present a new form of sensor construction which uses the PCB, also used for the rest of electronics, as a support for the temperature and heating probes (Section III). This is a great achievement as it will enable the industrial production of the sensor at a reduced cost.
- All calculations of the model used (Section II) are performed inside of the on-board microcontroller. The results of the calibration using agar (Section IV) showed good results of the model used.

The rest of this paper is organized as follows. Section II describes the models implemented for the calculation of the soil thermal properties and volumetric water content. Section III details all the fabrication process of the DPHP sensor, calibration method of the distance between heater and temperature sensor, and SDI-12 communication commands implemented. Section IV addresses the sensor calibration results and shows sensor prototypes. The acknowledgement and conclusions close the article.

## II. Theory

There are some models to describe the operation of sensors based on the DPHP method. The simpler model, described by Campbell [1], considers that the heat source is an infinite line and the heat pulse is released instantaneously. The other models [2] increase the constraints of the model of Campbell, considering that the heat pulse is finite, that the source line is finite and, finally, that it is not a source line, but a cylinder. Of these models the most common is the model which considers the finite heat pulse generated by an infinite source line [2]. In the present work, this will be the adopted model due to its precision and relative ease implementation in a microcontroller-based system. The solution for conducting radial heat from a short-duration, $t_0$ , heat pulse away from an infinite source line, for $t > t_0$ is

$$\Delta T(r,T) = \frac{q'}{4\pi\kappa\rho c}\left[\mathrm{E_i}\left(\frac{-r^2}{4\kappa(t-t_0)}\right) - \mathrm{E_i}\left(\frac{-r^2}{4\kappa t}\right)\right] \quad (1)$$

where, $\Delta T$ is change in temperature ($^\circ C$), $r$ is radial distance from the line source (m), $t$ is time (s), $q'$ is the energy input per unit length of heater per unit time ($\mathrm{W\,m^{-1}}$), $\rho c$ is the volumetric heat capacity ($\mathrm{J\,m^{-3}\,{}^\circ C^{-1}}$), $\kappa$ is the thermal diffusivity ($\mathrm{m^2\,s^{-1}}$) of the medium surrounding the heater, and $-\mathrm{Ei}(-x)$ is the exponential integral [20]. The thermal diffusivity ($\kappa$) and volumetric heat capacity ($\rho c$) can be determined from heat-pulse measurements using the single-point method [3], or a nonlinear curve fitting where (1) is fitted to measured $\Delta T(r,t)$ data [5]. It was showed that, accuracy in $\rho c$ will be limited by the accuracy of $r$, and accuracy in $\kappa$ will be limited by the accuracy of both $r$ and time of maximum temperature change, $t_{\mathrm{M}}$ [3]. The single-point method makes use of the fact that the temperature response at some distance $r$ from the heater displays a maximum, so that we can take the derivative of (1) with respect to time, set the result equal to zero, and obtain the time, $t_{\mathrm{M}}$, to the maximum temperature change ($\Delta T_{\mathrm{M}}$). This yields an expression for estimating $\kappa$ where

$$\kappa = \frac{r^2}{4}\left[\frac{\frac{1}{(t_{\mathrm{M}}-t_0)} - \frac{1}{t_{\mathrm{M}}}}{\ln\left(\frac{t_{\mathrm{M}}}{t_{\mathrm{M}}-t_0}\right)}\right] \quad (2)$$

which is a function of $r$, $t_{\mathrm{M}}$ and $t_0$. Rearrangement of (1) yields an expression for estimating $\rho c$, for $t > t_0$,

$$\rho c = \frac{q'}{4\pi\kappa\Delta T_{\mathrm{M}}}\left[\mathrm{E_i}\left(\frac{-r^2}{4\kappa(t-t_0)}\right) - \mathrm{E_i}\left(\frac{-r^2}{4\kappa t}\right)\right] \quad (3)$$

where $\kappa$ is obtained from (2). To minimize errors, the single-point method requires an accurate measurement of $r$ and times $t_{\mathrm{M}}$ and $t_0$. For $\rho c$ estimation, in addition to $\kappa$ from (2) and $r$, are needed accurate measurements of $q'$ and $\Delta T_{\mathrm{M}}$. Volumetric heat capacity $\rho c$ of soil can be determined as the sum of the heat capacities of the individual constituents and considering that the air is ignored and solids defined to include the mineral and organic matter fractions then soil water content $\theta_{\mathrm{v}}$ can be defined as a function of volumetric heat capacity [21],

$$\theta_{\mathrm{v}} = \frac{\rho c - \rho_{\mathrm{b}} c_{\mathrm{s}}}{(\rho c)_{\mathrm{w}}} \quad (4)$$

where $\rho$ is density, $c$ specific heat, $\theta_{\mathrm{v}}$ volumetric water content, and the subscripts b, s and w indicates bulk, average properties of the solids (minerals+organic matter), and water, respectively. Since $(\rho c)_{\mathrm{w}}$ is known, measurements of $\rho c$ obtained with the sensor can be used together with estimates (or preferably measurements) of soil bulk density ($\rho_{\mathrm{b}}$) and specific heat ($\rho_{\mathrm{s}}$) to obtain $\theta_{\mathrm{v}}$.

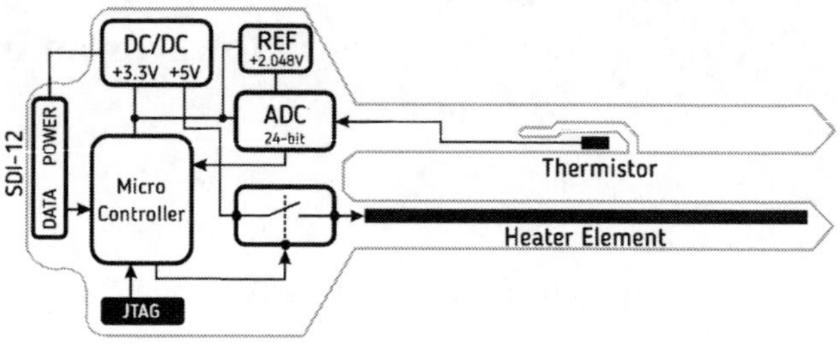


Figure 1. Sensor overview

## III. Materials and Methods

The developed sensor is a complete solution and this approach, together with the non-use of needles for the heating and temperature probes, is new. Next, all details of the sensor construction, as well as its firmware, the communication protocol and as referred to in the previous section the knowledge of the true value of $r$ ($r_{\mathrm{eff}}$) through calibration in agar, will be explained in detail.

### A. Sensor System Description

In Figure1 is depicted the electronic layout of the sensor system, the core unit is on-board 16 bit microcontroller (PIC24F32KA301) with very low power consumption, 12-channel 12 bit Analog-to-Digital Converter (ADC), serial communications modules (UART - Universal Asynchronous Receiver-Transmitter, SPI - Serial Peripheral Interface, and $\mathrm{I^2C}$ - Inter-Integrated Circuit), and hardware Real-Time Clock (RTC) Calendar with alarms. The temperature sensor probe consists of a $10\,\mathrm{k\Omega}$ (NCP15XH103F03RC) thermistor, a precision ($0.1\,\%$) voltage reference of $2.048\,\mathrm{V}$ (LM4128) and a 24 bit ADC (MCP3421). The heating probe consists of a series of 15 resistors of $1\,\Omega$, controlled by an electronic switch composed of transistors. The system power is from the SDI-12 power ($6\,\mathrm{V}$ to $12\,\mathrm{V}$) that feeds a dual DC regulator: $2\,\mathrm{V}$ to $5\,\mathrm{V}$ for powering the heat pulse (LM1117), and $3.3\,\mathrm{V}$ for the rest of the system (MIC5219).

The microcontroller controls the heat pulse through the transistors switch to enable/disable the power to the heater. To determine accurately the value of $q'$ (heat input per unit

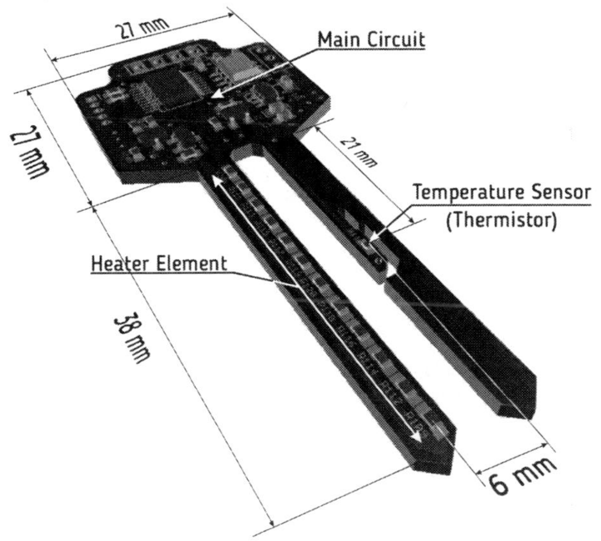


Figure 2. Sensor 3D view.

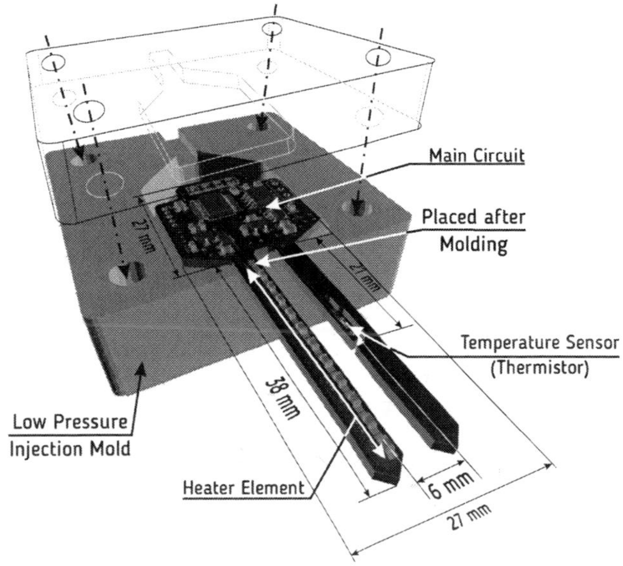


Figure 3. 3D view of the construction details.

length per unit time), average current through the heater was determined by sampling the voltage across a $0.18\,\Omega$ resistor ($1\,\%$) in series with the heater $15\,\Omega$ resistor ($15 \times 1\,\Omega$), and the voltage across resistance series of the heater and current measure resistor. The value $q'$ is determined by

$$q' = V_{\text{heater}} \times I_{\text{heater}} \times \frac{1}{l_{\text{heater}}} \quad (5)$$

where $V_{\text{heater}}$ is the measured voltage across the heater, $I_{\text{heater}}$ is the current through the heater given by $I_{\text{heater}} = V_{\text{R}=0.18}/0.18\,\Omega$ ($V_{\text{R}=0.18}$ is the measured voltage across the $0.18\,\Omega$ resistor), and $l_{\text{heater}}$ is the length of the heater ($0.0353\,\text{m}$). All voltages measured for $q'$ calculations, are performed by microcontroller internal ADC (12 bit). Temperature from the temperature probe was measured by sampling the voltage drop across the thermistor in series with a $10\,\text{k}\Omega$ ($0.1\,\%$) resistor. This was done on the 24 bit ADC to ensure sufficient sampling accuracy for determining temperature.

## B. Sensor Construction

The prototype of the developed sensor, as shown in Figure 2, is based on the printed circuit board (PCB) as substrate. In the PCB are welded all the components necessary for the operation of the sensor. The design of the PCB was made in the form of a fork with two 'rods' that form the heating probe and the temperature probe. The thermistor in the temperature probe is placed in a thermally insulated tab. The distance between these two elements were designed to be $6 \times 10^{-3}\,\text{m}$. However, this distance has to be calibrated because as previously described an error in this parameter contributed significantly to the error in the determination of $\kappa$ and $\rho c$ [4].

The process of mounting the sensor is as follows:

- Manufacture of PCB board;
- Assembly of all electric components, except for the first resistance of the heating element due to the mold;
- Sealing, using a mold as depicted on Figure 2, with thermoplastic molding resin to achieve high quality sealing and protection of components of the main circuit. Overtec 820 15 Hotmelt Glue Gun, from Techsil Limited, UK, was used with the respective polyamide resin OverTec 5 FR;
- Missing resistor placement;
- Placement of an epoxy adhesive in the heating element (in all resistors forming it) and in the thermistor.

As can be seen from the description of the process used for the elaboration of the prototype, it can be turned into an industrial process.

## C. Firmware

The developed firmware, after all the initialization, enters into sleep mode waiting for a SDI-12 command. After a `aM!` command the firmware will perform a complete measurement as presented on Figure III-C.

The presented values for the heater voltage ($5\,\text{V}$), the heating duration ($8\,\text{s}$) and the time allowed for the next measurement are the defaults. These values can be change as described next.

## D. Digital Communications

The sensor uses SDI-12 protocol for digital communication of sensor data and change sensor parameters. SDI-12 is a standard to interface battery powered data recorders with micro-processor based sensors designed for environmental data acquisition. All SDI-12 communications are transmitted using American Standard Code for Information Interchange (ASCII) at 1200 baud with 7 data bits and an even parity bit. The standard also specifies a communications protocol that allows sensors to remain in a low-power sleep state until awoken by a serial break signal sent by the master. The first character of each command is a unique sensor address, `a`, that specifies with which sensor the recorder wants to communicate. Table I lists

**repeat** ▷ Read soil temperature before applying heat
    $StartTemperature \leftarrow temperature$
**until** $time < 12\,\mathrm{s}$
HeatPulse ON (5 V)
**repeat** ▷ Read heat power
    $HeatVoltage \leftarrow voltage$
    $HeatCurrent \leftarrow current$
**until** $time < 8\,\mathrm{s}$
HeatPulse OFF
Calculate $q'$ using (5)
**repeat** ▷ Read Temperature Increase
    ▷ (3 samples/second)
    $\Delta T \leftarrow temperature - StartTemperature$
    DetectMaxTemperature ($\Delta T_{\mathrm{M}}$, $t_{\mathrm{M}}$)
**until** $time < 120\,\mathrm{s}$
Calculate $\kappa$ using (2)
Calculate $\rho c$ using (3)
Calculate $\theta_{\mathrm{v}}$ using (4)
Enter SLEEP mode (760 s)

Figure 4. Firmware algorithm

all the commands that the sensor will respond to. In addition to the standard commands it was necessary to implement a set of extended commands (with an `X` after the address) in order to configure the sensor and obtain individual readings of some parameters. These extended commands uses letter `G` after the `X` to get extra data from the sensor (heater voltage, heating power, heater current, spacing between heater and temperature sensor, maximum temperature rise, time of the maximum temperature rise, soil bulk density, and individual sensor parameters readings: soil volumetric water content, soil thermal diffusivity, and volumetric heat capacity), and a letter `S` to set new values for heater applied voltage and heat duration, to new spacing value, and to set new bulk density. Access to metadata is also available as presented in version 1.4 of the SDI-12 specification [22]. For calibration and whenever necessary, the raw values (16 bit unsigned floating point format) of the temperature curve can be requested using the High Volume Binary Command (`aHB!`).

### E. Probe Distance Calibration

The measurement of $\kappa$ and $\rho c$ are highly sensitive to effective separation distances, $r$, between the heater element on heater probe and the thermistor on temperature sensor probe [4]. Thus, calibration of this distance was crucial for accurate measurements. The calibration was performed by inserting the sensor in a gel that was made from a $4 \times 10^{-3}\,\mathrm{kg\,L^{-1}}$ agar solution, Figure 5. The agar has equal thermal properties as water, yet does not create heat convection as would occur by heating liquid water [1].

The measured temperature response in agar solution was used to calibrate the sensor separation distance for each thermistor by fitting the measured temperature change to (1) using known values of volumetric heat capacity ($4174\,\mathrm{kJ\,m^{-3}\,K}$) and thermal diffusivity ($1.436 \times 10^{7}\,\mathrm{m^2\,s^{-1}}$) of water.

## IV. Results and Discussion

Since this work is only about a description of the design and the construction of the sensor, only the results about the sensor assembly and the calibration of the distance between the probes will be discussed.

### A. Assembled Sensor

Figure 6 shows the assembled sensor without the thermoplastic molding resin and the final version of the sensor. The sensor is small in size, compact, robust and easy to use. The final product is comparable to commercial versions of other soil moisture sensors using other measuring methods, such as the EC-5, 5TE and 5TM probes from Decagon Devices Inc., USA.

This type of sensor (DPHP sensor) compares with capacitive type of sensor in terms of accuracy ($\pm 3\,\%$ [23]), and is very different from very low-cost resistive sensor. Resistive sensors give only qualitative estimation of the moisture content [23].

### B. Probe Distance Calibration

The probe distance calibration was determined by obtaining five sensor readings in agar solution with an interval of 1 h between readings and with heating power of $q' = 51.65\,\mathrm{W\,m^{-1}}$. Figure 7 presents the measured temperature response as a function of measurement time of one of these readings. The measured temperature data was fitted using the nonlinear least-squares Marquardt-Levenberg algorithm. There is a good agreement between measured and fitted data. The fitted values of effective separation distance, $r_{\mathrm{eff}}$, for all 5 readings are presented in Table II. The average value of $r_{\mathrm{eff}}$ is $5.534 \times 10^{-3}\,\mathrm{m}$. The differences between the designed PCB layout value ($6 \times 10^{-3}\,\mathrm{m}$) and effective distances are likely caused by unprecise placement of the components (heater

Figure 5. Probe distance calibration in agar solution

TABLE I. SDI-12 SENSOR COMMANDS

| *Command* | *Description* | *Command* | *Description* |
|---|---|---|---|
| ?! | Return address of the sensor | aI! | Return sensor identification |
| aAb! | Change actual address to new 'b' address | aXGQ! | Return heating power, $q'$, value |
| aM! | Start all measurements | aXGV! | Return heater applied voltage |
| aM1! | Start soil temperature measurement | aXSVn.n! | Assign heater voltage (from 2.0 to 5.0 V) |
| aD0! | Read measurements data | aXGT! | Return maximum temperature rise, $\Delta T_{\mathrm{M}}$ |
| aHB! | Raw data of temperature curve | aXGH! | Return heat duration, $t_0$ |
| aXGP1! | Return soil volumetric water content, $\theta_{\mathrm{v}}$ | aXGI! | Return heater current |
| aXGP2! | Return soil thermal diffusivity, $\kappa$ | aXGR! | Return spacing, $r$, value |
| aXGP3! | Return soil volumetric heat capacity $\rho c$ | aXSRn.nnn! | Assign new spacing value (from 5.500 to 6.500 mm) |
| aXGB! | Return soil bulk density, $\rho_{\mathrm{b}}$ | aXSHnn! | Change heat duration (from 6 to 30 s) |
| aXSBm.nn! | Set soil bulk density (from 0.90 to 2.00 $10^3$ kg m$^{-3}$) | | |

and/or thermistor) because they are hand welded. In an industrial process this error could be minimized and lead to two kinds of sensors: agar calibrated and uncalibrated lowering the costs.

It can also be observed in the Figure 7 that, compared to other works [3], [9], [24], just to mention a few, that uses datalogger for reading and control of the DPHP sensor, this prototype presents a better resolution (18 bit against 13 bit of must dataloggers) and a better sampling rate (1 sample/s against 3 samples/s). This will give a better precision on calculating $\Delta T_{\mathrm{M}}$ and $t_{\mathrm{M}}$. We can also observe a good signal to noise ratio ($\Delta T_{\mathrm{M}} = 0.3728\,°\mathrm{C}$ for a value of 100 % of $\theta_{\mathrm{v}}$, agar $\Rightarrow$ water) even for a lower heat power ($51.65\,\mathrm{W\,m^{-1}}$ against $60\,\mathrm{W\,m^{-1}}$ - minimum found in literature [3]). This low power (could be less and adjusted depending on $\theta_{\mathrm{v}}$ values - lower values less power) is very important in order to use the sensor in wireless systems (Internet of Things - IoT).

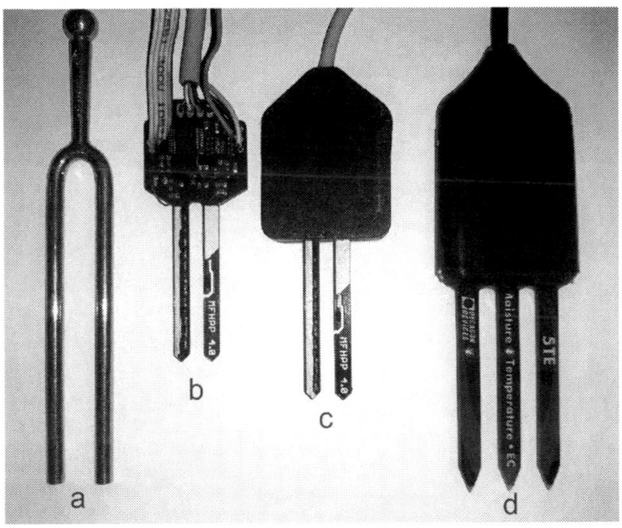


Figure 6. Developed prototypes of the DPHP sensor. a) Diapason; b) Prototype for debug without protective resin; c) Final prototype with protective resin; d) Decagon 5TE.

TABLE II. CALIBRATION OF THE EFFECTIVE SPACING, $r_{\mathrm{eff}}$

| *Sensor Readings* | $r$(m) | $r_{\mathrm{eff}}$(m) |
|---|---|---|
| #1 | | 0.005566 |
| #2 | | 0.005522 |
| #3 | 0.006 | 0.005521 |
| #4 | | 0.005512 |
| #5 | | 0.005551 |
| **Average** | | **0.005534** |

## V. CONCLUSION AND FUTURE WORK

This paper presents a novel design and an industrial process to build a DPHP sensor based on PCB board as substrate. The process is based on four steps and a calibration process in agar. Results also show that it is possible to build the multi-functional DPHP sensor in a low cost industrial process (PCB and assembly). This was the first time that a soil moisture sensor, based on heat-pulse method, was build using a PCB as support. Further work must be done to find out the sensor accuracy, test sensor readings variations with soil type, and perform in-field and long-term stability tests.

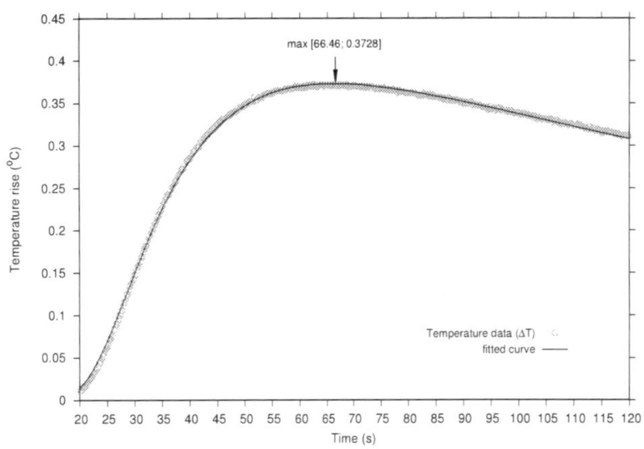


Figure 7. Measured temperature rise after the heat pulse in agar solution compared to the analytic modeled data (solid line).

In addition, as the sensor has a PCB as substrate, pads can be placed to measure soil moisture using the capacitive method and to measure soil Electrical Conductivity (EC).

## ACKNOWLEDGMENT

This work is financed by the ERDF European Regional Development Fund through the Operational Programme for Competitiveness and Internationalisation - COMPETE 2020 Programme within project "POCI- 01-0145-FEDER-006961", and by National Funds through the FCT - Fundação para a Ciência e a Tecnologia (Portuguese Foundation for Science and Technology) as part of project UID/EEA/50014/2013.

## REFERENCES

[1] G. S. Campbell, K. Calissendorff, and J. H. Williams, "Probe for measuring soil specific heat using a heat pulse method," Soil Sci. Soc. Am. j., vol. 55, 1991, pp. 291–293.

[2] G. J. Kluitenberg, J. Ham, and K. L. Bristow, "Error analysis of the heat-pulse method for measuring soil volumetric heat capacity," Soil Sci. Am. J., vol. 57, 1993, pp. 1444–1451.

[3] K. Bristow, G. Kluitenberg, and R. Horton, "Measurement of soil thermal properties with a dual-probe heat-pulse technique," Soil Sci. Soc. Am. j., vol. 58, 1994, pp. 1288–1294.

[4] G. J. Kluitenberg, K. L. Bristow, and B. S. Das, "Error analysis of the heat pulse method for measuring soil heat capacity, diffusivity, and conductivity," Soil Sci. Soc. Am. J, vol. 59, 1995, pp. 719–726.

[5] S. Welch, G. Kluitenberg, and K. Bristow, "Rapid numerical estimation of soil thermal properties for a broad class of heat-pulse emitter geometries," Measurement Science & Technology, vol. 7, no. 6, 1996, pp. 932–938.

[6] J. Tarara and J. Ham, "Measuring soil water content in the laboratory and field with dual-probe heat-capacity sensors," Agronomy Journal, vol. 89, no. 4, 1997, pp. 535–542.

[7] T. Ren, K. Noborio, and R. Horton, "Measuring soil water content, electrical conductivity, and thermal properties with a thermo-time domain reflectometry probe," Soil Science Society of America Journal, vol. 63, no. 3, 1999, pp. 450–457.

[8] K. Bristow, G. Kluitenberg, C. Goding, and T. Fitzgerald, "A small multi-needle probe for measuring soil thermal properties, water content and electrical conductivity," Computers and Electronnics in Agriculture, vol. 31, no. 3, 2001, pp. 265–280.

[9] Y. Mori, J. W. Hopmans, A. P. Mortensen, and G. J. Kluitenberg, "Multi-functional heat pulse probe for the simultaneous measurement of soil water content, solute concentration, and heat transport parameters," Vadose Zone Journal, vol. 2, no. 4, 2003, p. 561.

[10] T. Ren, T. E. Ochsner, and R. Horton, "Development of thermo-time domain reflectometry for vadose zone measurements," Vadose Zone Journal, vol. 2, 2003, pp. 544–551.

[11] Y. Mori, J. Hopmans, A. Mortensen, and G. Kluitenberg, "Estimation of vadose zone water flux from multi-functional heat pulse probe measurements," Soil Sci. Soc. Am. J., vol. 69, no. 3, 2005, pp. 599–606.

[12] W. Sheng, K. Rumana, M. Sakai, F. Silfa, and S. B. Jones, "A Multi-Functional Penta-Needle Thermo-Dielectric Sensor for Porous Media Sensing," IEEE Sensors Journal, vol. 16, no. 10, 2016, pp. 3670–3678.

[13] A. Valente, R. Morais, C. Couto, and J. Correia, "Modeling, simulation and testing of a silicon soil moisture sensor based on the dual-probe heat-pulse method," Sensors and Actuators A:Physical, vol. 115, no. 2-3, 2004, pp. 434–439.

[14] T. Kamai, G. J. Kluitenberg, and J. W. Hopmans, "Design and Numerical Analysis of a Button Heat Pulse Probe for Soil Water Content Measurement," Vadose Zone Journal, vol. 8, no. 1, 2009, pp. 167–173.

[15] A. Valente, J. Cunha, J. Correia, and C. Couto, "A silicon probe with integrated microelectronics for soil moisture measurements," in Proc. of WCCA 2001, 2001, pp. 440–446.

[16] A. Valente, C. Couto, and J. Correia, "On-chip integrated silicon bulk-micromachined soil moisture sensor based on the DPHP method," in Transducers '01: Eurosensors XV, vol. 1, 2001, pp. 316–319.

[17] A. Valente, R. Morais, C. Couto, and J. H. Correia, "Modeling and simulation of a silicon soil moisture sensor based on the DPHP method for agriculture," no. 2, 2003, pp. 564–567.

[18] A. Valente, S. Soares, R. Morais, J. M. Baptista, and M. Cabral, "Button heat-pulse sensor for soil water content measurements," Proceedings - 1st International Conference on Sensor Device Technologies and Applications, SENSORDEVICES 2010, 2010, pp. 180–182.

[19] A. Valente, R. Morais, J. Boaventura, and C. José, "A multi-chip-module micro-system for soil moisture," in EFITA 2003 Conference, no. July, Debrecen, Hungary, 2003, pp. 547–551.

[20] M. Abramowitz and I. Stegum, Handbook of Mathematical Functions. Dover Publ., 1972.

[21] G. Campbell, "Soil physics with basic, transport models for soil plant systems," Elsevier, 1985.

[22] SDI-12 Support Group, "SDI-12 a Serial-Digital Interface standard for microprocessor-based sensors," SDI-12 Support Group, Version 1.4, May 2017, [retrieved: January, 2018]. [Online]. Available: http://www.sdi-12.org/specification.php?file_id=1

[23] P. Aravind, M. Gurav, A. Mehta, R. Shelar, J. John, V. S. Palaparthy, K. K. Singh, S. Sarik, and M. S. Baghini, "A wireless multi-sensor system for soil moisture measurement," in 2015 IEEE SENSORS, Nov 2015, pp. 1–4.

[24] J. M. Tarara and J. M. Ham, "Measuring soil water content in the laboratory and field with dual-probe heat-capacity sensors," Agronomy Journal, vol. 89, no. 4, 1997, pp. 535–542.

# Analysis of Wireless and Internet Link Failure Effects on Open Loop Remote Control of Motors

Arpit Ainchwar, Jasmeet Singh Ladoiye, Dan Necsulescu
Department of Mechanical Engineering
University of Ottawa
Ottawa, Canada
Email: aainc092@uottawa.ca, jlado023@uottawa.ca, necsu@uottawa.ca

*Abstract*— **In the era of the Internet of Things (IoT), it is crucial to study the real-time dependencies of the Web, its failures, and the time delays. Wireless links widen the domain of applications of mixed, engineered systems such that computer integration includes remote nodes that are not wired to a central station. System integration requires addressing, monitoring and control issues resulting from link uncertainty. The performance of a real-time control system depends not only on the reliability of the hardware and software used but also on the time delay in estimating the output, because of the effects of computing time delay on the control system performance. New solutions are required based on distributed model predictive control, inverse problem solutions, and fractional order modeling. Remote monitoring and control contain wireless sensors and actuator networks that are stand-alone or embedded in an Internet of Things system. The focus of the paper is on enhancing continuity of operation of remote nodes considering random link failures. This is illustrated by the simulation results of Model Predictive Control (MPC) and Proportional-Integral-Derivative (PID). Mechatronic systems control is illustrated for the case of data loss in a remote motor closed loop operation.**

***Keywords-wireless links; internet; motors; experimental study; model predictive control.***

## I. Introduction

Wireless links permit to expand the domain of applications of mixed, engineered systems such that computer integration includes remote nodes, which belong to a network that is partly not wired to a central station.

Wireless mechatronic system integration requires addressing monitoring and control issues resulting from link uncertainty [1]- [4]. Mechatronic systems for remote monitoring and control contain wireless sensors and actuators consisting of standing-alone nodes of networks that can be embedded in an Internet of Things system. Systems integrated using wireless links expand the applications of wired links between components of various physical types (mechanical, electrical, fluid, thermal etc.) but also introduce uncertainty due to inherent effects of the environment of wireless communications. Remote nodes considered in this paper are part of sensor and actuator networks. The focus is on enhancing continuity of operation of remote nodes considering the random failure of links [5] - [8]. The effects of random discontinuities of links will be addressed for remote monitoring and control by developing autonomous features. Some of the important application fields are the network of mobile sensors and of vehicle formations. In case of functioning wireless network links, a central control station will generate sequences of optimal commands from distributed control. During link interruption, the remote nodes will switch to autonomous operation using the finite sequence of the last pre-computed optimal commands from distributed model predictive control, until the link is recovered [9]-[13].

This paper is the extension of paper, [14] "Determination of Cycle Time Constraints in Case of Link Failure in Closed Loop Control in the Internet of Things", which focused on the experimental setup for studying time delay and network losses in the open loop system. This paper analyses the data from a new experimental architecture and emphasizes on providing solutions for network interruption using MPC. A DC motor with an encoder is used as an actuator in our system for data analysis. A preliminary closed-loop solution for compensating for the time delay and losses in the recorded data is provided using MPC.

The paper is organized as follows: Section II describes the analysis of the delay components in detail. Section III presents the experimental setup and describes its various components. Section IV illustrates the experimental observations of our developed system implicating the rise in time delay and losses with an increase in the sampling intervals. Lastly, Section V shows preliminary results using MPC and a comparison is done with PID controller followed by discussion.

## II. Time Delay Analysis

Time delay at a single node along its route from source to destination is composed of: nodal processing time + queueing delay + transmission delay + propagation delay as shown in Figure 1. Delays are usually short, but packets can be dropped in the communication network. For reliable links, in case of loss, packet resending is required. For this purpose, stable data transfer protocols were developed [4] [14].

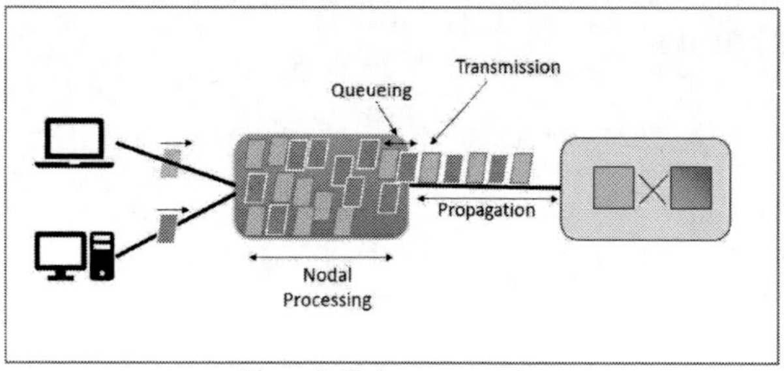


Figure 1. Delay components

The sampling rate must satisfy Shannon's sampling theorem [15] to accomplish the desired performance. A good example to confirm this is in [16] where series of robot control experiments were performed with different sampling rates. With the increase in the sampling rate time delay, computation becomes more evident. The effects of time delay cannot be neglected when the plant has a short time constant, and the order is high [17].

## III. EXPERIMENTAL SYSTEM

### *A. Experimental Setup*

The configuration of the experimental setup of open loop control system for the study of time delay and data losses in the given wireless network is shown in Figure 2. It consists of two different parts communicating with each other. The first part of the system consists of (Arduino Uno™ + Wi-Fi Shield™ + DC Motor) and the second part contains (Arduino Uno™ + Wi-Fi Shield™ + Encoder). There is a physical wired connection between (DC Motor + Encoder) of the first part to the Wi-Fi Shield of the second part of the system. The DC Motor can be operated remotely using the port forward method, which allows devices in a local network to be operated in a global environment, using an assigned IP address. The DC Motor attached to the Arduino Uno can be operated (from turning ON and OFF) continuously for regular time interval using the program uploaded on the Arduino through IDE software. The Encoder connected to the other part of the system senses the variations in the speed and sends the speed of the DC motor to the attached server, where it gets recorded and stored, subject to its time constraint. The recorded data further can be studied for the data delays and the link failure statistics. The timing of each recorded data will give the time delay in execution of the loop. If the time delay is greater than that of the sampling interval, there is a loss of data, which can be observed from the experimentally recorded data.

### *B. System Components*

The experimental setup components consist of two sets of Arduinos Uno™ and Arduino Wi-Fi Shield 101™ connected with each other in two separate parts. First part containing (Arduino Uno + Arduino Wi-Fi Shield) connected to a DC Motor, while the other part is connected to the Encoder.

DC motor's speed can be controlled over a wide range. The rotary encoder converts the motion or angular position of a shaft or axle to an analog signal and eventually, in a binary form. The signal can be further processed for obtaining the position and speed of the motor shaft.

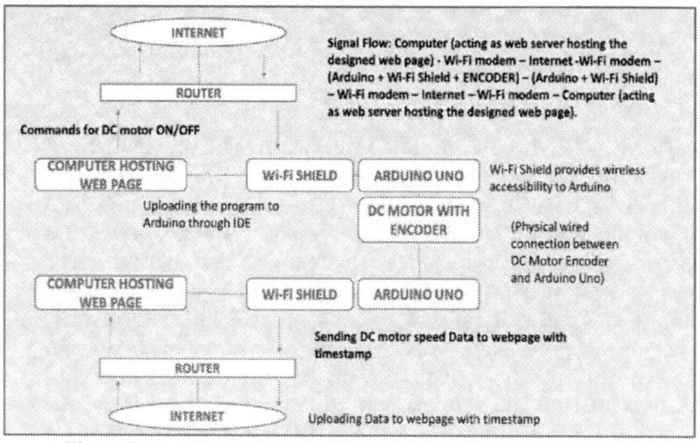


Figure 2. Experimental setup of open loop motor remote control

## IV. EXPERIMENTAL RESULTS

The increasing implementation of IoT has made it crucial to thoroughly analyze the effects of time delay and data losses for the given wireless environment to study the link failures and find out its cycle time constraints. This computing time delay differs from system time delay resulting from the execution of control programs.

Consequences of computing time delay are categorized as the delay and loss problems which can be analyzed for cycle time to link failure. The experimental setup described in this article concentrates on the development of the practical approach to study the closed-loop link failure problems and eventually find its randomness characteristics and cycle time of link failure for different time intervals. This study will help in determining the suitable time interval or frequency for performing the closed loop control accounting for data losses and link failures.

Figure 3 depicts the recorded data from the preliminary experiment. Time constraint is associated with each registered data which ultimately helps to find the delay and data losses and can be used in determining the suitable time interval for performing the closed-loop control with reduced effects of failures. In the graphs, the x-axis represents the time of the data recorded while the y-axis denotes the DC motor speed. The short horizontal lines on the x-axis indicate data losses when there is no data recorded at that time constraint.

Recorded data in Figure 3 has its time constraint. The collected data for the sampling interval shows the randomness throughout the period. From this figure, it can be observed that sometimes the time constraint of two continuous data is greater than the fixed sampling interval which shows the time delay, while for certain consecutive readings the time difference is in multiples of sampling intervals that shows the loss of data.

Figure 4-6 illustrates the experimentally recorded data for the 2, 5 and 15 seconds time intervals of DC motor operating (turn ON to OFF) respectively, and each recorded data has its time constraint. As can be observed from these figures the data delay and data loss are more evident in case of 2 seconds' time interval as compared to the other two graphs. As we compare the results of 5 seconds' and 15 seconds' time interval, data delay and loss are more apparent in 5 seconds' graph than the graph that represents the 15 seconds' time interval. This shows that as the time interval for the control system increases there are lesser chances of data delay and data losses resulting in fewer failures of the system.

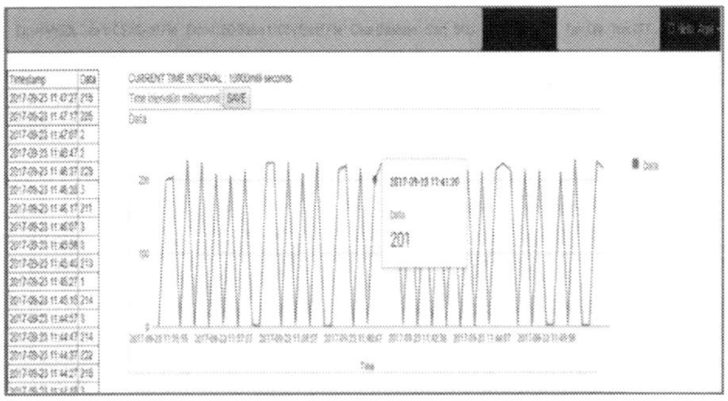

Figure 3. Experimental results with time constraints.

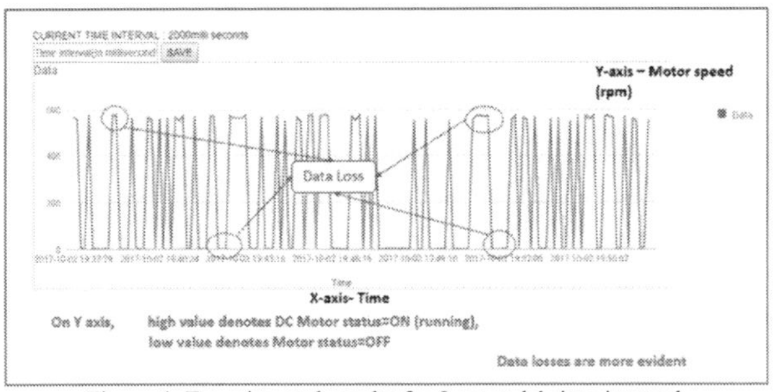


Figure 4. Experimental results for 2 seconds' time interval.

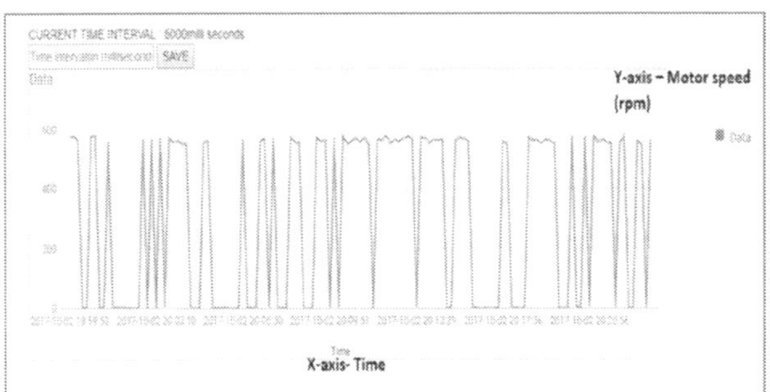


Figure 5. Experimental results for 5 seconds' time interval.

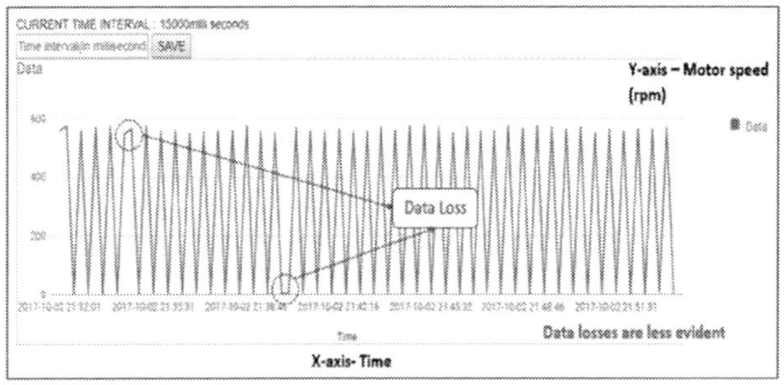


Figure 6. Experimental results for 15 seconds' time interval.

These experimental results show that, as the frequency of the open loop control system increases, more are the chances of failure of the system because of longer data delay and data loss as compared to the closed loop cycles of higher time intervals, i.e., lower frequency.

## V. Preliminary Results for Model Predictive Control

The wireless NCS (Network Control System) is a closed-loop system consisting of a plant consisting of an actuator and a sensor to provide feedback and a controller. The wireless input is communicating with the DC motor using the shared network. The wireless network is not a stable network as it always consists of delays and even data losses. To compensate the network latency and the data losses, Model Predictive Control (MPC) has been used, and the results are compared with the Proportional-Integral-Derivative (PID) controller. The property of the MPC to predict the future states will be exploited to compensate the losses in the network. In this system, as described in Figure 6, the delay is introduced when the Wi-Fi shield gets the signal from the webpage. Data packets also get lost when the latency exceeds a certain limit. We have introduced network delays and losses in the designed system imitating TCP/IP protocol considering average round trip delay of 70ms. The simulation results are produced and compared using MATLAB™ 2017b. Simulation results in Figure 7 show how MPC performs in case of network delays and losses.

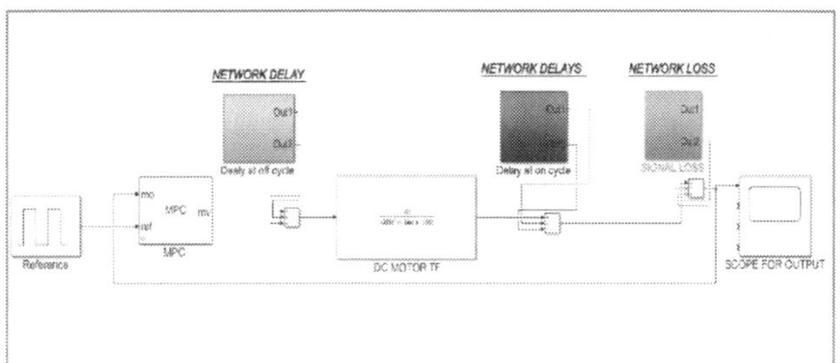


Figure 7. Closed loop network compensation using MPC

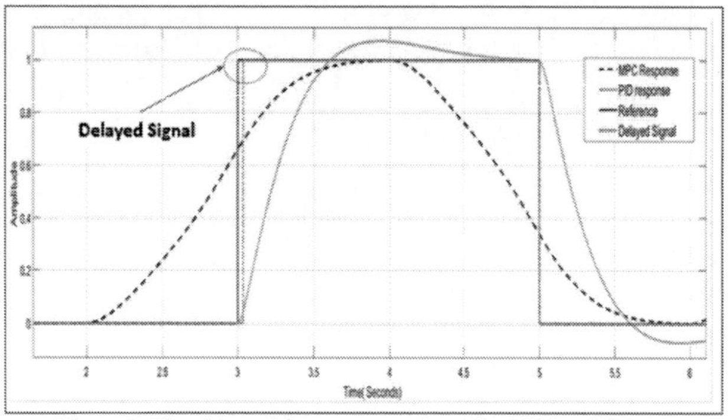

Figure 8. Closed loop delay compensation using MPC and PID.

Figure 8 describes the delay of 70ms during network interruptions. The network delays compensation was done using both MPC and PID stating the advantages of MPC over PID. MPC predicts the delay of its time as per its characteristic, unlike PID.

A sampling interval of 100ms was chosen for the simulation. Prediction horizon of 20 ms and control horizon as 3 ms were chosen such that the controller can look ahead at the behavior of the entire pulse. Reducing the sampling time will increase the performance of the system at the expense of the computational cost.

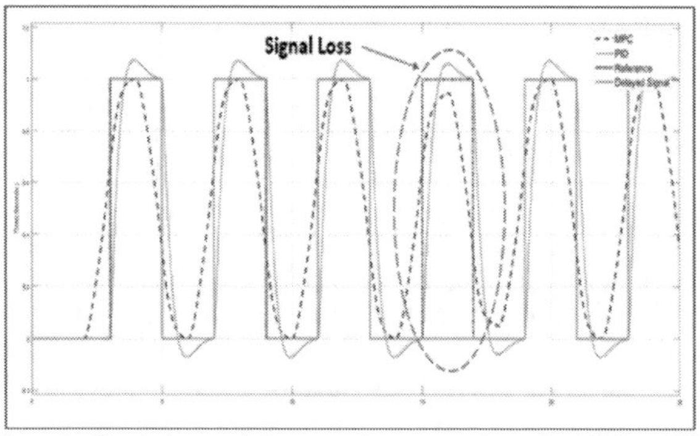

Figure 9. Simulation result for network compensation using MPC vs. PID.

The results obtained indicate that MPC can address the problems due to the delays and the losses such that in this initial investigation the output of the DC motor is unaffected by the network interruptions.

## VI. CONCLUSION AND FUTURE WORK

Wireless network control system depends heavily on the network protocol. The experimentally recorded data quantifies the randomness in the time delay and the data losses. Because of the time delays, wireless networks of sensors and actuators can become unstable. To stabilize the system, an appropriate controller must be used for the network delay and loss compensation.

In this paper, the various network delays and losses were verified using the custom-made experimental setup. The model predictive controller has been used to counter the effects of the time delay. MPC showed its robustness and prediction characteristics in the above results. The proposed scheme gives encouraging results and helps to operate remotely based sensor nodes and eventually record the sensor data accounting for the time delay and data loss problems.

In future work, the practical experimentation and evaluation with the constant and variable time delays will be done. Other delay compensation schemes can be applied and compared with the proposed ones. The future work will help present the intended experimental study of wireless networks of sensors and actuators for a remote velocity control, based on the approaches discussed in the paper.

## REFERENCES

[1] Y.-Q. Xia et al., Recent Progress in Networked Control Systems – A Survey, International Journal of Automation and Computing, Aug. 2015, pp. 343-367.

[2] I. F. Akyildiz and I. H. Kasimoglu, Wireless Sensor and Actor Network: Research Challenges. Ad-Hoc Networks, 2, 2004, pp. 351-367.

[3] I.F. Akyildiz et al., A Survey on Wireless Multimedia Sensor Networks, Computer Networks, 2006.10.002, pp. 1-40.

[4] C. Wang and K. Sohraby, A Survey of Transport Protocols for Wireless Sensor Networks, IEEE Network, May-June 2006, pp. 34-40.

[5] K. G. Shin and X. Cui. "Computing Time Delay and Its Effects on Real-Time Control Systems". IEEE transactions on control systems technology, vol. 3, no. 2, June 1995

[6] T. Strohmer and J. Tanner. "Implementations of Shannon's sampling theorem, a time-frequency approach." Vol. 4, No. 1, Jan. 2005, pp. 1-17 ISSN: 1530-6429.

[7] P. K. Khosla, "Choosing Sampling Rates for Robot Control," in front. IEEE Int. Conf 5 Robotics Automat., 1987, pp. 169-174.

[8] T. Mita, "Optimal digital feedback control systems counting computation time of control laws," IEEE Trans. Automat Contr., vol. AC-30, no. 6, pp. 542-547, June 1985

[9] S. Mansour, Using Model Predictive Control for Real-Time Control over the Internet, IEEE CCECE, Conf., Niagara Falls, May 2004, pp. 0827-0830.

[10] A. Fletcher et al., Estimation from Lossy Sensor Data: Jump Linear Modeling and Kalman Filtering, IEEE IPSN"04 Conf., Berkeley, Apr. 2004, pp. 251-258.

[11] A. Bemporad et al., Hybrid Model Predictive Control based on Wireless Sensor Feedback: An Experimental Study, Int. J. of Robust and Nonlinear Control, May, 2009, pp. 209-225.

[12] E. Henrikson, Predictive Control for Wireless Network Systems in Process Industry, Doctoral Thesis, KTH Royal Institute of Technology, 2014.

[13] W. Hu et al., Network Predictive Control over the Internet using Round-Trip Delay Measurement, IEEE Trans on I and M, no. 10, 2008, pp. 2231-2241.

[14] A. Ainchwar and D. Necsulescu. "Determination of cycle time constraints in case of link failure in closed loop control

in Internet of Things". Proceedings of the 4th International Conference of Control, Dynamic Systems, and Robotics (CDSR'17) Toronto, Canada – August 21 – 23, 2017 Paper No. 122 DOI: 10.11159/cdsr17.122.

[15] T. Strohmer and J. Tanner. "Implementations of Shannon's sampling theorem, a time frequency approach". Vol. 4, No. 1, Jan. 2005, pp. 1-17 ISSN: 1530-6429.

[16] P. K. Khosla, "Choosing Sampling Rates for Robot Control," in Proc. IEEE Int. Con. 5 Robotics Automat., 1987, pp. 169-174.

[17] T. Mita, "Optimal digital feedback control systems counting computation time of control laws," IEEE Trans. Automat. Contr., vol. AC-30, no. 6, pp. 542-547, June 1985.

# Indoor Navigation Control System for Visually Impaired People

Mohit Sain, Dan Necsulescu
University of Ottawa
161 Louis Pasteur, Ottawa, Canada
e-mail: msain064@uottawa.ca; dan.necsulescu@uottawa.ca

*Abstract* — **Blindness affects the perception of the surrounding environmental conditions. The primary requirement of any visual aid for mobility is obstacle detection. This work proposes an indoor navigation system for the visually impaired people. The system presented in this study is a robust, independent and portable aid to assist the user to navigate with auditory guidance. Computer-based algorithms developed in C sharp for the Microsoft Xbox Kinect 360 sensor allows to build a device for the navigational purpose. Kinect sensor streams both colour and depth data from the surrounding environment in real-time, which is then processed to provide the user with directional feedback using the wireless earphones. The effectiveness of the system was tested in experiments conducted with six blindfolded volunteers who successfully navigated across various indoor locations. Moreover, the user could also follow a specific individual through the output generated from the processed images.**

***Keywords - Indoor Navigation; Vision Assistance; Kinect Camera; Collision Avoidance.***

## I. INTRODUCTION

Visually impaired people often suffer from missing the perception of the environment, which affects them physiologically and psychologically. In the last few decades, many solutions have been proposed and were made available to the blind users through various means, such as white canes, laser canes, binaural sensing aids, Braille, and guide dogs.

The primary requirement is to detect the obstacles and help avoid a collision while navigating to a goal. To help the blind people navigate, the need is to find obstacles and hazards which the regular aids cannot notice. Navigation systems for blind people have been proposed to increase their mobility. However, they were only concerned with guiding the user along a predefined route as in the paper presented by Loomis et al. [1]. In their study, they evaluated the guidance performance in the virtual display mode that allows providing enhanced guidance.

Electronic Travel Aids (ETA) have been considered in the past, such as by Ram et al. [2] as an assistive device which transforms the environment surroundings sensing into signals for the blind. These aids brought a high level of confidence to help visually impaired people navigate. These devices helped to detect obstacles in the pathway of the user. The sensors, software interface, and a feedback mechanism are the three building blocks for any ETA. The sensors communicate the data to the system, where it is further processed using a specialised software and transmit to the user the required information as real-time feedback so that there are no hindrances in the user's way.

Borenstein et al. [3] and Dodds et al. [4] used ultrasonic sensors to augment the performance of the guidance cane. These sensors helped the user to detect barriers and steer accordingly, which proved to be better compared to traditional cane, given that the guide cane provided the path efficiently. Benjamin et al. [5] and Yuan et al. [6] used laser and vision sensors that enhanced user's confidence while navigating as a reasonable way for providing the information in real time using a laser triangulation system. S. T. Brassai et al. [7] provided an overview of the literature on assistive technologies for indoor and outdoor navigation in a dynamic environment. They also provided the list of solutions available for helping visually impaired people, such as navigation system, obstacle avoidance, and obstacle localisation.

The indoor auditory navigation system [8] presented by A. Zeb et al. assists visually impaired people in the surrounding environment using a computer vision technology which detects the markers. The user navigates using a webcam attached to the system which further provides the user with valuable audio assistance whenever it detects any markers in the environment that enables them to navigate independently in the environment.

C. K. Lakde et al. [9] reviewed and further improved a system [10] that guides blind people. This study presents an idea to make a person aware of the available pathway and the obstacles. The system proposed by the researchers here consists of sensors (depth and Red, Green and Blue (RGB) sensors) embedded in shoes, a control board and a communication system (vibration and voice assistance).

Another system, presented by T. Schwarze et al. [11], consists of a wearable assistance system for helping visually impaired people using a stereo camera and acoustic feedbacks. They used basic scene understanding, and head tracking, to make the user aware of the surroundings and allowing the user to walk in an unfamiliar environment and to avoid obstacles safely by sonic signals. There have been numerous solutions, but most of them are limited to specific situations and only for specific areas.

## II. METHODOLOGY

### A. System Design and Kinect Technology

In this study, a navigation system is proposed based on computer vision technology. The system is much more than a sensor itself; it includes three main components each having a specific functionality. First and the foremost is Microsoft Xbox 360 Kinect sensor, which is used for accumulating the environmental information from the data streams (both depth images and RGB images). The second is the image processing algorithm programmed using C sharp language, performed on a laptop, and the third component is a feedback system for guiding the user using the auditory information.

As soon as the system runs the algorithm, the Kinect sensor starts capturing the depth and RGB data from the video streams within the sensor range. The accumulated data is then directed to the processing unit, which, in this case, is a laptop running the Microsoft Visual Studio, which helps with real-time image processing without any noticeable time delay and provides the user with useful directional feedback. To achieve the best out of the Kinect device and to provide better viewing angles, the device is chest mounted using a GoPro chest mount [12]. Mounting the device right from the centre makes it more robust, and stable. The Kinect sensor is powered by a rechargeable 6000 mAh Li-Ion, 12V DC portable battery pack, which makes it portable and can run the system for about 8 to 10 hours.

The primary aim of this study is to provide better vision system as compared to the conventional low-priced sensors as those cannot produce the same quality output as compared to the much more advanced Kinect sensor. The prototype is a robust system comprising of an RGB camera, infrared sensor (IR), and an infrared projector. This device provides the user with an improved understanding of the environment. Moreover, it is a simple, reliable, and low-cost system which helps the user to navigate by providing the right amount of information.

Specific scenarios are tested using the Kinect, to help the user navigate [12].

Three main scenarios tested in this study are:

1. Navigating indoors, such as in classrooms and laboratories, guiding the visually impaired person through obstacles, such as tables, chairs, lab partitions, other individuals, and cabins.

2. Detection of the doors of the classrooms and labs by their names or numbers while in the hallways or corridors and recognition of the stairway going up or down.

3. Following a specific person out of a group of three in the lobby, with audio guidance through Bluetooth headphones.

For the above-mentioned testing scenarios, the system is designed for two different modes of guidance to fulfil the needs of the visually impaired people. First, the Normal Mode of guidance in which the user can roam independently indoors with the help of auditory feedback informing about the obstacles, persons in their way, as well as stairs. Moreover, if in some cases they do not receive precise information, they are backed up with Quick Response Code (QR) placed at various locations in the building. QR codes can be scanned by the Kinect sensor much faster, and these codes can store a substantial amount of data. Moreover, the user can be provided with some additional information such as stairs going down/up and the number of stairs, the location of an elevator, and level information. The other mode of guidance is the Follow Mode guidance in which the visually impaired people can follow a particular person for navigational help without any physical contact, and it would provide assistance which would not be altered even if anyone else is in the range of the sensor.

The depth of the obstacles or objects is measured using the triangulation method. The Prime sense chip sends a signal to the IR projector to start emitting an invisible electromagnetic light onto the object or the scene. It also sends the signal to IR depth sensor to initialise and capture the depth stream and this information is sent back to the chip where the frame by frame depth stream is created for the display.

The IR projector projects the laser pattern which gets reflected by the object in the sensing range and IR camera triangulates it for depth map by recapturing the emitted light, as shown in Figure 1.

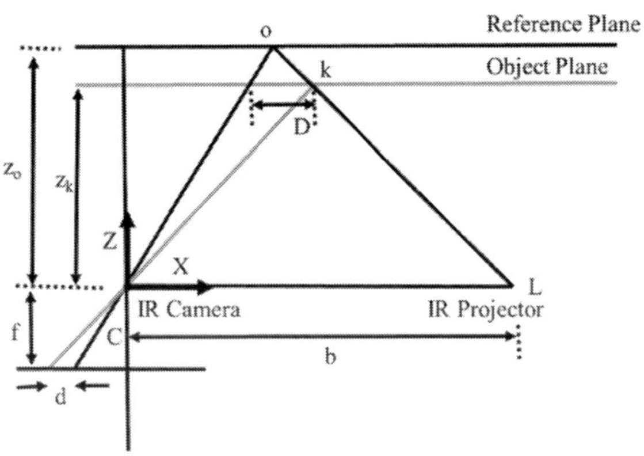


Figure 1. Schematic representation of triangulation method

The distance zk, from the camera to the reference plane is obtained from:

$$z_k = \frac{z_o}{1 + \frac{z_o}{f \times b} d} \quad (1)$$

where d is the depth distance/observed disparity, $z_o$ is the assumed position of the object on the reference plane, f is the focal length of the Infrared Camera, and b is the baseline between the IR camera and the IR projector. Equation (1) denotes the observed disparity where $z_o$, f and b can be determined by calibration.

### B. *System Initialization and Implementation*

Once the program starts, the very first step is to verify if the Kinect sensor is connected to the computer or laptop. If the system does not find any sensor connected, it will return the program with error and exits. If the Kinect sensor is connected to the system, the program proceeds normally. Once the system is connected and can interact with the Kinect, it will send a signal to both RGB and IR depth sensor to start the streams for colour and depth frames, Figure 2.

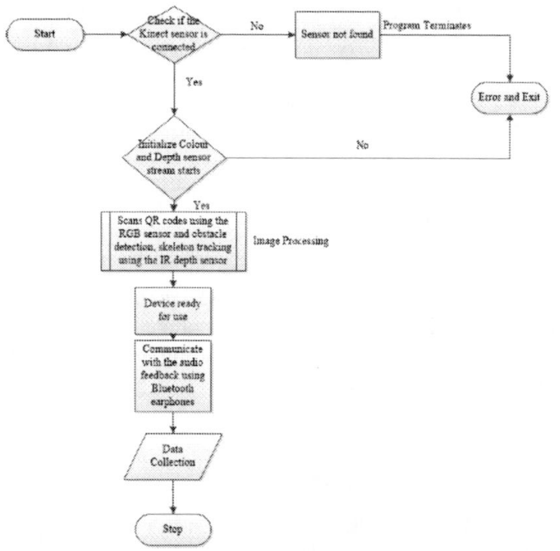


Figure 2. System data flow

If the Kinect sensor is connected to the system, the program proceeds normally. Once the system is connected and can interact with the Kinect, it will send a signal to both RGB and IR depth sensor to start the streams for colour and depth frames, Figure 2.

The RGB camera stream thus provides the QR code scanning for the audio output to the user which is done with the help of ZXing open source library that helps to scan the code and read the information stored. The depth camera stream uses the skeleton tracking and it also helps to provide information about obstacles. The image processing for the depth sensor is done using EmguCV, which is an open source library that helps to find different contours, skipping objects by different width ranges, can count people in the sensor range and take all the necessary decisions which help the user navigate. It also allows the speech synthesis which further provides the user with the necessary audio information. Then, finally, both the streams are displayed on the laptop screen running at 640 × 480 at FPS 30.

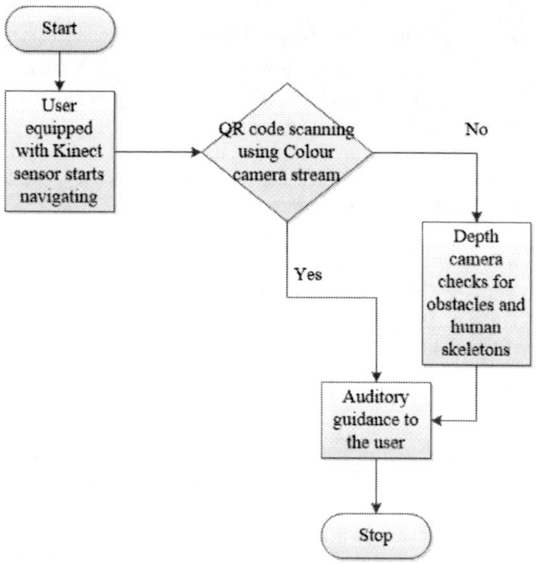


Figure 3. Free Mode of guidance

Figure 3 shows the data flow process for the free mode of guidance. Once the user starts navigating using this mode, the very first thing the program looks is the QR code. In case no QR code is detected by the colour camera, then the depth camera will start to look for the surrounding obstacles and provide the user with audio output necessary for the navigation. In case, the camera detects the QR code, then, it will communicate the information stored using the Bluetooth earphones.

## III. EXPERIMENTAL RESULTS

A total of six blindfolded sighted individuals participated in this experimental trials performed for both free mode and Follow Mode guidance. Each performed two trials on the specified path for the system testing and feedback. The blinded person starts from a lab on the level 2 on the free mode as shown in Figure 4 [12]. Then the individual must be able to avoid all the obstacles making their way out of the lab using the exit door. QR codes posted on the door gives the information to the user saying exit. Once the user exit the lab, they can either take the stairway or the elevators to reach down to the level 1. QR codes help assist the user with the number of stairs going up or down. The user then walks through the hallways which have many classrooms doors. QR codes posted will assist the user about their final destination.

In Follow Mode guidance, the user will just keep on following a particular person in the indoor environment. In this mode, a few assumptions are made such as no more than three individuals are walking in the hallway and following the designated guiding person. Directional feedback guiding the individual about every movement of the person being followed helps them to reach their destination. The red box highlights the person being followed, as shown in Figure 5. This lets the system guide the user accordingly and, at the same time, lets the user know about the obstacles.

For the Follow Mode of guidance, before iterations were done, it is assumed that there is no interference between the user and person being followed. In this case, the depth camera will help to locate the motion of the subject being followed using skeleton tracking and guide the user accordingly ignoring other humans in the surroundings. After the feedback from the blindfolded test subjects, another major iteration was done which improved the system.

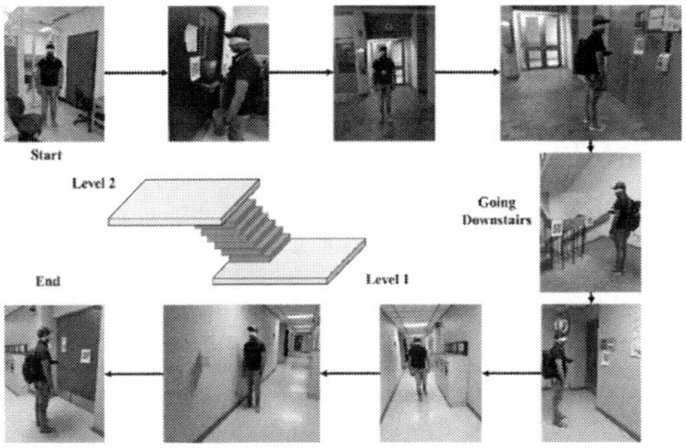


Figure 4. Experimental Environment for guidance

In this Follow Mode testing, instead of using the skeleton tracking, it was decided to follow a person with QR code at the back, and the sensor will keep on following that QR even if there is an interference of another human which would be ignored by the system. This change increased the capabilities of the proposed system; with further algorithm changes, it modified the way Follow Mode works as the part of iteration after the test results. In this iteration, the visually impaired person follows a QR code which was found to be more accurate for the Follow Mode of guidance. Results for this iteration are shown in Figure 5 and Figure 6. Whenever the sensor detects the QR code is saying 'Follow', it will keep on following that person even if any other person interferes or passes across.

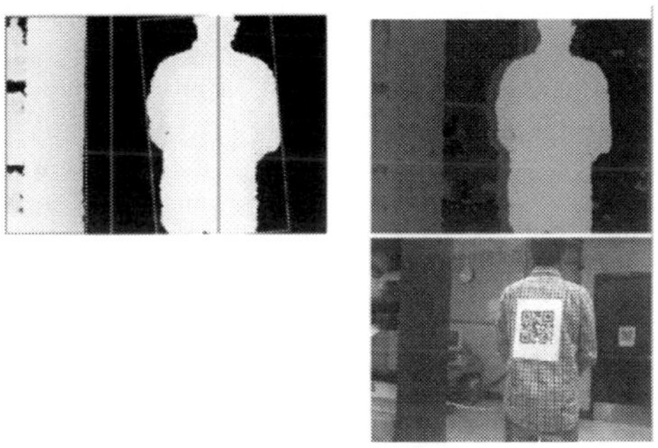

Figure 5. Follow Mode using QR code in a lab

Further experimentation with people interfering during the testing using Follow Mode was found to be better with the use of QR code, as shown in the Figure 7. The results below clearly show that the sensor is only tracking and following the person with the QR code which is highlighted with the red box and is not tracking the other two humans.

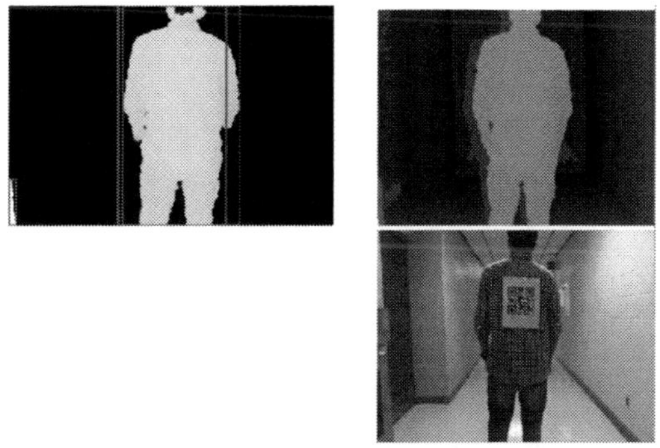

Figure 6. Follow Mode using QR code in hallway

Another scenario is shown in Figure 8, where there is another person in between the visually impaired person and the person being followed. In this case, the sensor highlights both the humans in the range for the normal Follow Mode, but with the iteration which was done with the use of QR for the following mode, now the sensor will guide the user to follow only the person with the QR code at the back. The accuracy of the test object through the test course helps to measure the effectiveness of our device.

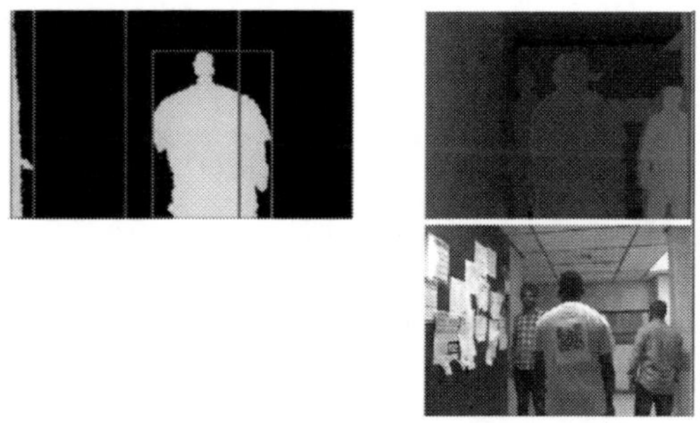

Figure 7. Follow mode with interference

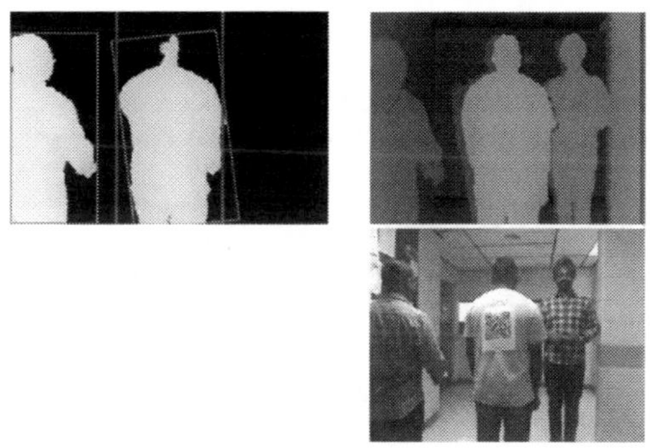

Figure 8. Follow Mode with another person in between user and the person being followed

The ability of the device in tracking all kinds of obstacles and providing auditory outputs was found to be noteworthy as compared to the previous studies discussed in the literature review section. The success of the system is in fact how it does the obstacle detection, avoidance, scanning QR codes and tracking humans as well as in providing audio information for the navigation purposes. The Kinect sensor helped to develop a novel approach for navigation as compared to the previously available devices in which there were more components used but for a specific use.

## IV. Conclusions and Future Work

This paper presented an indoor navigation system using a Kinect sensor, for the Free Mode and Follow Mode guidance. The prototype is durable, lightweight, and cost-effective, and anyone can use it with ease without any training because of its simple to operate. The real-time image processing, done with the help of computer vision algorithms, helped to detect all kinds of obstacles such as tables, chairs, humans, walls, doors, and stairs. The QR code helped to enhance the accuracy of the system and improved the results. Audio feedback is provided to the user whenever the system scans any obstacle or a QR code, and in case of the Follow Mode guidance, it provides directional information according to the movement of the person being followed. The system was evaluated by the feedback from six blindfolded users for both navigation modes. The results show the effectiveness and efficiency of the system in helping visually impaired users in the indoor environment, based on the navigation success of the users through the test course.

To add to the prototype that can assist the blind or visually impaired, further iterations and improvements can be made in the current system. The further scope of perfection and development can be achieved by designing a more stable mount for the camera, which can provide better viewing angles and even help in calibration. The current Kinect sensor can be replaced by the newer version of Kinect which has all new technology and better sensor quality outputs. These changes would increase the scanning range of the obstacles. There is also a possibility of using multiple Kinect sensors that might help to provide more independence while navigating. Further changes in the algorithm can be made to make it more robust. Radio-frequency identification (RFID) technology can also be incorporated into the current system for better results in outdoor areas which will provide another solution to help to navigate through public places using RFID tag grids, canes or other various devices.

## References

[1] J. M. Loomis, R. G. Golledge, and R. L. Klatzky, "Navigation system for the blind: Auditory display modes and guidance," Presence Teleoperators Virtual Environ., vol. 7, no. 2, pp. 193–203, 1998.

[2] S. Ram and J. Sharf, "The people sensor: a mobility aid for the visually impaired," presented at the Wearable Computers, 1998. Digest of Papers. Second International Symposium on, 1998, pp. 166–167.

[3] J. Borenstein and I. Ulrich, "The guidecane-a computerized travel aid for the active guidance of blind pedestrians," presented at the Robotics and Automation, 1997. Proceedings., 1997 IEEE International Conference on, 1997, vol. 2, pp. 1283–1288.

[4] A. G. Dodds, "The Sonic Pathfinder: An Evaluation.," J. Vis. Impair. Blind., vol. 78, no. 5, pp. 203–6, 1984.

[5] J. Benjamin, N. Ali, and A. Schepis, "A laser cane for the blind," presented at the Proceedings of the San Diego Biomedical Symposium, 1973, vol. 12.

[6] D. Yuan and R. Manduchi, "Dynamic environment exploration using a virtual white cane," presented at the Computer Vision and Pattern Recognition, 2005. CVPR 2005. IEEE Computer Society Conference on, 2005, vol. 1, pp. 243–249.

[7] S. T. Brassai, L. Bako, and L. Losonczi, "Assistive technologies for visually impaired people," Acta Univ. Sapientiae Electr. Mech. Eng., vol. 3, pp. 39–50, 2011.

[8] A. Zeb, S. Ullah, and I. Rabbi, "Indoor vision-based auditory assistance for blind people in semi controlled environments," presented at the Image Processing Theory, Tools and Applications (IPTA), 2014 4th International Conference on, 2014, pp. 1–6.

[9] C. K. Lakde and P. S. Prasad, "Review paper on navigation system for visually impaired people," Int. J. Adv. Res. Comput. Commun. Eng., vol. 4, no. 1, pp. 2278–1021, 2015.

[10] C. K. Lakde and P. S. Prasad, "Navigation system for visually impaired people," presented at the Computation of Power, Energy Information and Commuincation (ICCPEIC), 2015 International Conference on, 2015, pp. 0093–0098.

[11] T. Schwarze, M. Lauer, M. Schwaab, M. Romanovas, S. Böhm, and T. Jürgensohn, "A camera-based mobility aid for visually impaired people," KI-Künstl. Intell., vol. 30, no. 1, pp. 29–36, 2016.

[12] M. Sain, "Portable Monitoring and Navigation Control System for Helping Visually Impaired People. Diss. Université d'Ottawa/University of Ottawa, 2017." https://ruor.uottawa.ca/handle/10393/36869.

# Detection and Cancellation of Motion Artifact in fNIRS Device Using Kalman Filter and Discrete Fourier Transform

Kensuke Uesugi
Graduate School of Science and Engineering
Doshisha University
Kyotanabe, Japan
e-mail: uesugi0410@gmail.com

Masafumi Hashimoto, Kazuhiko Takahashi
Faculty of Science and Engineering
Doshisha University
Kyotanabe, Japan
e-mail: {mhashimo, katakaha}@mail.doshisha.ac.jp

*Abstract*—**This paper presents a method for detecting and cancelling motion artifacts related to standing and walking in a functional near-infrared spectroscopy (fNIRS) signal. Our fNIRS device has 22 channels. The motionless fNIRS signal from each channel is represented by a fourth-order autoregressive (AR) model, and the related parameters are estimated based on the motionless fNIRS signal using the Yule Walker equation. The motion artifacts included in the fNIRS signal are cancelled using the Kalman filter constructed from the AR model. However, the cancellation may be insufficient when the motion artifacts are strong. To determine in which fNIRS channels the motion artifacts are cancelled insufficiently, we apply a measurement prediction error related to the Kalman filter and a discrete Fourier transform. The brain activity of the user is then recognized from those fNIRS channels in which the motion artifacts are cancelled sufficiently. To evaluate the proposed method, a mobile robot is controlled using an fNIRS devise as worn by 10 subjects while standing, walking, or sitting. The experimental results show the performance of the proposed method.**

***Keywords-fNIRS; Motion artifact; Detection and cancellation; AR model; Kalman filter; Discrete Fourier transform***

## I. INTRODUCTION

Human brain activity is being measured in fields, such as automobile driving, rehabilitation, and computer interfaces [1][2][3]. Various devices have been developed for measuring human brain activity, such as electroencephalography (EEG), functional magnetic resonance imaging (fMRI), and functional near-infrared spectroscopy (fNIRS).

fNIRS devices measure the brain activity from changes in the hemoglobin concentration (fNIRS signals). This has the advantage of being less restrictive compared with EEG or fMRI devices [4] [5]. However, the disadvantage with fNIRS devices is that they can be disturbed by artifacts due to body movement, fatigue, and anxiety, for example [5]. Such artifacts have to be removed before the brain activity can be evaluated correctly using an fNIRS signal.

Many methods have been proposed for removing motion artifacts from an fNIRS signal [6][7][8]. Cooper et al. [6] proposed a method that removes motion artifacts using spline interpolation, wavelet analysis, Kalman filter, or principal component analysis. Izzetoglu et al. [9] proposed a method that identifies a motionless fNIRS signal using an autoregressive (AR) model, and then constructed an AR model-based Kalman filter to remove the motion artifacts. Admian et al. [10] applied an autoregressive moving-average (ARMA) model to identify a motionless fNIRS signal.

However, the aforementioned methods removed only motion artifacts due to head motion while sitting. Such methods are expected to be ineffective for large motion artifacts caused by body movements, such as standing or walking. Hiroyasu et al. [11] attached an accelerometer to the head. Because acceleration and the fNIRS signal are largely correlated during head motion, they were able to remove the motion artifacts by using an independent component analysis. This method enables motion artifacts to be removed easily, however, it required an additional sensor other than the fNIRS device.

In this paper, we consider motion artifacts that occur in the fNIRS signal during standing and walking. We propose a method of detecting and cancelling such motion artifacts using the Kalman Filter and the discrete Fourier transform. We verify our proposed method experimentally with a mobile robot controlled by human brain activity.

The remainder of this paper is organized as follows. In Section II, we give an overview of our experimental system. In Section III, we present our method for detecting and removing motion artifacts from an fNIRS signal. In Section IV, we describe a method for controlling a mobile robot via human brain activity. In Section V, we conduct experiments on mobile-robot control to verify the proposed method, followed by conclusions in Section VI.

## II. Experimental System

Figure 1 shows the configuration of our experimental system. The fNIRS signal obtained from the fNIRS device is transmitted to a control personal computer (PC) via a wireless LAN and a data-capture PC. The control PC recognizes the brain activity (as either active or inactive) and then sends a command (either run or stop) to the mobile robot according to the brain activity.

As shown in Figure 2, the fNIRS device has 22 output channels, each of which measures an fNIRS signal in the human prefrontal cortex every 0.2 s using near-infrared light (700–900 nm). The fNIRS signal comprises an oxygenated hemoglobin (OxyHb) concentration and a deoxygenated hemoglobin (DeoxyHb) concentration. When the brain is active, OxyHb increases and DeoxyHb decreases. In this paper, we use only the OxyHb concentration as the fNIRS signal.

## III. Method for Detecting and Cancelling Motion Artifacts

### A. Reducing Motion Artifacts Using Kalman Filter

When body movement (e.g., jaw, eyes (blinking), and head) occurs, contact between the fNIRS device and the scalp becomes unstable and thus motion artifacts appear in the fNIRS signals. Such motion artifacts cause the brain activity based on the fNIRS signal to be recognized incorrectly, and so need to be removed.

We use the following fourth-order AR model to reduce the motion artifacts in an fNIRS signal [8]:

$$x_k = a_3 x_{k-1} + a_2 x_{k-2} + a_1 x_{k-3} + a_0 x_{k-4} + w_k \quad (1)$$

where $k-i$ ($i$ = 0–4) denotes a time step, $x_{k-i}$ denotes an fNIRS signal that contains no motion artifacts, and $a_j$ ($j$ = 0–3) denotes a coefficient. $w_k$ denotes the model error, which is assumed to be a normal white-noise sequence with zero mean and variance $q$. We set $q = 5.0 \times 10^{-4}$ (mM × mm)$^2$ in the experiments in Section V.

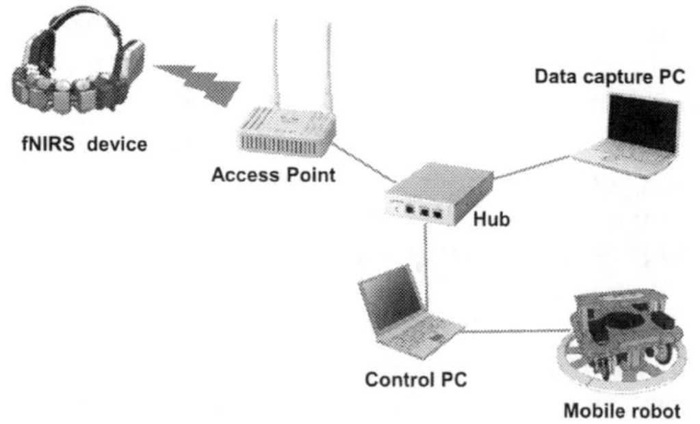


Figure 1. Overview of experimental system.

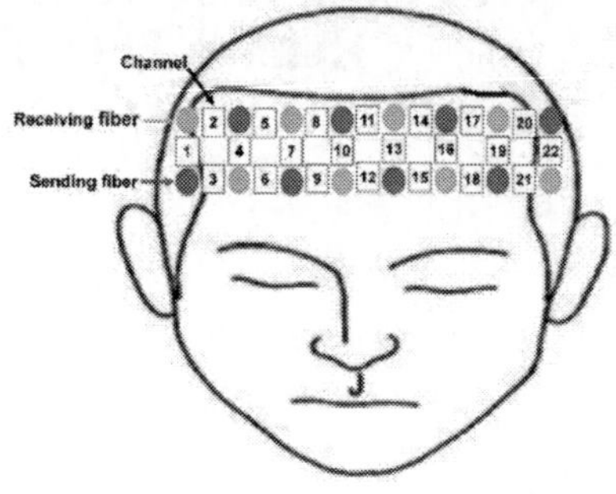


Figure 2. Output channels of fNIRS device.

We obtain the values of coefficient $a_j$ ($j$ = 0–3) from the fNIRS signal measured while sitting and hence including no motion artifacts. The following state equation is obtained from (1):

$$\begin{aligned} \boldsymbol{x}_k &= \boldsymbol{A}\boldsymbol{x}_{k-1} + \boldsymbol{B}w_k \\ &= \begin{pmatrix} a_3 & a_2 & a_1 & a_0 \\ 1 & 0 & 0 & 0 \\ 0 & 1 & 0 & 0 \\ 0 & 0 & 1 & 0 \end{pmatrix} \boldsymbol{x}_{k-1} + \begin{pmatrix} 1 \\ 0 \\ 0 \\ 0 \end{pmatrix} w_k \end{aligned} \quad (2)$$

where $\boldsymbol{x}_k = \begin{pmatrix} x_k & x_{k-1} & x_{k-2} & x_{k-3} \end{pmatrix}^T$.

The measurement equation is given by

$$\begin{aligned} z_k &= \boldsymbol{H}\boldsymbol{x}_k + v_k \\ &= \begin{pmatrix} 1 & 0 & 0 & 0 \end{pmatrix} \boldsymbol{x}_k + v_k \end{aligned} \quad (3)$$

where $z_k$ denotes the fNIRS signal that includes motion artifacts in the current time step $k$. $v_k$ denotes the measurement noise, which is assumed to be normal white-noise sequence with zero mean and variance $r$. We set $r = 1.0 \times 10^{-5}$ (mM × mm)$^2$ in the experiments in Section V.

When we apply the Kalman filter [12] based on (2) and (3), the estimate $\hat{x}_k$ and its associated covariance $\boldsymbol{P}_k$ for an fNIRS signal that does not contain motion artifacts can be obtained from the following algorithms:

- Prediction algorithm

$$\begin{cases} \hat{\boldsymbol{x}}_{k/k-1} = \boldsymbol{A}\hat{\boldsymbol{x}}_{k-1} \\ \boldsymbol{P}_{k/k-1} = \boldsymbol{A}\boldsymbol{P}_{k-1}\boldsymbol{A}^T + \boldsymbol{B}\boldsymbol{B}^T q \end{cases} \quad (4)$$

- Estimation algorithm

$$\begin{cases} \hat{\boldsymbol{x}}_k = \hat{\boldsymbol{x}}_{k/k-1} + \boldsymbol{K}_k (z_k - \boldsymbol{H}\hat{\boldsymbol{x}}_{k/k-1}) \\ \boldsymbol{P}_k = \boldsymbol{P}_{k/k-1} - \boldsymbol{K}_k \boldsymbol{H}\boldsymbol{P}_{k/k-1} \end{cases} \quad (5)$$

where $\boldsymbol{K}_k = \boldsymbol{P}_{k/k-1}\boldsymbol{H}^T / S_{k/k-1}$ and $S_{k/k-1} = \boldsymbol{H}\boldsymbol{P}_{k/k-1}\boldsymbol{H}^T + r$.

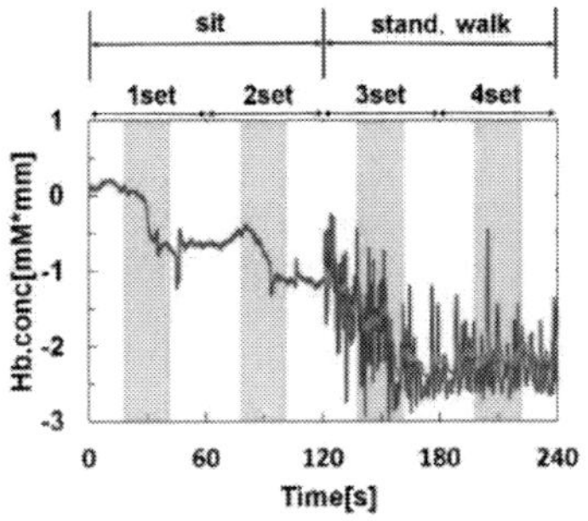


Figure 3 fNIRS (red) and efNIRS (blue) signals.

It should be noted that the coefficient estimation for the AR model and the Kalman-filter-based estimation for the fNIRS signal are performed in every channel of the fNIRS device.

Figure 3 shows an example of fNIRS signal (red lines) with and without motion artifacts. The subject wearing the fNIRS device remains seated for sets 1 and 2 and then stands up at the start of set 3 and walks until the end of set 4. During the task, the subject alternates between concentrating on moving the mobile robot (in the green areas in Figure 3) and not (in the white area). One set of 60 s comprises 15 s of rest prior to executing the task (pre-rest), 30 s of task activity, and then 15 s of rest (post-rest).

As shown in Figure 3, no motion artifacts appear in the fNIRS signal while sitting (sets 1 and 2), whereas motion artifacts contain while walking (sets 3 and 4). We estimate the AR-model coefficients at the end of set 2 using the Yule Walker equation [13] based on the fNIRS signal without motion artifacts during sitting (sets 1 and 2). We then apply the Kalman filter based on (4) and (5) and obtain an estimated fNIRS signal (hereinafter referred to as the efNIRS, blue line in Figure 3) from which motion artifacts have been removed. It is clear from this that the AR model can reduce the motion artifacts caused by walking.

### *B. Detecting and Removing Motion Artifacts*

Sufficiently large motion artifacts in the fNIRS signal cannot be removed effectively even by applying the Kalman filter. Therefore, we execute the following process to identify whether the brain is in a state of activity or inactivity.

(a) Determine whether the fNIRS signal contains large motion artifacts;

(b) If so, determine whether they have been removed from the efNIRS signal sufficiently by the Kalman filter.

To achieve process (a), we use the measurement prediction error that is obtained using the Kalman filter. To achieve process (b), we use a discrete Fourier transform to obtain the power spectrum of the efNIRS signal.

The measurement prediction error $\tilde{z}_k$ can be defined as

$$\tilde{z}_k = z_k - \boldsymbol{H}\hat{\boldsymbol{x}}_{k/k-1} \tag{6}$$

where $z_k$ denotes the fNIRS signal measurement, and $\hat{\boldsymbol{x}}_{k/k-1}$ denotes the fNIRS signal prediction obtained by the Kalman prediction algorithm given by (4).

We set the threshold value for the measurement prediction error as 0.4 from a preliminary experiment. If $|\tilde{z}_k| < 0.4$, we deem the fNIRS signal not to include large motion artifacts, and we use its estimate to recognize the brain activity. In contrast, if $|\tilde{z}_k| \geq 0.4$, we deem the fNIRS signals to include large motion artifacts, whereupon process (b) is applied.

To achieve process (b), we use the power spectrum $PS$ of the efNIRS signal obtained by a discrete Fourier transform. We set the frequency and threshold values for the $PS$ as 0.07 Hz and $2.0 \times 10^{-4}$, respectively, which were obtained from a preliminary experiment. If $PS < 2.0 \times 10^{-4}$ for a frequency of 0.07 Hz or greater, we deem large artifacts to have been removed sufficiently from the efNIRS signal, whereupon it is used to recognize the brain activity.

In contrast, if $PS \geq 2.0 \times 10^{-4}$ for a frequency of 0.07 Hz or greater , we deem large motion artifacts to be still present in the efNIRS signal, and we do not use the efNIRS signal to recognize the brain activity. For the discrete Fourier transform, we use 512 measurements and a Hamming window function.

## IV. CONTROL METHOD FOR MOBILE ROBOT USING EFNIRS SIGNAL

We will conduct experiments on controlling a mobile robot (moving or stopping) in the following section to evaluate the proposed method. In this section, we describe the control method.

Any channel, whose output includes large motion artifacts, is not used for recognizing the brain activity. We perform this process for all 22 channels of the fNIRS device. Two appropriate output channels are selected from those that can be used to recognize the brain activity. Their efNIRS signals are used to recognize the brain activity and to control the robot. We refer to these two selected output channels as the control channels.

If channels that output a small fNIRS signal are used as the control channels, it is difficult to recognize the brain activity accurately. To use channels with high levels of brain activity as the control channels, firstly, we calculate two average values for the efNIRS signal, namely the average resting value in the rest section and the average task value in the task section. We obtain the difference between these average values and then use the two channels with the largest difference as the control channels.

Saika et al. [14] proposed a distance-type fuzzy reasoning method to recognize the brain activity from an fNIRS signal. In their study, subjects wore the fNIRS device while sitting, so that motion artifacts did not occur. In our study, we recognize the brain activity by applying the distance-type fuzzy reasoning method to the efNIRS signal containing motion artifacts. We outline this method below; further details can be found in [14][15].

The Kalman filter is used to estimate the output fNIRS signals of the control channels. Because an fNIRS signal would increases in the presence of brain activity, we introduce following three rules for robot control, in which the fluctuation in the efNIRS signal is used as the antecedent part and the switching of the robot control signals (output signals) as the consequent part:

· Rule 1: If the efNIRS signal increases compared with the previous state, turn the control signals on;

· Rule 2: If the efNIRS signal changes minimally or not at all compared with the previous state, maintain the current control signals;

· Rule 3: If the efNIRS signal decreases compared with the previous state, turn the control signals off.

Also, to compare the efNIRS signal in the current time step with that in the previous time step, we use the efNIRS signal from five time frames, namely the current one and those 0.4 s, 0.8 s, 1.2 s, and 3.0 s previously.

The distance-type fuzzy reasoning method is used to recognize the brain activity in each of the two control channels. Thus, when the output results from these two channels coincide, they are sent to the robot as the output signals. When the output results are different, the output signals are turned off.

## V. EXPERIMENTAL RESULTS

To verify the proposed method, we compare the results of robot control in two cases: using the efNIRS signal obtained by the proposed method and using the original fNIRS signal. The subjects are nine men and one woman in their 20's, to whom we explain the experiment outline and from whom we acquire informed consent prior to the experiments.

Figure 4 shows the flow of the experimental process. Each experiment comprises 10 sets, each of which consists of 15 s of pre-rest, 30 s of task, and 15 s of post-rest (a total of 60 s). Each subject performs the experiment twice. The subjects are instructed to concentrate during the task time (i.e., focus on moving the robot) and rest during the rest time.

During the preparation stage shown in Figure 4, the subjects perform tasks and rest while sitting without controlling the robot. During the robot-controlling stage, they control the robot while standing, sitting, and walking. The subjects avoid moving their heads while transitioning from sitting to standing and vice versa. They also walk at a normal speed. In the experiments, the robot moves if the brain activity is recognized as being active, and it stops if the brain activity is recognized as being inactive.

To verify the efficacy of the proposed method, the robot is controlled using the proposed method during sets 3–5, 9, and 10. In contrast, the robot is controlled using the original fNIRS signal during sets 6–8. It should be noted that the subjects do not know during which sets the proposed method will be applied.

The AR-model coefficients are estimated based on the fNIRS signal acquired during the preparation stage (sets 1 and 2), and two control channels are selected at the end of set 2. In sets 3–5, the robot is controlled by the efNIRS signals of the selected control channels. Because the robot is controlled using the original fNIRS signal during sets 6–8, we select two control channels at the end of set 5 using the original fNIRS signal during set 5.

Because the subjects become fatigued as the experiment progresses, the control channels and AR-model coefficient estimates acquired during sets 1 and 2 tend to differ from those found during sets 9 and 10. To address this problem, we estimate the AR-model coefficients during the robot control and again select two channels at the end of set 8. In sets 9 and 10, the robot is controlled by the efNIRS signals of the selected control channels.

As an example, we show the experimental results for subject "A". Channels 1–4 and 20–22 in the fNIRS device are not used because of their relatively low S/N ratios; therefore, the experiment is performed using only the remaining 15 channels. The proposed method is used to select the control channels: channels 9 and 12 during sets 3–5, channels 7 and 12 during sets 6–8, and channels 6 and 12 during sets 9 and 10.

Figure 5 shows the results obtained using the proposed method during sets 3–5 (120–300 s). Figure 5 (a) shows the output signals for channel 12 of the fNIRS device, and Figure 5 (b) shows the corresponding robot control signals. The efNIRS signals are also shown in Figure 5 (b). The robot moves while the control signal output is "ON", and it stops while the control signal output is "OFF".

We can see from these figures that the robot is controlled in accordance with the changes in the efNIRS signal. The control output signals turn on when the estimate shows an increasing trend, and turn off when that trend is a

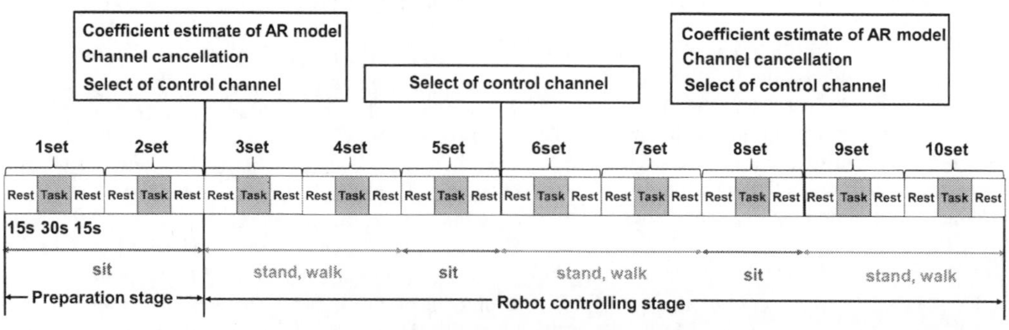


Figure 4. Experimental flow.

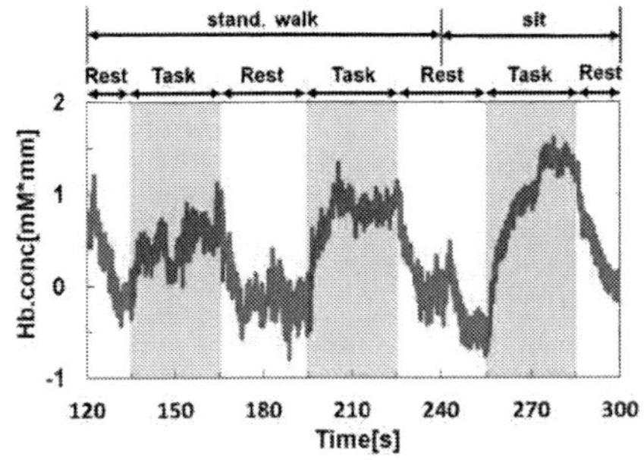


(a) fNIRS signal (12ch).

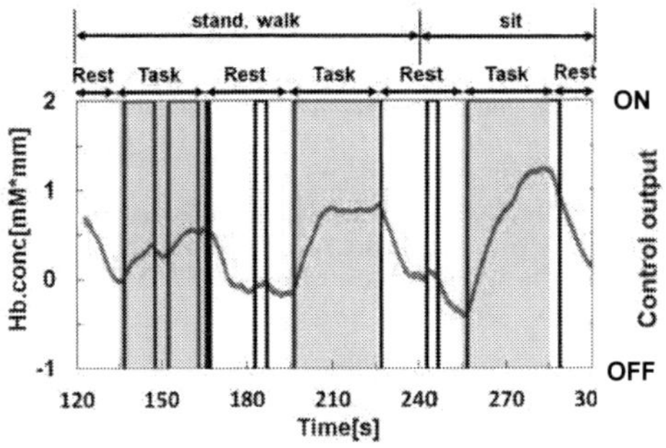


(b) efNIRS signal and control output (12ch).

Figure 5. fNIRS and efNIRS signals and control output by the proposed method during sets 3–5.

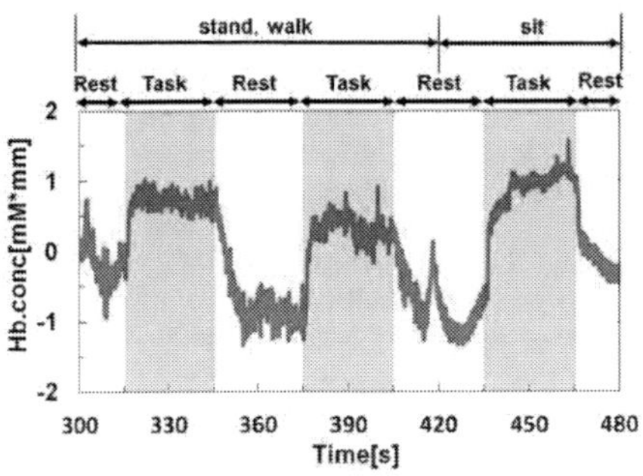


(a) fNIRS signal (12ch).

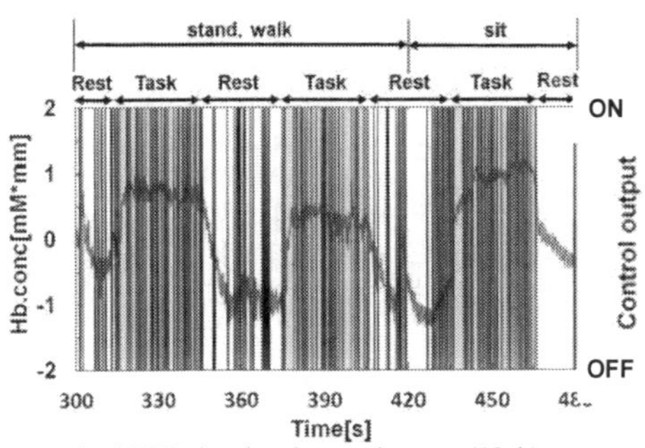


(b) fNIRS signal and control output (12ch)

Figure 6. fNIRS signal and control output without the proposed method during sets 6–8.

decreasing one. However, the output signals turn on at 180–190 s and 240–250 s because the estimates then exhibit extremely small increasing trends during the rest time.

Figure 6 shows the results without the proposed method during sets 6–8 (300–480 s). Figure 6 (a) shows the output signals for channel 12 of the fNIRS device, and Figure 6 (b) shows the corresponding robot control signals. The fNIRS signals are also shown in Figure 6 (b). Because the fNIRS signals contained motion artifacts are fluctuated over short periods of time, the robot-control output signals are switched frequently and repeatedly between on and off. Therefore, the robot cannot be controlled correctly.

To compare quantitatively the recognition performance with and without the proposed method, we calculate the average recognition success rate of the brain activity for the 10 subjects. The average recognition success rate indicates the success rate for controlling the robot and is defined as follows:

$$\text{Average recognition success rate} = \frac{1}{2}(\text{Rest recognition success rate} + \text{Task recognition success rate}) \quad (7)$$

where the rest (task) recognition success rate is defined as

$$\text{Rest recognition success rate} = \frac{\text{Time while control signals are off during rest time}}{\text{Rest time}} \quad (8)$$

$$\text{Task recognition success rate} = \frac{\text{Time while control signals are on during task time}}{\text{Task time}} \quad (9)$$

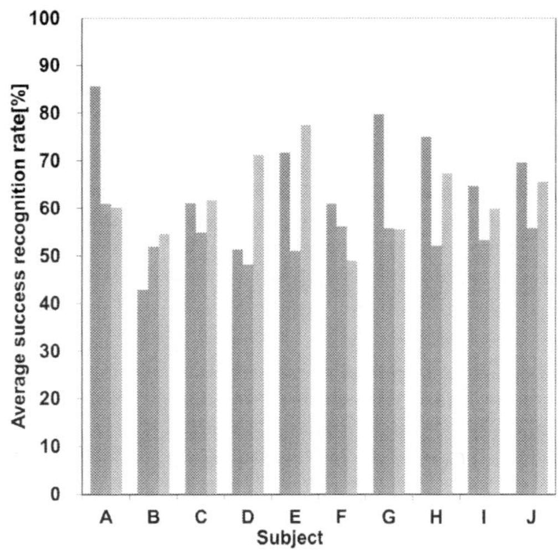


Figure 7. Average success recognition rate of 10 subjects.

Figure 7 shows the results. Blue bar indicates the result by the proposed method (sets 3–5). Green bar indicates the result by the proposed method (sets 9 and 10). Orange bar indicates the result without the proposed method (sets 6–8).

When using the proposed method, 8 of the 10 subjects have an average recognition success rate of 60% or greater during sets 3–5, and 7 of the 10 subjects have an average recognition success rate of 60% or greater during sets 9 and 10. In contrast, when the proposed method is not used, only one of the 10 subjects has an average recognition success rate of 60% or greater during sets 6–8. When the proposed method is used, the average recognition success rate for the 10 subjects is 66.3% during sets 3–5 and 62.2% during sets 9 and 10. In contrast, when the proposed method is not used, it is only 54% during sets 6–8.

## VI. CONCLUSIONS

In this paper, we proposed a method for detecting and cancelling motion artifacts due to standing and walking in the fNIRS signals acquired by a multi-channel fNIRS device.

We identified the motionless fNIRS signal (while sitting) using a fourth-order AR model, and then reduced the motion artifacts due to standing and walking in the fNIRS signals using an AR-model-based Kalman filter. We used the measurement prediction error to assess whether large motion artifacts were present in the fNIRS signals. In addition, we also used the power spectrum of the efNIRS signal estimated with the Kalman filter to determine whether the efNIRS signal could be used to recognize brain activity.

The experimental results of controlling a mobile robot based on the brain activity verified that the proposed method provides better recognition of the brain activity than that without the proposed method.

In the experiments, five parameters were set at the same values for 10 subjects: the variances of $5.0\times10^{-4}$ and $1.0\times10^{-5}$ for $w$ in (1) and $v$ in (2), the threshold value of 0.4 for the measurement prediction error in (6), and the frequency of 0.07 Hz and threshold value of $2.0\times10^{-4}$ for the power spectrum. These values were obtained from a preliminary experiment by one of authors (he was not a subject in the experiments shown in Section V). The optimal values of these parameters would depend on the subjects. In future work, we intend to improve our present abilities to detect and cancel motion artifacts by learning the optimal values of these parameters according to the subjects. In the experiments, the subjects were in 20's. Experiments by subjects from other aging ranges are also our future work.

## ACKNOWLEDGMENT

This work was supported in part by the MEXT-Supported Program for the Strategic Research Foundation at Private Universities, 2014–2018, Ministry of Education, Culture, Sports, Science and Technology, Japan.

## REFERENCES

[1] P. M. Arenth, J. H. Ricker, and M. T. Schultheis, "Applications of Functional Near-Infrared Spectroscopy (fNIRS) to Neurorehabilitation of Cognitive Disabilities," The Clinical Neuropsychologist, vol. 21, pp. 38–57, Jan. 2007, doi: 10.1080/13854040600878785.

[2] T. Kojima, H. Tsunashima, T. Shiozawa, H. Takada, and T. Sakai, "Measurement of Train Driver's Brain Activity by Functional Near-Infrared Spectroscopy (fNIRS)," Optical and Quantum Electronics, vol. 37, pp 1319–1338, Dec. 2005, doi:10.1007/s11082-005-4202-9.

[3] N. Naseer and K. S. Hong, "fNIRS-based Brain-Computer Interfaces: A Review," Frontiers in Human Neuroscience, vol. 9, pp.1–15, Jan. 2015, doi:10.3389/fnhum.2015.00003.

[4] M. Ferrari and V. Quaresima, "A Brief Review on the History of Human Functional Near-Infrared Spectroscopy (fNIRS) Development and Fields of Application," Neuro Image, vol. 63, pp. 921–935, Nov. 2012, doi:10.1016/j.neuroimage. 2012.03.049.

[5] Y. Hoshi, "Functional Near-Infrared Spectroscopy: Current Status and Future Prospects," J. Biomedical Optics, vol. 12:062106, Nov. 2007, doi:10.1117/1.2804911.

[6] R. J. Cooper, et al., "A Systematic Comparison of Motion Artifact Correction Techniques for Functional Near-Infrared Spectroscopy," Frontiers in Neuroscience, vol. 6, pp.1–10, Oct. 2012, doi:10.3389/fnins.2012.00147.

[7] S. Brigadoi, et al., "Motion Artifacts in Functional Near-Infrared Spectroscopy: A Comparison of Motion Correction Techniques Applied to Real Cognitive Data," Neuroimage, vol. 85, pp. 181–191, Jan. 2014, doi:10.1016/j.neuroimage.2013. 04.082.

[8] B. Molavi and G. A. Dumont, "Wavelet-based Motion Artifact Removal for Functional Near-Infrared Spectroscopy," Physiological Measurement, vol. 33, pp.259–270, Feb. 2012, doi:10.1088/0967-3334/33/2/259.

[9] M. Izzetoglu, P. Chitrapu, S. Bunce, and B. Onaral, "Motion Artifact Cancellation in NIR Spectroscopy Using Discrete Kalman Filtering," BioMedical Engineering Online, pp.9–16, March. 2010.

[10] M. Amian and S. K. Setarehdan, "Motion Artifact Reduction in fNIRS Signals by ARMA Modeling based Kalman Filtering," Int. J. Scientific Engineering Research, vol. 4, pp. 2280–2285, July 2013.

[11] T. Hiroyasu, Y. Nakamura, and H. Yokouchi, "Method for Removing Motion Artifacts from fNIRS Data Using ICA and an Acceleration Sensor," Proc. 35th Annu. Int. Conf. IEEE Engineering in Medicine and Biology Society (EMBC), pp.6800–6803, July 2013.

[12] B. Yaakov, X. Li, and T. Kirubarajan, "Estimation with Applications to Tracking and Navigation", John Wiley & Sons, Inc., 2001.

[13] T. Nakamizo, "Signal Analysis and System Identification," Corona Publishing, p. 58, 1988 (in Japanese).

[14] H. Saika, N. Miura, and S. Wang, "Recognition of Brain Activity Using Fuzzy Reasoning for NIRS-based BCI," IEICE-NC, vol.109, pp.55–58, Nov. 2009 (in Japanese).

[15] K. Takahashi, S. Maekawa, and M. Hashimoto, "Remarks on Fuzzy Reasoning-based Brain Activity Recognition with a Compact Near Infrared Spectroscopy Device and its Application to Robot Control Interface," Proc. Int. Conf. Control, Decision and Information Technologies (CoDIT), pp.615–620, Dec. 2014, doi:10.1109/CoDIT.2014.6996966.

# Wireless Printed System for Humidity Monitoring

José F. Salmerón, Andreas Albrecht, Silmi Kaffah,
Markus Becherer, Almudena Rivadeneyra
Institute for Nanoelectronics
Technical University of Munich
Munich, Germany
e-mail: jf.salmeron@tum.de, silmi.kaffah@tum.de,
andreas.albrecht@tum.de markus.becherer@tum.de,
almudena.rivadeneyra@tum.de

Paolo Lugli
Faculty of Science and Technology
Free University of Bolzano
Bolzano-Bozen, Italy
e-mail: paolo.lugli@unibz.it

*Abstract*— **In this work, we present a complete wireless sensory system based on a chipless strategy in the sensor part. Instead of characterizing individually the sensor element, we show the response seen by the reader antenna through inductive coupling with respect to the detection parameter, in our case, moisture content. The wireless chipless sensor consists of an LC circuit fabricated by printed techniques on a flexible substrate. This substrate is actually the element sensitive to humidity by changes in its electrical permittivity. We show the differences in the frequency response depending on the measurement point: the variation in frequency is reduced more than 3 times when measuring at the reader antenna with 10 mm distance between elements.**

***Keywords-cantennas coupling; flexible substrate; printed electronics; reader; resonance frequency.***

## I. INTRODUCTION

A recent trend in sensor design is to remotely access the desired information via a wireless link, facilitating the monitoring of hazardous environments or under harsh conditions. This trend is known as wireless sensors. Typical wireless sensors can be differentiated into optical sensors, surface acoustic wave sensors, intermodulation sensors and radiofrequency (RF) sensors. Among RF sensors, we can distinguish electromagnetically coupled sensors and devices working on the far or near field regions, depending on the operating frequency. In the latter case, the coupling mechanism is inductive using typically LC resonant circuits [1]-[5]. This paper focuses on the LC-type passive sensors, which offer several advantages such as simple structure, easy to integrate and inexpensive to manufacture [6]. Furthermore, the sensor is acting highly energy-efficient due to the low operating frequency and the smaller coupling distance [7]-[9]. Based on the positive characteristics, recent researchers have investigated passive LC sensors in various environmental applications: temperature [7][9], humidity [5] and pressure in the human body [10]. The core sensing system consists of an LC circuit, which is powered and interrogated remotely by a reader coil antenna. Variations in the physical or chemical conditions lead to changes in electrical properties, such as conductance or inductance, leading to a variation in the near field coupling properties. In order to obtain the resonant frequency wirelessly, an additional coil at the readout circuit is inductively coupled to the inductor of the LC circuit. The resulting frequency shift is measured by the change in the impedance of the reader coil [11]-[13]. As a consequence, parameters of interest are monitored remotely and the sensing system in the harsh environment is passively powered. Some authors have already studied the sensing capabilities of this kind of systems [13][14], demonstrating that minimal losses of the sensor is crucial to develop a wireless sensor system based on a coupled LC resonator. Moreover, the fabrication techniques employed are a critical factor because they define the performance and the cost of the sensor. In this sense, one of added value to this kind of sensors is to be manufactured by printed electronics (PE). This emerging technology can produce thin, flexible, wearable, lightweight, ultra-cost-effective, and environmentally friendly structures [15]. The combination of PE technology with wireless chipless sensors is a promising alternative to develop sensors with low-cost process and provide to this circuitry all the mentioned characteristics. In a previous work, we presented printed resonant structures on a flexible substrate for humidity detection [16]. The devices consist of a screen-printed spiral inductor working as radio frequency identification (RFID) antenna and two different inkjet-printed planar capacitive structures forming LC resonators, being the substrate the sensitive layer [16]. In the same direction, Wang et al. [17] reported a wireless humidity sensor label manufactured by screen-printing and dry-phase patterning. The sensor label includes a planar antenna, a tuning capacitor and a printed sensor-capacitor head, where changes in humidity are detected as a shift of the resonant frequency. The printed sensor head is working as a resistive-type sensor between 150 kHz and 250 kHz with a frequency shift of about 80 kHz between dry condition (10%RH) and high humidity (90% RH).

In this work, we have looked into the real operation of LC printed structures acting as humidity sensors, considering all the elements of a full wireless sensor system. In Section II the fabrication and characterization of the wireless sensor system is described. In section III, the response of the wireless sensor is studied from the reader side because this element will be in charge of collecting all the sensor information in any real scenario. We conclude the paper in Section IV.

## II. Materials and Methods

### A. Working Principle

The global idea of this work is to develop wireless and chipless sensors capable of being read out by smart devices, making use of the common frequencies and technologies already in use (i.e. Wi-Fi, Bluetooth). To better understand our global approach, let us look at the high frequency (HF) band and implemented by Near Field Communication (NFC) and some RFID protocols. At this frequency, the working principle is based on the coupling between two coil antennas, one of them acting as reader (i.e. coil inductor included in the smartphones to implement NFC) and the other one acting as tag (element that provides the reader with some desired information). Nopper et al. demonstrated that only two independent parameters of the sensor circuit, i.e. quality factor and resonance frequency, can be extracted from a wireless measurement [13]. Normally, RFID tags include a silicon chip to establish the communication and send the requested information. The input impedance of these chips is capacitive (several hundreds of pF). Therefore, in the resonant circuit, this impedance represents the C-component, while the fabricated antenna corresponds to the inductive part (L). But, in the strategy that we are going to follow, no chip is going to be included, making our sensor tag chipless. So, the capacitive part of the circuit will be defined by the designed capacitive sensor. This sensing material will change the frequency response of the tag, providing the information in an analog way. We have already proved the feasibility of this approach for humidity sensing [16]. The elements of the system (reader and wireless LC sensor) were designed to resonate at HF band with ADS software (Keysight EEsof EDA, USA) [18]. The antenna design has been focused on the optimization of the antenna quality factor because it offers a longer read range and a better reading of the sensor information [19][20].

### B. Fabrication process

The selected materials were DGP-40LT-15C ink (ANP, Korea) with a solid content of 35% of silver nanoparticles dispersed in TGME (triethylene glycol monoethyl ether) for inkjetted patterns and silver conductive paste (Sigma Aldrich, USA) with a solid content higher than 75% for the screen printed ones. All the patterns were printed on a polyimide substrate with 75 µm thickness (Kapton® HN, Dupont™, Wilmington, DE, USA) taking advantage of the fact that its electrical permittivity varies with the relative humidity, as already shown in [16][21]. In order to obtain a compromise in the tag performance, the capacitive array was defined by inkjet printing to reduce the distance between consecutive fingers and, therefore, to increase the sensitivity without occupying more area whereas the coil inductor was screen printed because of its better performance with respect to the inkjetted antenna [18]. Then, the capacitive structures were defined with a DMP-2831™ Dimatix printer (Fujifilm Dimatix Inc, Santa Clara, USA) by only one printing layer. The substrate temperature was fixed at 60 °C during printing. A drop space of 40 µm was settled in the printer for 80 µm landed diameter drops followed by a drying step at 120 °C for 1 h. The inner and outer ends of the coil have been connected through a small "bridge" manufactured by ink-jet printing and attached using the adhesive epoxy EPO-TEK H20E (Epoxy Technology, Inc., Billerica, USA). A 100 Nylon threads per centimeter (T/cm) mesh were used to manufacture the screen printed patterns. The tags consisted of one printed layer with a manual screen printing machine (FLAT-DX 100 from Siebdruck-Versand, Germany). Finally the curing process took place at 120 °C for 5 min. As reader, we fabricated a coil inductor milled in Flame-Retarded class 4 (FR-4) copper clad laminate rigid substrate from Cirqoid (Latvia) with a metallization layer of 35 µm copper using a prototyping machine from Cirqoid (Latvia). A surface mount device (SMD) capacitor was soldered to resonate at 13.56 MHz. In particular, the inductance is 5.9 µH and the capacitance 31 pF.

### C. Characterization

The AC electrical characterization for the different fabricated tags was performed by measuring their impedance, both magnitude and phase, using the four-wire measurement technique with a precision Impedance Analyser E4294A and an impedance probe kit (4294A1) (Agilent Tech., Santa Clara, CA, USA). The stationary humidity and temperature responses of the tags were measured in a climatic chamber VCL4006 (Vötsch Industrietechnik GmbH, Germany). The excitation voltage applied in all measurements was $V_{DC} = 0$ and $V_{AC} = 500$ mV from 5 MHz to 30 MHz. We considered this frequency range because it contains the work frequency of the RFID chip (13.56 MHz) and enough frequencies around it to perceive shifts on the resonance frequency due to variations in the relative humidity. The distance between the reader and the sensors was defined with a spacer manufactured with a 3D printer (EntresD UP Plus2, Germany). The height of this custom frame was checked with a digital calliper (DIN 862) with a resolution of 0.01 mm. Coils of sensor and reader were aligned during measurements in order to maximize the coupling factor ($M \approx 1$).

## III. Results and Discussion

### A. Reader characterization

Figure 1 depicts the prototypes used as reader and as wireless sensors. As can be observed, both elements present a coil inductor and a capacitor. In the case of the reader, there is only one SMD capacitor to tune the resonance frequency to the band of interest, whereas we defined an array of capacitive IDEs in the case of the wireless sensor. This array forces the sensor not only to work in the HF band but also to be the sensitive element to RH variations. The electrical permittivity of the sensing element changes with moisture content, leading to a change in the total capacitance of this array, and therefore, the resonance frequency of this wireless sensor is directly shifted.

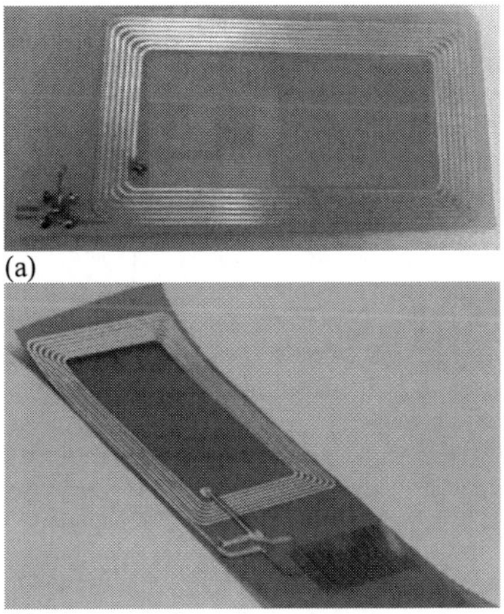

(a)

(b)

Figure 1. (a) Reader and (b) wireless sensor.

The first study carried out was the frequency response of the reader. Figure 1 shows the impedance seen by the reader when there is no tag in its vicinity and when a tag is placed at 10 mm of it. In the former case (no sensor tag in the surroundings), the reader resonates at almost 14.5 MHz, whereas when the tag is approximated, the resonance of the reader decreases 0.5 MHz. This can be explained by the fact that real and imaginary parts of reader impedance are equal at resonance condition. Thus, when a tag is in the vicinity of the reader antenna, the measured input impedance changes [13], giving as a result the shift on frequency observed in Figure 2.

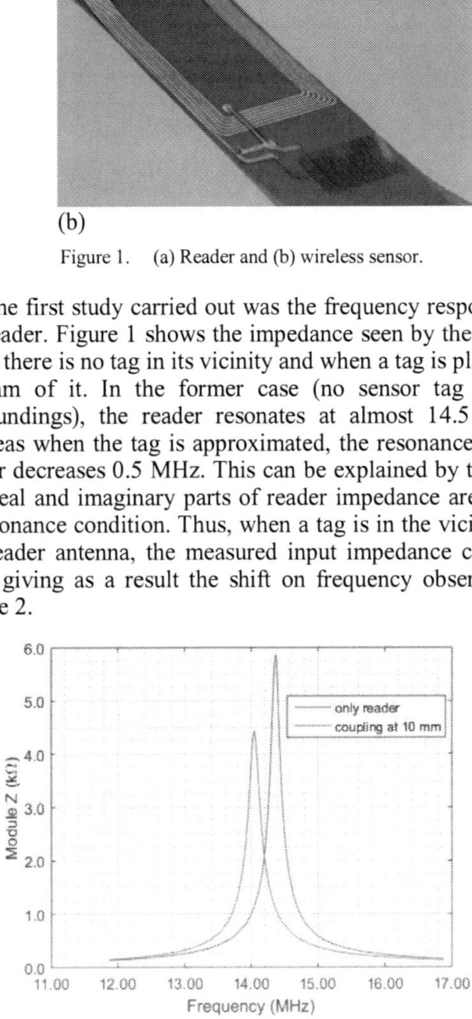


Figure 2. Module the reader and coupling between reader and wireless sensor.

It should be noticed that this relationship depends on the coupling factor, and consequently, on the distance between the two elements. Therefore, all the characterization must be done at a fixed distance. Next, we present the results for 3 different distances. It is important to clarify that in a real environment not only the reader antenna is important to define the whole systems, but also the full electronic design of the reader. One solution is to use a reader capable of detecting the resonance frequency [22][23].

### B. *Wireless humidity measurements*

In our previous work, we already showed that the impedance of the coil inductor presents almost no variation with respect to humidity (less than 0.02% in the studied RH range), proving that the element responsible of the variation of the LC structure response is the capacitive element of the circuit, in our case an array of interdigitated capacitors placed in parallel in order to increase the global capacitance of the system and its sensitivity [16]. We tested the response of the sensor at 3 different distances between reader and wireless device. In particular, we placed the wireless sensor at 10, 15 and 20 mm from the reader and measured the impedance in the reader side. Due to the fact that the capacitance increases when the moisture content is higher, the resonance frequency decreases at higher RH values. This trend can be observed in the three scenarios, although the effect of the distance is clearly appreciated: At the lowest distance, the effect of the humidity level in the resonance frequency is much more noticeable than at the other two tested distances. A shift of about 150 kHz is achieved at 10 mm, whilst this shift is ten times lower when the distance is doubled.

Looking at the change in the resonance frequency at the different RH levels (see figure 34), we have also noticed that the linearity of the response degrades when the distance between the two elements is too big, reducing the detection range of the system. Table 1 summarizes the variation in the resonance frequency at the RH range studied together with the calculated sensitivity for the different distances. The sensitivity is defined as follows:

$$S_{RH}(dist.) \equiv \frac{\partial freq_{T=cte}(RH)}{\partial\, RH} \tag{1}$$

Comparing these resonance values with the one presented in [16], a reduction in the frequency shift of about 70% (~500 kHz) is observed when, instead of measuring directly the response of the wireless sensor, the measurement point is fixed at the reader side. This reduction highlights the importance of performing the characterization at the reader side when a wireless sensory system is described. This loss of sensitivity can be associated to the coupling factor (M) that is inversely related to the distance between the elements [13]. Therefore, the larger the distance between reader and sensor tags, the poorer their coupling factor and, thus, the lower the sensitivity of the wireless sensor.

TABLE I. RESONANCE FREQUENCY OF THE READER WHILE COUPLING THE WIRELESS SENSOR AT THE MINIMUM (20%) AND MAXIMUM (80%) RH LEVEL TESTED FOR DIFFERENT DISTANCES.

| Distance (mm) | Freq. Change (kHz) | Sensitivity (Hz/%RH) |
|---|---|---|
| 10 | 148 | $-2.60\cdot10^3$ |
| 15 | 21 | $-0.30\cdot10^3$ |
| 20 | 14 | $-0.20\cdot10^3$ |

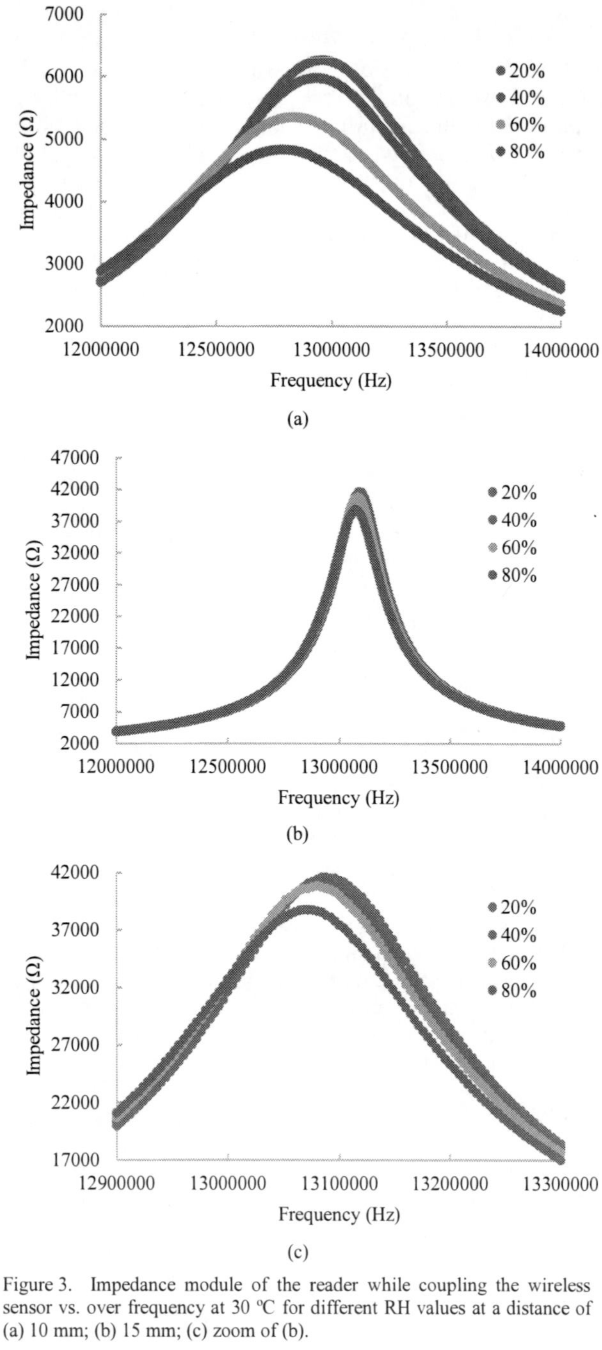


Figure 3. Impedance module of the reader while coupling the wireless sensor vs. over frequency at 30 ºC for different RH values at a distance of (a) 10 mm; (b) 15 mm; (c) zoom of (b).

## IV. CONCLUSIONS

In this work, we present the characterization of a wireless chipless system focusing our interest on the reader side. Normally, this kind of systems is described by showing only the frequency response of the sensor to the magnitude of interest but it is forgotten what happens in a real environment where a reader element needs to extract the sensor information. For this reason, we have shown the coupling characteristics of the chipless sensory system at the reader side, varying the distance between the two antennas: reader and sensor one. To do that, a wireless chipless device sensitive to moisture content have been fabricated by printed techniques on a flexible substrate and placed in the vicinity of a reader in FR-4 technology, showing how important is the influence of the distance between the devices is critical for the proper and ubiquitous use of the system. In particular, a sensitivity of -2.6 kHz/%RH is observed at 10 mm distance while this value decreases more than 10 times when the separation between the reader and the wireless sensor is doubled.

## ACKNOWLEDGMENT

This work was partially supported by the European Union through FP7-PEOPLE-2012-ITN 316832-OLIMPIA and FP7-PEOPLE-2013 607896-OrgBIO. Also, this work was partially funded by the TUM Graduate School. We thank the TUM Institute for Cognitive Systems for the use of the inkjet printer.

## REFERENCES

[1] A. A. Babar, S. Manzari, L. Sydanheimo, A. Z. Elsherbeni, and L. Ukkonen, "Passive UHF RFID Tag for Heat Sensing Applications," *Antennas and Propagation, IEEE Transactions on,* vol. 60, pp. 4056-4064, 2012.

[2] R. Bhattacharyya, C. Floerkemeier, and S. Sarma, "Low-cost, ubiquitous RFID-tag-antenna-based sensing," *Proceedings of the IEEE,* vol. 98, pp. 1593-1600, 2010.

[3] M. J. Cazeca, J. Mead, J. Chen, and R. Nagarajan, "Passive wireless displacement sensor based on RFID technology," *Sensors and Actuators a-Physical,* vol. 190, pp. 197-202, Feb 1 2013.

[4] X. Yi, C. Cho, J. Cooper, Y. Wang, M. M. Tentzeris, and R. T. Leon, "Passive wireless antenna sensor for strain and crack sensing—electromagnetic modeling, simulation, and testing," *Smart Materials and Structures,* vol. 22, p. 085009, 2013.

[5] C. Zhang, L.-F. Wang, J.-Q. Huang, and Q.-A. Huang, "An LC-type passive wireless humidity sensor system with portable telemetry unit," *Journal of Microelectromechanical Systems,* vol. 24, pp. 575-581, 2015.

[6] Q.-A. Huang, L. Dong, and L.-F. Wang, "LC Passive Wireless Sensors Toward a Wireless Sensing Platform: Status, Prospects, and Challenges," *Journal of Microelectromechanical Systems,* vol. 25, pp. 822-841, 2016.

[7] C. Li, Q. Tan, W. Zhang, C. Xue, and J. Xiong, "An embedded passive resonant sensor using frequency diversity technology for high-temperature wireless measurement," *IEEE Sensors Journal,* vol. 15, pp. 1055-1060, 2015.

[8] L. Chen, T. Qiu-Lin, X. Chen-Yang, Z. Wen-Dong, L. Yun-Zhi, and X. Ji-Jun, "Wireless contactless pressure measurement of an LC passive pressure sensor with a novel antenna for high-temperature applications," *Chinese Physics B,* vol. 24, p. 048801, 2015.

[9] Q. Tan, Z. Ren, T. Cai, C. Li, T. Zheng, S. Li, *et al.,* "Wireless passive temperature sensor realized on multilayer HTCC tapes for harsh environment," *Journal of Sensors,* vol. 2015, 2015.

[10] Q. Shi, J. Wang, D. Chen, J. Chen, J. Li, and K. Bao, "In Vitro and In Vivo characterization of wireless and passive micro system enabling gastrointestinal pressure monitoring," *Biomedical microdevices,* vol. 16, pp. 859-868, 2014.

[11] H. Zhang, Y. Hong, B. Ge, T. Liang, and J. Xiong, "A novel readout system for wireless passive pressure sensors," *Photonic Sensors,* vol. 4, pp. 70-76, 2014.

[12] S. Bhadra, W. Blunt, C. Dynowski, M. McDonald, D. J. Thomson, M. S. Freund, *et al.*, "Fluid embeddable coupled coil sensor for wireless pH monitoring in a bioreactor," *IEEE Transactions on Instrumentation and Measurement,* vol. 63, pp. 1337-1346, 2014.

[13] R. Nopper, R. Niekrawietz, and L. Reindl, "Wireless readout of passive LC sensors," *Instrumentation and Measurement, IEEE Transactions on,* vol. 59, pp. 2450-2457, 2010.

[14] R. Nopper, R. Has, and L. Reindl, "A wireless sensor readout system—Circuit concept, simulation, and accuracy," *IEEE Transactions on Instrumentation and Measurement,* vol. 60, pp. 2976-2983, 2011.

[15] K. Suganuma, *Introduction to printed electronics* vol. 74: Springer Science & Business Media, 2014.

[16] J. Fernandez-Salmeron, A. Rivadeneyra, M. A. Carvajal Rodriguez, L. F. Capitan-Vallvey, and A. J. Palma, "HF RFID Tag as Humidity Sensor: Two Different Approaches," *Sensors Journal, IEEE,* vol. 15, pp. 5726-5733, 2015.

[17] X. Wang, O. Larsson, D. Platt, S. Nordlinder, I. Engquist, M. Berggren, *et al.*, "An all-printed wireless humidity sensor label," *Sensors and Actuators B: Chemical,* vol. 166, pp. 556-561, 2012.

[18] J. F. Salmerón, F. Molina-Lopez, D. Briand, J. J. Ruan, A. Rivadeneyra, M. A. Carvajal, *et al.*, "Properties and Printability of Inkjet and Screen-Printed Silver Patterns for RFID Antennas," *Journal of Electronic Materials,* vol. 43, pp. 604-617, 2014.

[19] J. F. White, *High frequency techniques: an introduction to RF and microwave engineering*: John Wiley & Sons, 2004.

[20] G. Haobijam and R. P. Palathinkal, *Design and Analysis of Spiral Inductors*: Springer, 2014.

[21] Dupont™, " Kapton Datasheet, (Kapton® polyimide film datasheet)," ed.

[22] G. T. Le, T. V. Tran, H.-S. Lee, and W.-Y. Chung, "Long-range batteryless RF sensor for monitoring the freshness of packaged vegetables," *Sensors and Actuators A: Physical,* vol. 237, pp. 20-28

[23] C.-F. Huang and Y.-F. Huang, "Design of RFID reader antenna for exclusively reading single one in tag assembling production," *International Journal of Antennas and Propagation,* 2012.

# Multi-Layer Printed Shear Force Sensor on Flexible Substrates

Andreas Albrecht, Mauriz Trautmann, Markus Becherer, and Almudena Rivadeneyra
Institute for Nanoelectronics
Technical University of Munich
Munich, Germany
e-mail: Andreas.Albrecht@tum.de

Paolo Lugli
Free University of Bozen-Bolzano
Bozen-Bolzano, Italy
e-mail: Paolo.lugli@unibz.it

***Abstract*— Printed electronics technology is a promising way of fabricating low-cost electronics without the need for masking and etching. In recent years, additive printing techniques, such as inkjet and screen printing, have been adopted to fabricate low-cost and large-area electronics on flexible substrates. In this work, the design of a 3-axial normal and shear force sensor was developed, that consists of four miniaturized printed capacitors. The partially overlapping electrodes are arranged in a manner so that force sensitivity in orthogonal directions is achieved. The base unit of this sensor has been fabricated using inkjet-printing and characterized. The force response of this sensor was investigated in a force range from 0.1 N to 8 N, the normal-force sensitivity was determined to be $S_z$ = 5.2 fF/N and the shear-force sensitivity was $S_y$ = 13.1 fF/N. Due to its sensing range, this sensor could be applicable in tactile sensing systems.**

***Keywords-Capacitive sensor; inkjet printing; normal force; PDMS.***

## I. INTRODUCTION

Printed electronics possess the advantage to reduce the number of production steps by applying several components with similar process technologies. In contrast to conventional electronics, sensors can be printed instead of assembled. The present work deals with the development, fabrication, and characterization of a capacitive normal and shear force sensor. Such sensors could be used for basic force and pressure measurements. They could also be part of a tactile sensing system in robotics. Advanced robotic systems need reliable information about friction and strain when interacting with the environment and handling objects [1]. Additionally, the ability of printed electronics to fabricate devices on flexible substrates could bring us a step closer to an artificial skin, which can be wrapped around the robot surface [2].

In a previous work, we studied inkjet printing and photonic sintering for low-cost printing of electrodes and wiring [3]. Chase et al. [4] showed a parallel plate capacitor approach with four capacitances that change in the overlapping area for exposure to shear forces and in distance for normal forces. Khan et al. [5] presented an all screen printed flexible pressure (normal force) sensor with a piezoelectric sensing principle. Silver (Ag) based paste serves as a conductor, and the piezoelectric material was polyvinylidene fluoridetrifluoroethylene (P(VDF-TrFE)), which is a ferroelectric polymer that exhibits efficient piezoelectric and pyroelectric properties. The force response was characterized by the voltage readout.

A thin-film normal and shear force sensor was designed by Chase and Luo [4]. Their capacitive device senses normal and shear forces simultaneously. The operation is based on the deflection of a compressible filler material, which is sandwiched between two electrodes of a plate capacitor. Making a few adjustments, this design could be implemented using printing technologies. A more advanced sensor design was reported by Dobrzynska and Gijs [6] using conventional semiconductor technology. Their capacitive approach is based on the deflection of an elastic dielectric spacer. Especially for shear force sensing, they used multiple small capacitor areas leading to a higher sensitivity. However, the fabrication of similarly small features is a challenging task using printed-electronics techniques.

In the present work, the basic idea of their sensor was adopted for printed electronics. The rest of the paper is structured as follows. In Section 2, we present the materials, the printing process, the elastic dielectric and its application as well as the characterization tools used to produce the presented results. Section 3 discusses the design, a theoretical model thereof as well as the evaluation of the print quality and the measured electromechanical behavior of out sensors. In Section IV, we summarize the main findings and conclude the paper.

## II. MATERIALS AND METHODS

### *A. Materials*

The shear-force sensors were fabricated on the transparent coated Polyethylene Terephthalate (PET) film Screenfilm Waterbased (Colorgate Digital Output Solutions GmbH, Germany). The film was developed for inkjet printing and has a nano-porous surface coating and has a grammage of 210 g $m^{-2}$ and a thickness of 170 μm.

For inkjet printing, we used the nanoparticle-based silver ink DGP 40LT-15C (ANP Co., South Korea). The ink contains 35 % silver nanoparticles dispersed in TGME ($C_8H_{18}O_4$), which is a polar solvent. The dispersion was carefully shaken by hand prior to filling into the cartridge. The curing temperature is indicated with 120 – 150 °C and the specific resistivity is 11 - 12 μΩ cm. As the dielectric spacer of our sensor, we used a two-component screen-printable silicone paste, Alpatec 30191 (CHT R. Beitlich GmbH). The two components were mixed equally (1:1) in a small dish. After mixing, the paste can be used for one hour before hardening. Both components are highly transparent.

## B. Inkjet-printed electrodes

The printer used in this work is a Dimatix DMP-2850 (Fujifilm Dimatix Inc., Santa Clara, USA). The cartridge and plate temperature was set to 55°C with a drop-spacing of 30 μm. With these settings, the fabrication of one electrode took about ten minutes. By using more than one nozzle, the printing time can be reduced, but the probability of a failure due to a blocking in one of the nozzles is much higher. Through the heat of the platen, the pattern was quickly dried. To make sure that all the solvents evaporated, the samples were additionally cured in an oven for 60 min at 60 °C.

To improve the conductivity of the electrodes, we employed Intense Pulsed Light (IPL) sintering using a Sinteron 2010 (Xenon, US). A double pulse (period of 3 s) at 2.5 kV was used. The pulse lengths were 500 μs for the first pulse and 1000 μs for the second pulse, which was identified as a good value in previous work [3]. The manufacturer measured a light intensity of 2.6 - 3.28 J $mm^{-2}$ for a single pulse at 830 J.

## C. Elastic spacer

The Polydimethylsiloxane (PDMS) spacer was applied onto the inkjet-printed silver layer on the PET film using a stencil made of 75 μm thick Kapton film. After applying PDMS on both electrodes, they were placed on each other, aligned using alignment marks and baked on a hot plate at 60 °C for about 30 min. To make sure that the electrodes did not detach, a slight pressure was exerted on the sample using a glass slide. In this way, we effectively used the PDMS both as an adhesive as well as a dielectric spacer of our sensor.

## D. Characterization

Optical microscope images were taken with a Zeiss Germany Axio.Lab A1, equipped with a digital camera Axiocam 105. These images were used to assess the quality of the printed electrodes and to determine their lateral and longitudinal dimensions. Further, the drop diameter of the silver ink on the PET and Kapton substrate were identified.

The thickness of our printed electrodes and PDMS layer were measured with a DektakXT stylus surface profiler (Brucker Corporation, USA).

To generate the normal and shear force, we used the voice coil linear actuator V-275 PIMag (Physikinstrumente, Germany) with an integrated force sensor. Figure 1(a) shows the actuator mounted to a movable stage for the normal force application. The fabricated sensor was fastened to the table using double-sided adhesive tape. To reduce parasitic capacitive coupling, a 2.5 mm x 2.5 mm glass slide was put between the metallic bar of the motor and the sensor. The capacitance of a fabricated sensor was continuously monitored using an Agilent E4980A Precision LCR Meter(100 kHz, 0 V bias, 1 V AC voltage). The characterization was automated by a LABVIEW program.

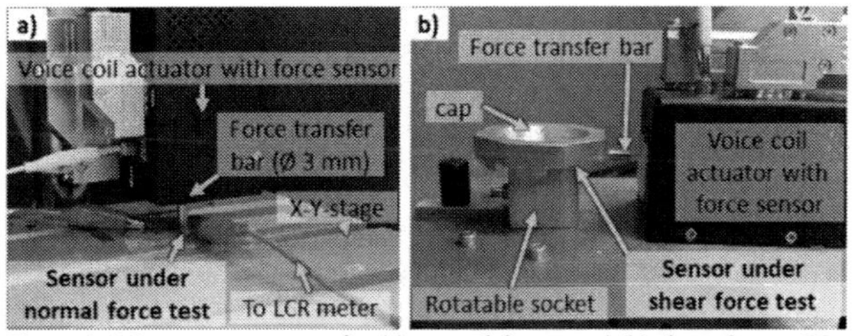


Figure 1. Measurement setup for (a) normal forces and (b) shear forces. The metallic bar transfers the force generated by the voice coil actuator to the sensor and the cap where the sensor is fixed, respectively.

For the shear force characterization, a different setup was developed and built using the same voice coil actuator. Figure 1(b) shows the measurement setup. The force is applied precisely on the sensor plane, thus parasitic forces are minimized. To characterize the samples from all directions, the socket can be rotated from -90 to +90. One side of the sensor is fixed (double-sided tape) to the socket and the other side to the cap. To route the wiring out, small grooves are milled into the bottom of the cap.

For the electro-mechanical characterization, we loaded the sensors with forces from 0.1 N to 8 N with incremental steps of 20 % every five seconds, and subsequently, the force was reduced by the same factor. This was repeated three times. The time-force-signal is shown in Figure 2. For evaluation of the hysteresis, we differentiated between the rising and the declining edges of the profile. In the following, the rising edges are labeled with R and the declining edges are denoted with D.

# III. RESULTS AND DISCUSSION

## A. Sensor design

The design of the sensor was defined by the requirements and technical capabilities described in the previous sections. Thus, we were looking for a sensor, which can be fabricated on flexible substrates, like Kapton and PET using inkjet and screen printing. In literature, different capacitive sensors were demonstrated. For example, Chase et al. [3] presented a shear and normal force sensor where four squared electrodes form the bottom and a single squared electrode the top of the sensor. The operation was based on the deflection and compression of the filler layer between top and bottom electrodes.

The shear force and direction were then determined by calculating the ratios of the four single capacities. The

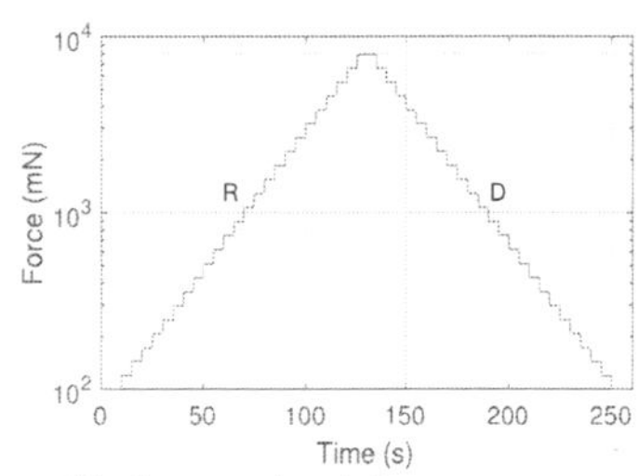


Figure 2. Force profile for normal and shear response measurements with increasing (R) force from 100 mN in steps of 20 % up to 8 N and decreasing (D) force with the same values.

downside of this configuration is that one only obtains very small delta in the capacity, especially when measuring shear force. Therefore, the basic principles of the four individual capacitors had to be modified to achieve an improvement in sensitivity.

So, instead of using square electrodes, we chose an 'E'-shaped pattern for both the top and the bottom electrode. This approach was firstly presented by Dobrzynka and Gijs in 2013 [4]. Figure 3 shows the proposed design of our sensor. The benefit of these 'E'-shaped structures is that one obtains multiple edges, so that a deflection leads to a change in the parallel area of the capacitor. The top and bottom electrode are displaced by half of the finger width, so the initial capacity amounts to 50% of the maximum capacity. Two of the capacitors are x-axis-sensitive, and the other two are y-axis sensitive.

### *B. Theoretical Model*

The sensor was modeled using a simple parallel-plate capacitor approach according to (1). The design of the sensor uses identical areas A and distances d of the parallel plates for all capacitances in the relaxed position with no applied force.

$$C_0=\varepsilon_0\varepsilon_r\frac{A}{d} \tag{1}$$

A force in z-direction reduces the distance by $\Delta d_z$, thus, increasing the capacitance of all capacitances. The design of the sensor assures that an x-force increases the area $\Delta A_x$ of $C_1$ to the same extent it reduces the area of $C_3$ according to (2) and does not influence $C_2$ and $C_4$. Similarly, a y-force increases the area of $C_2$ and decreases the area of $C_4$ by $\Delta A_y$.

$$C_{1/3}=\varepsilon_0\varepsilon_r\frac{A\pm\Delta A_x}{d-\Delta d_z} \qquad C_{2/4}=\varepsilon_0\varepsilon_r\frac{A\pm\Delta A_y}{d-\Delta d_z} \tag{2}$$

The average of all the capacitor values cancels out all area changes due to x- and y-forces and, thus, only depends on the change of the distance of the parallel plates. The z-force can be determined by the change of $C_z$.

$$C_z=\frac{1}{4}\sum_{n=1}^{4}C_n=C_0\cdot\frac{d}{d-\Delta d_z}\approx C_0\cdot(1+\frac{\Delta d_z}{d}) \tag{3}$$

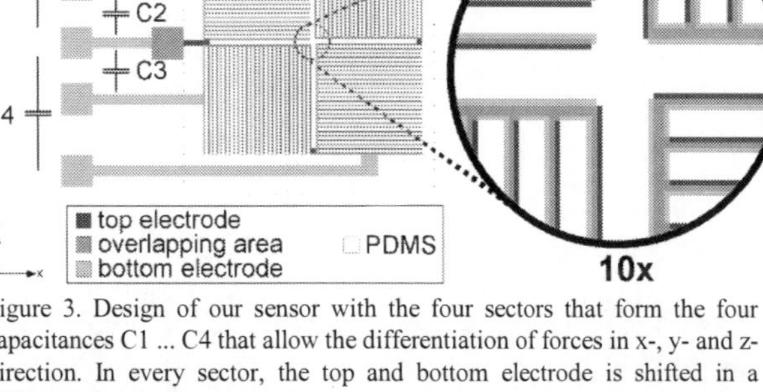


Figure 3. Design of our sensor with the four sectors that form the four capacitances C1 ... C4 that allow the differentiation of forces in x-, y- and z-direction. In every sector, the top and bottom electrode is shifted in a different direction.

A shear force exerted in positive x-direction causes an increase in capacity $C_1$ and a decrease of $C_3$ and can be expressed by (4).

$$C_{1/3}=\left(1\pm\frac{\Delta A_x}{A}\right)\cdot C_z \tag{4}$$

A subtraction of these two capacitances leads to an expression that reduces the z-dependence and can serve as an indicator for the applied x-force. Similarly, an expression for the
y-force can be derived from $C_2$ and $C_4$ that remain constant for any x-force.

$$C_x=\frac{(C_1-C_3)}{2\cdot C_z}=\frac{\Delta A_x}{A} \qquad C_y=\frac{(C_2-C_4)}{2\cdot C_z}=\frac{\Delta A_y}{A} \tag{5}$$

One capacitor consists of 31 fingers with a width of 60 µm and a length of 5950 µm, the connecting bridge has an area of 1.22 µm$^2$, the distance between the two electrodes is presumed at 40 µm and the dielectric constant of PDMS is taken as 2.5 [7]. A theoretical modeling of our sensor is shown in Figure 4.

For a normal force, an increase in all four capacitors is expected according to (5) since the dielectric spacer is then compressed. Figure 4(a) shows a slightly above-linear relation between the reduction of the distance between the parallel plates of the capacitor and the normalized change of capacitance. Figure 4(b) shows the four capacitance values for shear forces in x-direction. $C_1$ and $C_3$ change linearly in opposite directions with the displacement of the electrodes that lead to an increase and decrease in the overlapping area of the electrodes, respectively. The change of $C_2$ and $C_4$ is remaining zero as the overlapping area of these capacitors do not change. Similarly, for shear force in y-direction, $C_2$ and $C_4$ are increasing and decreasing, respectively, whereas $C_1$ and $C_3$ remain constant. A clear separation of the three force directions seems to be possible. However, a change in the normal force affects the change of the shown shear-force behavior.

Figure 5 highlights the influence of the normal displacement on the individual capacitor values. Previous work by Dobrzynka and Gijs [6] neglected this effect. However, already small normal forces that compress the dielectric layer by a few percent can lead to a large error, especially when measuring small shear forces. This work suggests calculating the $C_x$ and $C_y$ values according to (5) to reduce this effect.

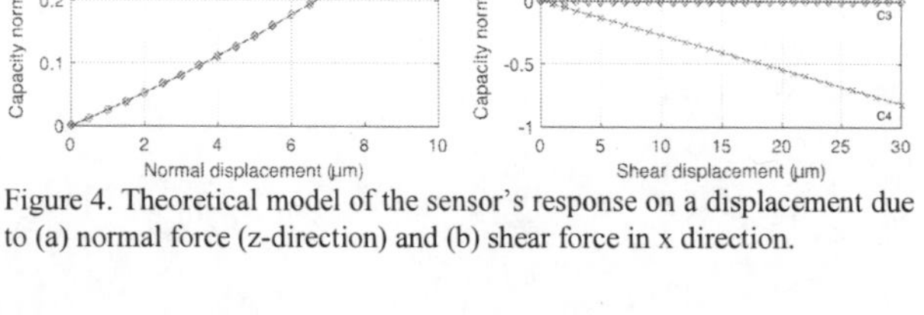


Figure 4. Theoretical model of the sensor's response on a displacement due to (a) normal force (z-direction) and (b) shear force in x direction.

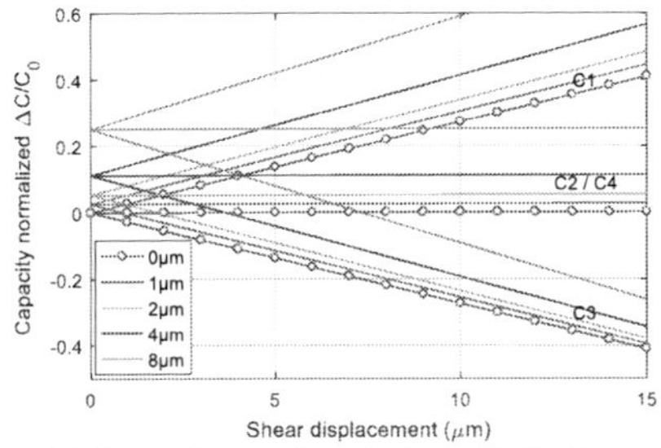

Figure 5. Calculated capacitance values for the individual capacitances for a shear load in x-direction at different constant z-forces.

### C. Print Characterization

The silver ink printed on the PET film resulted in drops with a size of 60 µm, thus we chose a drop spacing of 30 µm to achieve a good line formation. Optical images of the printed electrodes in Figure 6 show a consistent pattern for two different finger widths of 60 µm and 210 µm. The printing of the very fine patterns proved to be too sensitive to nozzle failures that interrupt parts of the fingers. Furthermore, the alignment of the top and bottom electrodes turned out to be more difficult than initially assumed. So, we continued the work with the 210 µm fingers. The sensitivity is similar, but the total area of the sensor is increased.

The profile measurement shown in Figure 7 was recorded perpendicular to the printing direction. We measured an average thickness of 412 nm. The green markers indicate drop rows where nozzle failure occurred and the thickness of the film is much lower. Since these gaps only appear locally, we expect them to have a small influence on the conductivity of the electrodes. However, the thickness of the silver layer greatly affects the conductivity of the electrodes. At this point, we were not aware of the fact that the conductivity could be a problem for the performance of the sensor.

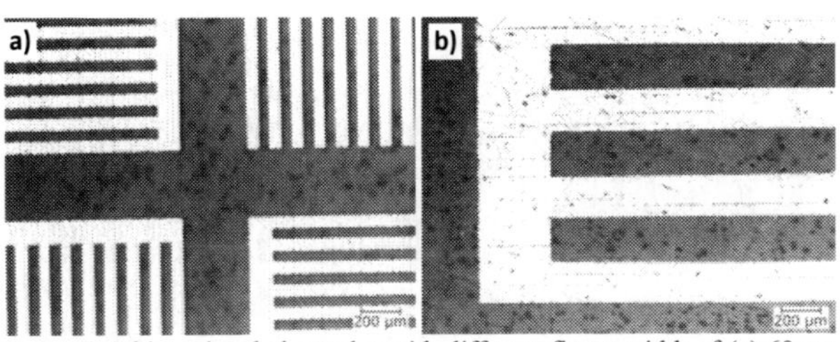

Figure 6. Inkjet printed electrodes with different finger width of (a) 60 µm and (b) 210 µm. The silver can be seen bright while the substrate is dark. The individual droplets form small bulges on the edges.

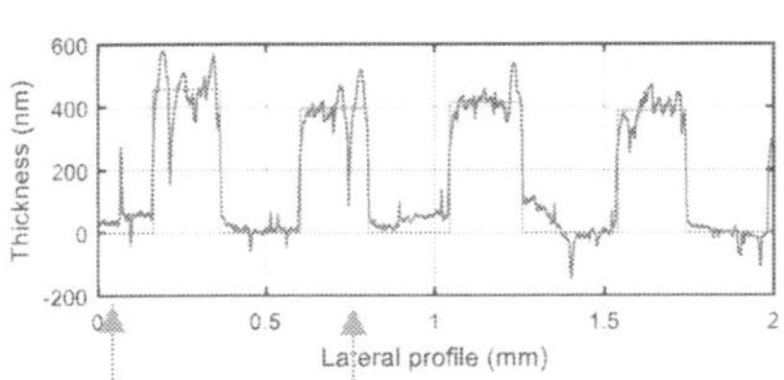

Figure 7. Profile of an inkjet-printed electrode. An average thickness of 412 nm was measured within the red marked areas. The spikes marked by green arrows may lead to an interruption of the conductive path.

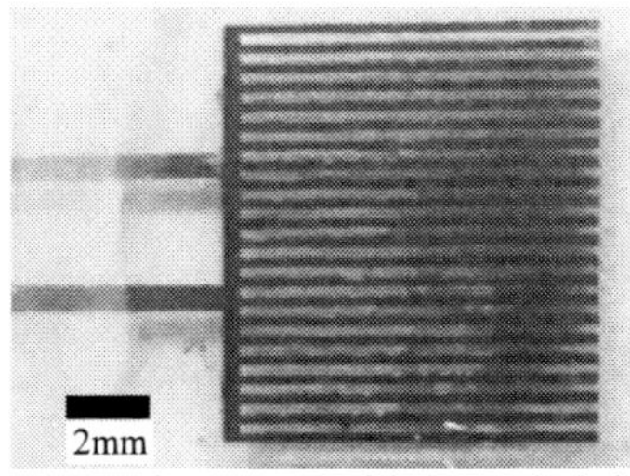

Figure 8. Optical image of one quarter of the sensor including wiring.

The fabricated sensor was then contacted at the rectangular contact-pads. Therefore, the overhanging PET foil was cut off and the contact-pads were uncovered. Figure 8 depicts the contacted sensor. To plug the sensor to the LCR meter, two small wires were attached by conductive epoxy.

### D. Electro-Mechanical Characterization

The results of the normal force sensing experiments are depicted in Figure 9. The data is collected from a characterization cycle, including three rising and declining force ramps. The blue lines represent the reference force signal and the orange lines represent the capacity signal. In Figure 9(b), the solid line represents a shear force in -y-direction and the dashed lines a shear force in +y-direction. The sensor responses occur almost simultaneously with the application of a normal force.

Due to the viscoelastic relaxation of the PDMS, the capacitance during unloading of the force is slightly higher than at loading. Furthermore, a permanent part is remaining that takes more time to vanish. This viscoelastic behavior ismore pronounced for shear forces, for which the capacitance signal shows a small delay to the force signal. Especially for the unloading, the capacity follows tens of seconds after the force signal. Again, a remaining part of the capacitance signal can be observed.

The response of the capacitance to different forces is investigated in the following. For all the following plots, the solid lines represent the loading of the sensor and the dashed lines show the unloading response. To minimize errors in measurements and reduce noise, the 16 capacity values which were measured immediately before a change in applied force have been considered in the analysis. Figure 10 shows that the response of the sensor is linear to the normal force, and it can be seen that the hysteresis is small. The sensitivity is approximately 5.2 fF/N, which is very small. The reason lies at the large area of the sensor. The area where the PDMS was printed is approximately 2.5 x 2.5 cm$^2$ large, so the maximal

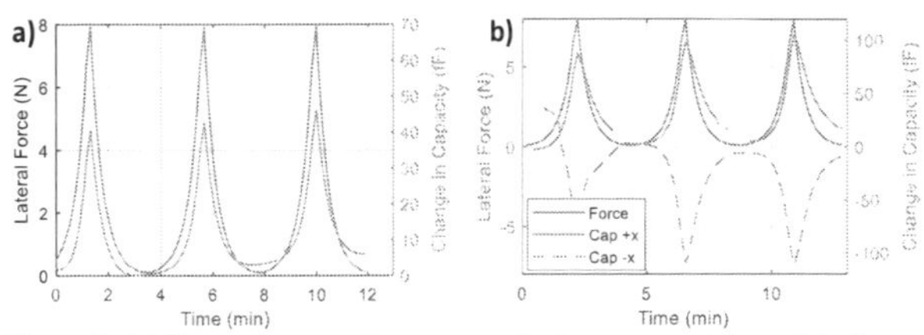

Figure 9. (a) Shows the capacity response (red) to a normal force (blue) over time. In (b) the solid red line corresponds to the capacitance change due to a force in −x-direction and the dashed line to the +x-direction.

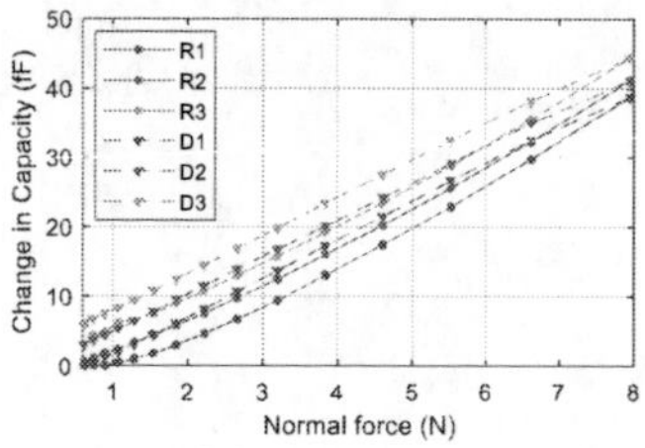


Figure 10. Characteristic of the sensor to three increasing (R, solid) and decreasing (D, dashed) cycles of normal force. A linear behavior was found. The drift of the signal can be explained by viscoelastic behavior of the PDMS and is reversed after a longer resting time.

pressure was only about 12.8 kPa. Thus, the sensitivity to pressure is about 3.25 fF/kPa.

Figure 11 shows the shear force response of the sensor for the two opposite shear directions. The shear response shows a symmetry for the two opposite directions, since the area of the capacitor is equally reduced or increased for a certain force. The slope of both curves is linear over the whole force range. Thus, the sensor is very close to the theoretical model. Thus, it can be seen that a positive or negative force results in the same absolute change in capacity. We measured a large hysteresis that is most probably related to the mechanical properties of the PDMS spacer. Due to the design of the sensor, its response for shear forces is considerably better than for normal forces. The sensitivity lies between 12.3 fF/N and 13.8 fF/N. Comparing our sensor to the sensitivity values of Dobrzynska and Gijs [4], we came very close to their results for the shear response while our sensor was three times less sensitive to normal forces (about 11 fF/kPa [4]).

The capacity values of the sensors are considerably lower than the theoretical values. From the profilometer measurement, we know that the thickness of the PDMS layer is about 40 µm and the area of the electrodes is about 44.4 mm$^2$. The theoretical capacity value for 50 % overlap is 12.3 pF. Our measured capacitance value was 6.82 pF and only half of the theoretical value. This capacitance would correspond to a distance of 96.8 µm. When checking the overlap of our sensor, we found that the overlap in resting state of about two thirds (67 %) was slightly higher than the desired value. This should lead to an even higher capacitance value of 16.5 pF. This significant deviation of the capacitance value originates most probably from some trapped air between the top electrode and the stencil-printed PDMS layer. Such trapped air bubbles are colored in red in Figure 12 and

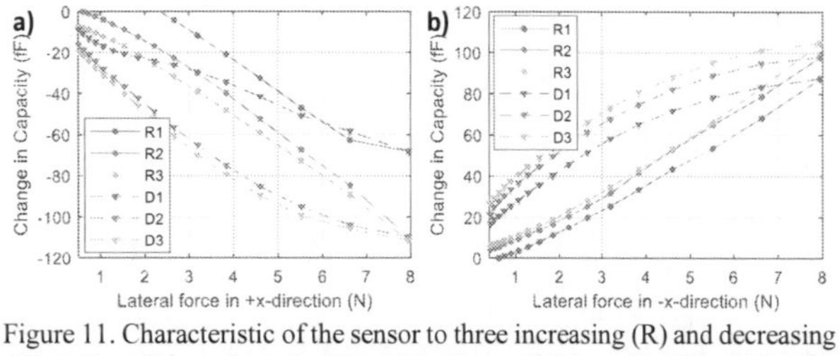


Figure 11. Characteristic of the sensor to three increasing (R) and decreasing (D) cycles of shear force in (a) +x direction and (b) –x direction. After the first force application, a linear behavior with a large hysteresis was found. The drift of the signal can be explained by viscoelastic behavior of the PDMS and is reversed after a longer resting time.

TABLE I: COMPARISON OF THE THEORETICAL AND MEASURED CAPACITY VALUES, THE THICKNESS OF THE DIELECTRIC SPACER $D_0$ AND THE DEFLECTION $\Delta D$. BOLD VALUES ARE CALCULATED FROM THE OTHER COLUMNS.

| | $C_0$ (pF) | Overlap | $\varepsilon_r$ | $d_0$ (µm) | Δd (nm) |
|---|---|---|---|---|---|
| Ideal 50 % | **12.3** | 50 % | 2.5 | 40.0 | **146** |
| Ideal 67 % | **16.5** | 67 % | 2.5 | 40.0 | **109** |
| Sensor | 6.82 | 67 % | 2.5 | **96.8** | **635** |
| S. (25 % air) | 6.82 | 67 % | **1.8** | **69.7** | **457** |

increase the average distance, but do not explain a factor of 2.5. Additionally, the lower relative permittivity of air (compared to PDMS) decreases the overall capacity. The trapped air acts like a second capacity connected in series. The capacity as a function of the fraction of air $\chi = d_2/d$ and $d = d_1 + d_2$ is:

$$C = \frac{\varepsilon_0 \varepsilon_r A}{d(1-\chi+\varepsilon_r \chi)} \quad (6)$$

Here, d is the total distance of the electrodes, $d_1$ denotes the thickness of the PDMS layer and $d_2$ is the thickness of the air gap. For example, if the spacer contains 25 % air and 75 % PDMS the capacity is reduced to 72.8 % of its ideal value ($\chi = 0$, no trapped air). The combination of the higher distance due to trapped air and a lower effective permittivity leads to a reasonable relation of capacitance and distance.

The change in capacitance is originated by a displacement Δd of the top electrode with respect to the bottom electrode. Using the distances in Table I, we calculated the change in distance for each of the four possibilities that results in the measured change in capacitance of about 45 fF. The range of the calculated distance changes of less than a micrometer is reasonable since PDMS has a Poisson's ratio of almost 0.5. Therefore, the PDMS is only little compressible as the lateral expansion is limited.

## IV. CONCLUSIONS

In this work, a fully flexible, capacitive force sensor for two-axial force measurements has been developed by acquiring printed electronic technologies on a polymeric film. We successfully fabricated structured silver-based electrodes on PET foil by inkjet printing. We achieved a resolution with lines below 60 µm and an average thickness of about 500 nm. For a conducting layer, the inkjet-printed samples required an additional post-production treatment. With photonic sintering, an ultra-fast, selective, and cheap method was used to

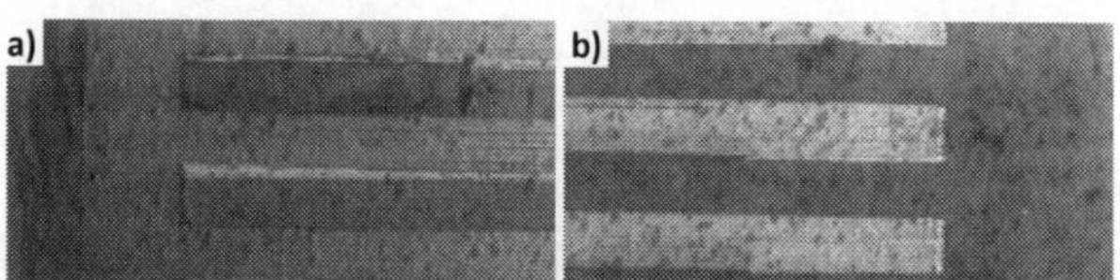


Figure 12. (a) Overlapping area of the electrodes colored in red onto an optical microscope picture and (b) trapped air in the PDMS layer colored in red as well for better visibility.

functionalize the thin-films. PDMS, which was chosen for its good processability and elastic properties, was found unsuitable for direct inkjet printing. Oxygen plasma treatment could be an effective way to overcome the hydrophobic surface properties of PDMS. But further research is required here. The most challenging task was to fabricate the stacked structure of a printed bottom electrode, a dielectric spacer, and a printed top electrode. The method of gluing the two printed sheets together to solve the problem was the best available. The main objective of this report to fabricate a printed normal and shear force sensor was achieved. By integrating this sensor into a 2-by-2 arrangement of four sensors, simultaneous normal and shear forces (three-axial) can be measured. Due to trapped air in the dielectric spacer, the experimental capacitive values were distinctly lower than the theoretical predictions.

The shear force response was characterized using a self-made setup, which was developed to minimize parasitic normal forces when exerting shear forces. The sensor exhibits a linear response to exerted shear and normal forces, operating in a range of 100 - 8000 mN. Under shear load operation the sensor shows hysteresis effects which can be ascribed to the mechanical properties of the PDMS layer. Through the design of the sensor, the sensitivity for shear forces was about twice that for normal forces. We calculated a shear force sensitivity of around $S_x$ = 13.1 fF/N and a normal force sensitivity of $S_z$ = 5.2 fF/N. All of the materials and methods used here are low-cost and cause a very small amount of chemical waste, especially when compared to conventional semiconductor processes.

## ACKNOWLEDGMENT

This work was partially supported by the Deutsche Forschungsgemeinschaft (DFG) within the German Excellence Initiative through the cluster of excellence "Nanosystems Initiative Munich" (NIM) and the TUM Graduate School. The authors want to thank Prof. Cheng of the Technical University of Munich (TUM) for the use of their lab to produce the inkjet-printed patterns used in this work.

## REFERENCES

[1] E.-S. Hwang, J. Seo, and Y.-J. Kim, "A Polymer-Based Flexible Tactile Sensor for Both Normal and Shear Load Detections and Its Application for Robotics," *J. Microelectromechanical Syst.*, vol. 16, no. 3, pp. 556–563, Jun. 2007.

[2] R. S. Dahiya, G. Metta, M. Valle, and G. Sandini, "Tactile sensing-from humans to humanoids," *IEEE Trans. Robot.*, vol. 26, no. 1, pp. 1–20, 2010.

[3] A. Albrecht, A. Rivadeneyra Torres, J. F. Salmerón, A. Abdellah, and P. Lugli, "Inkjet Printing and Photonic Sintering of Silver and Copper Oxide Nanoparticles for Ultra-Low-Cost Conductive Patterns," *J. Mater. Chem. C*, Mar. 2016.

[4] T. A. T. A. Chase and R. C. R. C. Luo, "A thin-film flexible capacitive tactile normal/shear force array sensor," in *Proceedings of IECON '95 - 21st Annual Conference on IEEE Industrial Electronics*, 1995, vol. 2, pp. 1196–1201.

[5] S. Khan, L. Lorenzelli, and R. S. Dahiya, "Screen printed flexible pressure sensors skin," *ASMC (Advanced Semicond. Manuf. Conf. Proc.*, pp. 219–224, 2014.

[6] J. A. Dobrzynska and M. A. M. Gijs, "Polymer-based flexible capacitive sensor for three-axial force measurements," *J. Micromechanics Microengineering*, vol. 23, no. 1, p. 15009, Jan. 2013.

[7] J. E. Mark, *Polymer data handbook.* Oxford University Press, 2009.

# Design and Simulation of Out-of-Plane Nanomaterial-Based Thermocouples

Aniello Falco
Paolo Lugli
Faculty of Science and Technology
Free University of Bolzano - BozenBolzano – Bozen, Italy
email: {Aniello.falco, paolo.lugli}@unibz.it

Florin-Cristian Loghin
Almudena Rivadeneyra
Institute for Nanoelectronics
Technical University of Munich
Munich, Germany
email: {florin.loghin, almudena.rivadeneyra}@tum.de

Luca Larcher
Alessandro Bertacchini
Dipartimento di Scienze e Metodi dell'Ingegneria
University of Modena and Reggio Emilia
email: {luca.larcher, Alessandro.bertacchini}@unimore.it

*Abstract*— **Our contribution indicates a novel solution for the development of the field of low-cost, printed thermocouples for energy harvesting and autonomous thermal sensors. Particularly, our work stems from the observation that the totality of printed thermocouples presented in literature relies on the conversion of a thermal gradient parallel to the plane of material deposition. This strategy is inherently inefficient and rarely applicable in real life scenarios. To overcome these issues, we introduced a novel concept of printed thermocouples, which use 3D-printing to define a vertical structure, upon which an out-of-plane thermal gradient can form and be harvested. Here, we perform thermoelectrical multi-physics simulations, employing parameters of nanomaterials extracted from literature, to show how this approach can lead to generate hundreds of microwatt in typical work conditions. Given their elevated thermopower, these structures could be employed both as autonomous sensors and energy harvesters in Internet of Things applications.**

***Keywords - 3D Printing; Spray-Deposition; Thermocouple; Nanomaterials; Nanotubes; Low-Cost Electronics***

## I. INTRODUCTION

As the concept of Internet of Things (IoT) has been steadily rising in importance and interest, the world of electronics found itself facing many complex and very exciting challenges. If, on one hand, the IoT might account for an economic impact of more than $10 trillion by 2025, on the other hand there is still a number of barriers – socio-ethical and technological - to overcome [1]. One of the main areas of needed technical progress is represented by the realization of low-cost and low-power sensors, able to provide the necessary information to the computer-centralized data-analysis structures [1][2]. Amongst the many quantities to measure and to collect, temperature is certainly one of the most important: its applications range from smart cities [3] to agriculture [4], from healthcare [5] to industrial processes [6].

However, as in autonomous or semi-autonomous IoT nodes the power supply of the sensing system is a major issue, conventional thermoresistive systems cannot be employed.

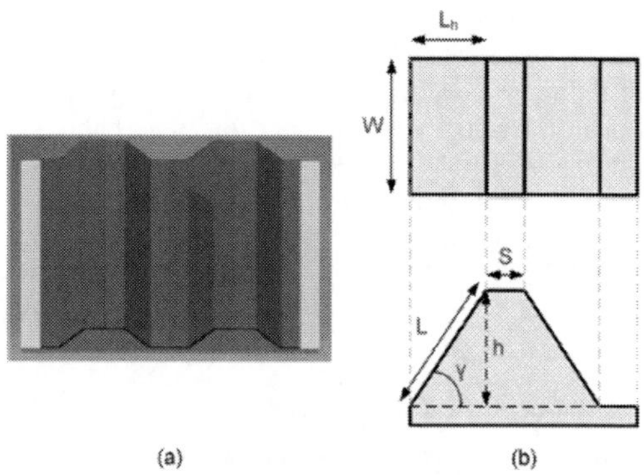


Figure 1. Concept of a 3D-Printed support for planar printed thermocouples, where the light colored material is a printable thermoplastic (e.g., ABS), the red and blue bands represent p- and n-type thermoelectric (a) The diagrams in (b) show the most important geometrical parameters

One of the strongest candidates to solve this issue is represented by printed thermoelectric devices. Differently from thermoresistors, thermocouples are able to generate a voltage across junctions of p-type and n-type thermoelectric materials. As a result, they can be employed as both differential temperature sensors and energy harvesters. Furthermore, printed thermocouples, similarly to most printed devices [7], are characterized by facile production, low-cost and arbitrary shapes [8]. Classical printed thermocouples are composed of a number of junctions between p-type and n-type thermoelectric materials, printed on a plastic (or paper) surfaces [9][10]. This system, however, presents a significant drawback: in order to function properly, they need a thermal gradient parallel to the deposition plane. Although this condition is easy to fulfill in laboratory conditions, it is far from real life applications, where typical thermal gradients are transverse to the deposition plane. Examples include, and are not limited to, heat emitted from a living body, or the temperature inside the engine of a vehicle. The solution we

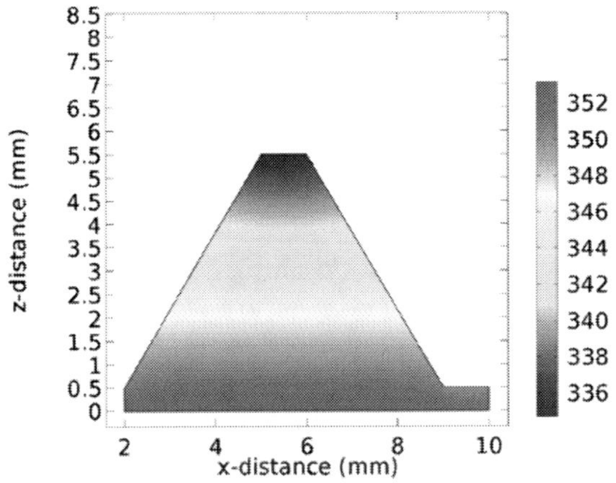


Figure 2 COMSOL simulation of the thermal profile for a 3D-printed object in ABS, with W = 25 mm, $L_h$ = 3 mm, h = 5 mm, when the difference between the hot side and room temperature is set to 60 K.

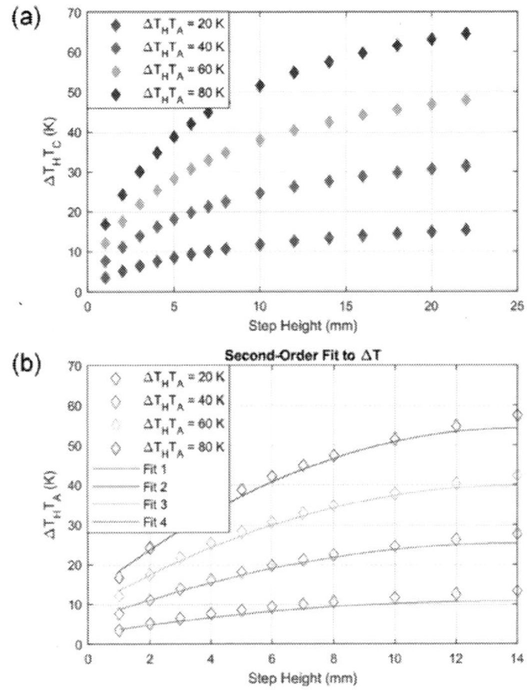


Figure 3. Panel (a) presents the simulated temperature gradient between hot side and cold side of the 3D-printed structures, as a function of the step height h and parametrized with the temperature of the hot side. Panel (b) is a reduced version of the same curves, considering showing that the considered polynomial fit is sufficiently accurate, when the step height is below 12 mm

recently proposed to use an out-of-plane thermal gradient, while retaining the benefits of printed electronics, is the development of printed thermocouples with unneglectable vertical dimension [11]. This result can be achieved depositing thin film thermoelectric materials upon thick 3D printed vertical structures, as presented in Figure 1. With this approach, the insulating thick structure will help retaining a temperature separation between top and bottom side ($\Delta T_H T_C$), and the thermoelectric material will be able to generate a proportional thermovoltage. In this contribution, we systematically investigate the voltage and power, which can be potentially generated by such structures, using as active thin film thermoelectric nanocomposites explored in recent literature. The rest of this paper is structured as follows. In Section II, we briefly describe the methods employed for the thermal and electrical simulations. Subsequently, in Section III we describe the evaluation of an explicit function for the thermal gradient (III.A), followed by a calculation of the theoretical power (III.B) and by the comparison of results for different active materials.

## II. Methods

### A. Thermal Simulations

The geometrical structures have been drawn in a commercial multi-physics simulation toolbox (COMSOL Multiphysics®). The material considered for the bulk 3D substrate is Acrylonitrile Butadiene Styrene (ABS), as it is commonly employed in desktop 3D-printers. The simulations were performed sweeping the temperature of a *hot-side* (i.e., the bottom of the structure depicted in Figure 1b), considering conduction and convection heat dissipation on all the surfaces, given an ambient temperature of 293 K.

### B. Electrical Power Estimation

The generated power was estimated utilizing the theoretical formula conjunctly with the semi-empirical model described in the "Discussion and Results". The electrical and thermoelectrical characteristics of the considered materials were extracted from the works of Suemori et al. [12], Montgomery et al. [13], Lu et al. [14] and our own laboratory measurements.

## III. Discussion and Results

### A. Evaluation of the thermal gradient

The multiphysics simulations show how the thermal gradient across the 3D structure is strongly dependent on the difference between room temperature and the hot side $\Delta T_H T_A$, and the step height h. A typical result is presented in Figure 2, with a width of the structure equal to 25 mm and a step height of 5 mm, when $\Delta T_H T_A = 60K$. The gradient retained by the structure is circa 28 K, which is a remarkable value. On the other hand, Figure 3 (a) shows the variation of $\Delta T_H T_C$ as a function of the step height, and parametrized to the gradient $\Delta T_H T_A$ . Albeit an exact analytical representation of the phenomena might require a more in-depth analysis, by restricting the domain to small step height (i.e., h < 14 mm), it is possible to effectively approximate the behavior of the gradient with respect to h with a family of second order polynomial curves:

$$\Delta T_H T_C = \Delta T_H T_A * (a_2 h^2 + a_1 h + a_0) \qquad (1)$$

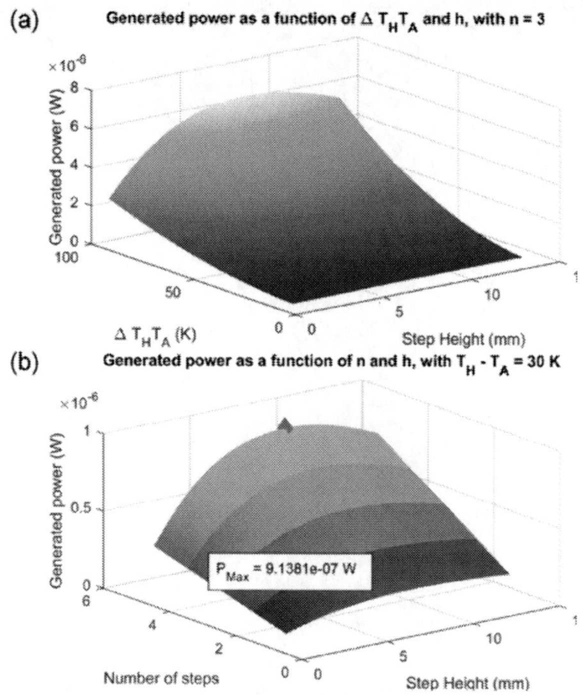


Figure 4. The output of the calculations using the theoretical formula and the semi-empirical model are collected in a series of plots, summarizing the theoretically acheivable power as a function of the step height versus $\Delta T_H T_A$ (a) and the number of steps (b)

with $a_2 = -0.0029, a_1 = 0.0796$ and $a_0 = 0.1680$, yielding an adjusted $R^2 = 0.99$.

*B. Calculation of the Generated Power*

First, given the electrical, thermoelectric and geometrical characteristics of the system, we calculated an analytical formula to describe the dissipated power in the considered structures. Electrical power will simply be:

$$P = \frac{V^2}{R_T} \tag{2}$$

where $R_T$ is the total resistance of the thin film, and V is the generated thermovoltage between the left and the right side. Defining an effective Seebeck Coefficient α, as the average between the coefficients of the p-type and the n-type material, and n, as the number of periodic cells, it is possible to write:

$$V = n\,\alpha\,\Delta_T(h) \tag{3}$$

Concerning the overall resistance, it can be evaluated as the sheet resistance of the thin film, multiplied by the total length and divided by the width W. The latter is a design parameter, while the former can be evaluated as 2n times the sum of the horizontal connecting steps and the oblique walls. In formulas:

$$L_T = 2n\left(\frac{h}{\sin(\gamma)} + S\right) \tag{4}$$

$$R_T = \frac{R_{sh} L_T}{W_T} \tag{5}$$

Combining (2) – (5), a final expression for the electrical power can be derived as:

$$P = \frac{2\,n\,\alpha^2\,W\sin(\gamma)}{R_{sh}(h + S\sin(\gamma))}\Delta T^2(h) \tag{6}$$

This formula highlights a linear dependency of the power from the number of periodic cells, and a proportionality to the square of the temperature gradient. As shown in the previous section, however, the temperature gradient can be approximated with sufficient accuracy by a second order polynomial curve. By plugging (1) in (6) it is possible to have an approximation of the theoretical generated power as a function of all the geometrical, thermoelectric and electrical parameters. The resulting equation (not shown, as it is just as informative as (6)) can then be used for a simple calculation or for parameters optimization purposes.

*C. Comparison of different nanomaterials*

In order to find the effectiveness of such structure, a series of different nanomaterials from previous literature was considered. Since, as we previously showed [15], solution-processable nanomaterials can be deposited in-situ on 3D-printed objects, we selected the most promising thermoelectric nanomaterials considered in current literature [11]–[14]. In the first three works, the materials are employed by the respective research groups for the realization of planar devices, while the last work is our preliminary proof-of-concept of 3D-printed out-of-plane thermocouples. In every case, the sheet resistance was calculated as the ratio of the conductivity to a layer thickness of 1 $\mu m$. The outputs of our calculation script are shown in Figure 4, which presents the generated power as a function of $\Delta T_H T_A$ and h, with fixed n (a) and power as a function of n and h with given $\Delta T_H T_A$ (b). The curves provide a useful toolbox for the choice of the optimal geometrical parameters. For instance, combining the results, it is possible to estimate the optimal h and the minimum number of periodic cells to achieve a target power, with a constraint on the temperature difference.

Calculations performed on the different nanomaterials yield a complete picture on the efficiency of the different materials, when employed in the proposed out-of-plane configuration. Particularly, as presented in Figure 5 (a), among the Carbon Nanotubes (CNT)-based nanocomposites, the top performer resulted to be the one presented by Suemori et al. [12], because of its elevated conductivity, due to high-purity Single Walled Carbon Nanotubes. The best performances, however, would be obtained employing the aqueous dispersion of $(Sb,Bi)_2(Te,Se)_3$ nanowires, as presented by Lu et al. [14]. Finally, to evaluate the maximum power generated by this material, the simulations were re-iterated for different thickness of the thermo-active layer (1 $\mu m$ to 5 $\mu m$). While still keeping the thickness below a

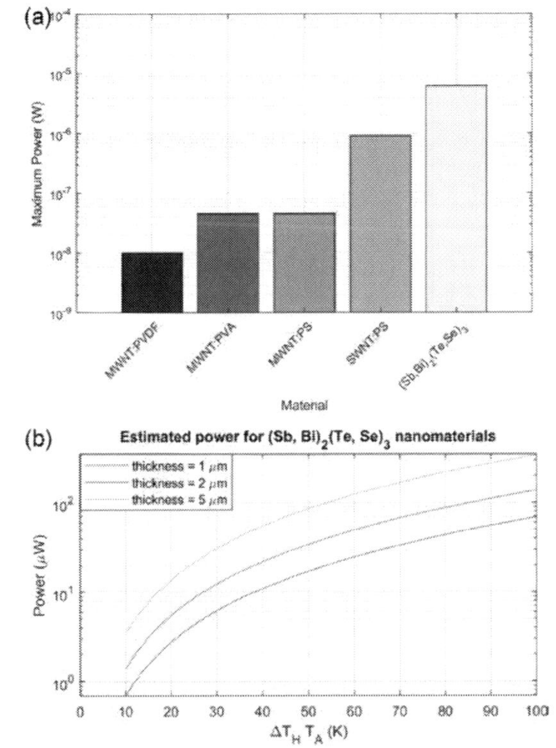


Figure 5. Panel (a) presents the maximum theoretical power for the different materials, estimated for a structure made of 5 periods at a temperature difference between the room and the hot side equal to 30 K. The bottom figure (b) presents an estimate of power for different active layer thickness.

reasonable target for common deposition methods, such as spray-deposition, this approach would yield even superior results: the generated power, with $\Delta T_H T_A = 100\ K$, can easily exceed the hundreds of microwatts.

## IV. Conclusion

In this contribution, we introduced further advances towards the obtainment of a fully printed, cost-effective, out-of-plane thermocouple. In our previous work, we presented three different 3D geometries, choosing the one with the best trade-off between the ability to keep the thermal gradient, and the overall produced voltage. Here, we present a comprehensive theoretical calculation of the maximum power that can be generated by such structures, applied to some known nanomaterials. The final results show how most of the CNT-based nanocomposites could generate few microwatts with a very limited temperature gradient. They, however, underperform, when compared to $(Sb,Bi)_2(Te,Se)_3$ nanowires. Although these values are smaller than what previously reported in literature for printed thermocouples, the scenarios in which out-of-plane thermal gradients are required (e.g., body temperature, vehicle engine) are much more likely than for the planar counterparts. Finally, these sensors can be employed either as harvesters to power up sensor modules, or as energy-autonomous temperature sensors.

For this reason, we believe this novel approach will be a significant step forward in the realization of cost-effective, energy-efficient and environmental-friendly sensor nodes for the Internet of Things.

## Acknowledgement

The authors acknowledge the support of ASK Industries SpA. The project was partially funded by the Ministry of Economic Development through the "Vehicle Active Sound Management" project.

## References

[1] McKinsey & Company, "The Internet of Things: Mapping the Value beyond the Hype," 2015.

[2] H. Bauer, M. Patel, and J. Veira, "The Internet of Things: Sizing up the opportunity," *McKinsey&Company - High Tech*, 2014. .

[3] A. Zanella, N. Bui, A. Castellani, L. Vangelista, and M. Zorzi, "Internet of Things for Smart Cities," vol. 1, no. 1, pp. 22–32, 2014.

[4] J. Roberts, N. Jackson, and M. Smith, *Tree roots in the built environment*. TSO (The Stationery Office), 2006.

[5] W. Honda, S. Harada, T. Arie, S. Akita, and K. Takei, "Wearable, human-interactive, health-monitoring, wireless devices fabricated by macroscale printing techniques," *Adv. Funct. Mater.*, vol. 24, no. 22, pp. 3299–3304, 2014.

[6] C. Perera and C. H. I. H. Liu, "The Emerging Internet of Things Marketplace From an Industrial Perspective : A Survey," *IEEE Trans. Emerg. Top. Comput.*, vol. 3, no. 4, pp. 585–598, 2015.

[7] A. Falco, J. F. Salmerón, F. C. Loghin, P. Lugli, and A. Rivadeneyra, "Fully Printed Flexible Single-Chip RFID Tag with Light Detection Capabilities," *Sensors*, vol. 17, no. 3, p. 534, 2017.

[8] K. Suemori, S. Hoshino, and T. Kamata, "Flexible and lightweight thermoelectric generators composed of carbon nanotube-polystyrene composites printed on film substrate," *Appl. Phys. Lett.*, vol. 103, no. 15, pp. 153902-1-153902–4, 2013.

[9] Z. Lu *et al.*, "Fabrication of flexible thermoelectric thin film devices by inkjet printing," *Small*, vol. 10, no. 17, pp. 3551–3554, 2014.

[10] A. Albrecht *et al.*, "Transparent Thermocouples based on Spray-coated Nanocomposites," in *IEEE Sensors 2017 (in press)*, 2017.

[11] A. Falco, P. Lugli, F. C. Loghin, and A. Rivadeneyra, "Design, Simulation and Fabrication Strategies for Printed Out-of-Plane Thermoelectric Devices," in *IEEE Sensors 2017 (in press)*, 2017.

[12] K. Suemori, Y. Watanabe, and S. Hoshino, "Carbon nanotube bundles/polystyrene composites as high-performance flexible thermoelectric materials," *Appl. Phys. Lett.*, vol. 106, no. 11, pp. 113902-1-113902–5, 2015.

[13] D. S. Montgomery, C. A. Hewitt, R. Barbalace, T. Jones, and D. L. Carroll, "Spray doping method to create a low-profile high-density carbon nanotube thermoelectric generator," *Carbon N. Y.*, vol. 96, pp. 778–781, 2016.

[14] Z. Lu *et al.*, "Aqueous solution synthesis of (Sb, Bi)2(Te, Se)3 nanocrystals with controllable composition and morphology," *J. Mater. Chem. C*, vol. 1, no. 39, p. 6271, 2013.

[15] A. Falco, M. Petrelli, E. Bezzeccheri, A. Abdelhalim, and P. Lugli, "Towards 3D-Printed Organic Electronics: Planarization and Spray-Deposition of functional layers onto 3D-printed objects," *Org. Electron.*, vol. 39, pp. 340–347, 2016.

# Flexible Laser-Reduced Graphene Oxide Thermistor for Ubiquitous Electronics

Francisco J. Romero, Noel Rodriguez, Diego P. Morales,
Francisco G. Ruiz, Encarnación Castillo

Dept. Electronics and
Computer Technology
Facultad de Ciencias
University of Granada
Email: franromero@ugr.es, noel@ugr.es,
diegopm@ugr.es, franruiz@ugr.es,
encas@ugr.es

Almudena Rivadeneyra

Institute for Nanoelectronics
Technische Universität München
Email: almudena.rivadeneyra@tum.de

*Abstract*—**This work presents a versatile sensing platform, intended for ubiquitous and flexible electronics based on a laser reduced-Graphene-Oxide thermistor. This technique enables the fast and ecological production of reduced Graphene Oxide without the need of masks or expensive lithography processes. The final transducer is fabricated on a flexible plastic substrate in order to use it as a superficial patch. Finally, a full demonstrator, which integrates this flexible thermistor with a low power System on Chip with wireless transmission, is presented.**

*Keywords–Graphene; rGO; flexible; sensor; thermistor; SoC.*

## I. INTRODUCTION

After the Nobel Prize in Physics 2010 was awarded jointly to Andre Geim and Konstantin Novoselov for the isolation of single Graphene flakes, Graphene has become one of the most studied materials in all the fields of technology, in both theoretical and application lines. This interest is due to its unique spectrum of physical, chemical and electrical properties [1]. However, the expectations have not been yet materialized into end-user applications due to, among other reasons, the difficulty to obtain high quality samples with the current mass production techniques. The research activity related to Graphene has awaken the interest in other Graphene-like materials. One of them is the reduced-Graphene-Oxide (rGO) which, although it is far from achieving the unique properties of Graphene, capitalizes part of its unique features (e.g., flexibility, transparency or electrical and thermal conductivity) together with the great advantage of an easier and simpler synthesis process. Several works have demonstrated the potential of reduced-GO as a sensor [2][3]. In this work, the rGO's linear conductivity-temperature dependence is exploited to develop a flexible temperature transducer (thermistor). Finally, as a demonstrator of the potential of this technology, we present a complete ultra-low power temperature monitoring solution based on a reduced Graphene Oxide thermistor. After the introduction, the manuscript is divided in four sections Sections as follows: Section II introduces the process to obtain rGO from the GO colloid. Section III presents the design of a thermistor based on rGO as well as its electrothermal behavior. Sections IV exemplifies the use of rGO flexible sensors in end-applications. Finally, the main conclusions are drawn in Section V.

## II. GRAPHENE OXIDE REDUCED BY LASER

The first step in the rGO-based thermistors fabrication process is to synthesize the Graphene Oxide colloid (GOc). This synthesis has been based on a fast and reliable production technique which is a modified version of the Hummers and Offeman method [4] which consists on the oxidation and sonic exfoliation of graphite powder. The GOc can be deposited as a thin and uniform film on any non-porous surface (structurally flexible or not) and turned into rGO through a reduction process. The alteration of the crystallographic network of carbon atoms after the oxidation process turns the GO into an electrical insulator. However, the GO reduction process removes the functional groups and restores partially the crystallographic structure [5], returning the electrical conductivity. The reduction procedure selected is the laser photothermal reduction [6], which offers the following advantages:

- Environmental friendly.
- High precision patterns without the use of mask.
- Conductivity control through the laser power control.

Based on this third point, we studied the sheet resistance of the lasered-rGO as a function of the laser photothermal power. First, the GO was deposited on a polyethylene terephthalate (PET) film in order to provide flexibility to the sample. After that, it was reduced at a wavelength of 550 nm, which as confirmed by Raman spectroscopy is capable to reduce the GO, using different values of the laser power. As seen in Figure 1, the results obtained show that an increase of the photothermal power implies a sheet resistance exponential decay. Therefore, once the power exceeds 90 mW, the sheet resistance remains almost constant.

According to these results, the selection of a laser photothermal power in the range [90, 115] mW would reduce the variability among different samples for power shifts due to the stability of the sheet resistance in this range.

## III. FLEXIBLE TEMPERATURE SENSOR BASED ON REDUCED GRAPHENE OXIDE

There are a lot of works focused on the study of the conductivity of the rGO using different substrates and reduction methods. However, it is most difficult to find works about end-use applications based on this technology. Because of it, this

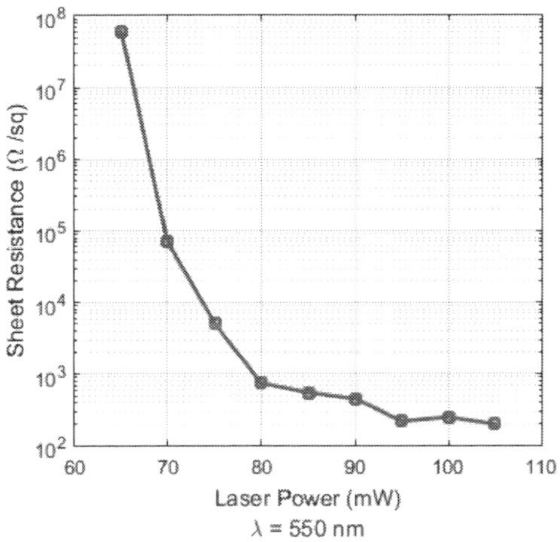


Figure 1. Lasered-rGO sheet resistance as a function of the laser power ($\lambda = 550\ nm$) for a GO concentration of 70 $\mu g/cm^2$.

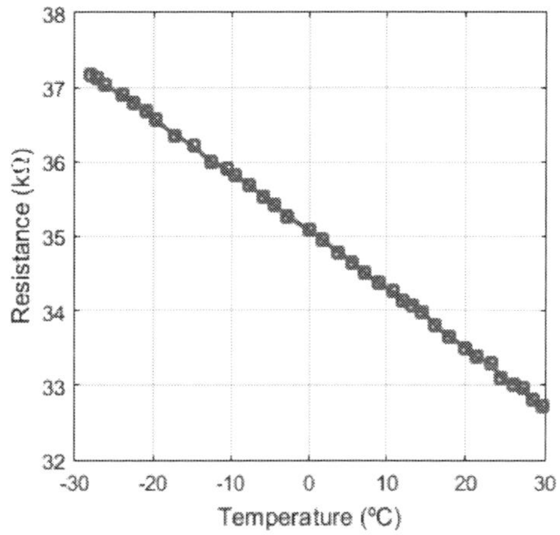


Figure 3. Representation of the flexible transducer resistance as a function of the temperature. Heating and cooling cycles are shown.

paper presents a rGO flexible temperature sensor on the basis of its conductivity dependence with respect to the temperature.

The developed transducer, shown in Figure 2, presents a total resistance which depends on both sheet resistance and pattern physical dimensions (width ($W$) and length ($L$)) as follows:

$$R_T = \rho_s \cdot (L/W) \quad (1)$$

where $R_T$ is the total resistance of the sensor and $\rho_s$ is the sheet resistance of the rGO.

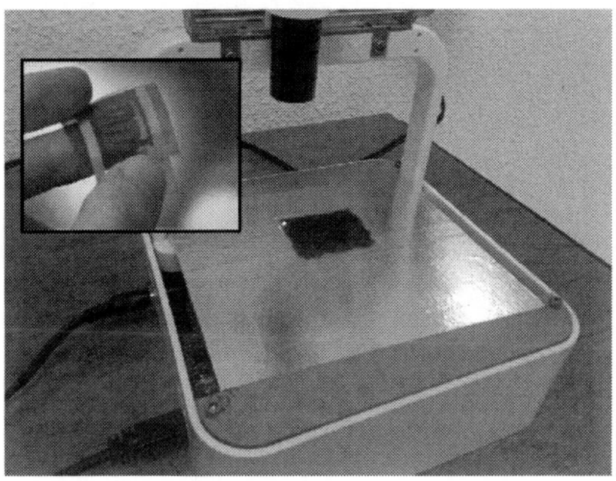

Figure 2. Image of laser reduction of GO deposited on PET film. Inset: Final flexible temperature sensor.

Once GO is deposited on the PET flexible film and patterned using the laser, a second PET film is used to seal the sensitive layer in order to avoid any undesired effect due to the contact with the the atmosphere. In the middle of this stack, two copper strips allow the access to the sensitive layer.

The dependency of the developed flexible transducer resistance with respect to the temperature is shown in Figure 3. As seen in this figure, the response is almost linear and does not present hysteresis. On the other hand, the sensitivity obtained in this prototype is $-77.43\Omega/^oC$ for the range of temperature studied.

## IV. A Simple Application: Ultra-Low Power Sensor Platform

As a demonstrator of the potential of this technology, a device to monitor the ambient temperature has been developed based on the rGO sensor previously detailed. This device, shown in Figure 4, combines the rGO sensing capabilities with the versatility that the System-on-Chip (SoC) devices offer. This prototype, whose controller is the low power version of the Programmable System-on-Chips (PSoCs) by Cypress [7], has also wireless data transmission capability. Then, the measured temperature can be sent by Bluetooth Low Energy (BLE, or Bluetooth 4.0) to a master device, e.g., a smartphone.

Figure 4. Prototype developed.

## V. Conclusion

Graphene Oxide has been suited as a flexible sensing platform ready to be exported to certain end-user applications as it was shown in this work. Once the GO is deposited on a flexible substrate, a simple process of reduction based on laser gives to the GO the conductivity needed to constitute a thermal transducer whose conductivity is completely linear with respect to the temperature. Therefore, we advocate that once the SoC systems become available on flexible substrates, the rGO-based sensors will take a big step forward expanding to multiple ubiquitous applications.

## ACKNOWLEDGMENT

This work has been partially supported by the Spanish Ministry of Education, Culture and Sport (MECD) through the pre-doctoral grant FPU16/01451 , the National Excellence Research Project TEC2017-89955-P and the University of Granada through the scholarship "Initiation to Research".

## REFERENCES

[1] A. K. Geim and K. Novoselov, "The rise of graphene," Nature Materials, vol. 6, 2007, pp. 183–191.

[2] Y. Wang et al., "Ammonia gas sensors based on chemically reduced graphene oxide sheets self-assembled on au electrodes," Nanoscale Research Letters, vol. 9:251, 2014.

[3] D. Acharyya and P. Bhattacharyya, "Highly efficient room-temperature gas sensor based on tio2 nanotube-reduced graphene-oxide hybrid device," IEEE Electron Device Letters, vol. 37, 2016, pp. 656–659.

[4] W. S. H. Jr. and R. E. Offeman, "Preparation of graphitic oxide," Journal of the American Chemical Society, vol. 80 (6), 1958, pp. 1339–1339.

[5] S. Pei and Hui-MingCheng, "The reduction of graphene oxide," Carbon, vol. 50, 2012, pp. 3210–3228.

[6] E. Kymakis, C. Petridis, and T. D. Anthopoulos, "Laser-assisted reduction of graphene oxide for flexible, large-area optoelectronics," IEEE Journal of Selected Topics in Quantum Electronics, vol. 20, 2014, pp. 106–115.

[7] PSoC® 5LP: CY8C52LP Family Datasheet, Cypress Semiconductor.

# Sensor-Based on $PbZrO_3/PbTiO_3$ with $La_2O_3$ for Measuring the Absorbed Dose in Disinfection of Food Products by Electron Beam in the Agricultural Industry

Paulo E. Cruvinel
Embrapa Instrumentation
Brazilian Agricultural Research Corporation, São Carlos, SP, Brazil
Email: paulo.cruvinel@embrapa.br

*Abstract*— **This paper presents a thermal detector using an inorganic crystal based on a chemical compound prepared with $PbZrO_3/PbTiO_3$ with 1% of $La_2O_3$. It has been designed for measuring the absorbed dose due the use of an electron beam applied for the disinfection of food products. The measuring arrangements for validation of the sensor were all carried out based on the use of incident doses up to 10 kGy, i.e., using several exposure times from a linear electron accelerator source with selective voltage in the range of 200 kV to 10,000 kV. For a given energy, the detector has a linear response with beam intensity and an inverse response with chopping frequency. A calibration curve which reports the relation of the absorbed dose (kGy) versus the sensor's amplified output voltage is also presented. The detector may be used over a wide range of energies either inside or outside vacuum, and it does not require an external bias field. Results have shown the usefulness of such agricultural sensor in applications related to food safety.**

***Keywords- sensor in agriculture; pyroelectric sensor; thermal detector; radiation in food; radiation measurements; pulsed electron deposition.***

## I. INTRODUCTION

The use of radiation in the food industry consists of subjecting the product to a dose of radiation from a radioactive ionizing source, such as the radioactive isotopes Cobalt-60 ($Co^{60}$) and Cesium-137 ($Cs^{137}$), or equipment capable of producing such energy. In this context, the elimination of microorganisms, as well as the food disinfection can be achieved. Today, such procedures have been widely used in the agroindustry, in order to improve public health, i.e., for reducing the number of people who acquire diseases caused by microorganisms. In addition, it can help to gain a competitive advantage, i.e., since the radiation extends the useful life of the food favoring the logistics to distant places. Besides, since radiation extends the shelf life of irradiated foods, it is also useful to reduce losses, and operates as an inhibitor of the germination capacity of foods that were intended for human consumption.

Food irradiation has always been carried out in a controlled manner, to avoid contamination and damage to consumers. In general, the foods that are most susceptible to radiation are fruits, vegetables, cereals and animal products, i.e., products based on poultry, fish and beef.

According to Fan et al. [1], the application of food irradiation is recognized worldwide as an effective method in food preservation. This technique became known in the 1950s by the US Atomic Energy Commission, because of the US military's use in conserving food for use by troops in war. The first patent for the use of food irradiation was in 1905 by J. Appleby and A. J. Banks for use in cereals using alpha, beta or gamma rays, for reducing the incidence of disease [2]. Over a long period, irradiated foods were evaluated by the Food and Drug Administration (FDA) and the United States Department of Agriculture (USDA) [3][4]. Since the 1960s, the World Health Organization (WHO) and the Joint Expert Committee on Food Irradiation (JECFI) have been adopting the use of methods base on the absorbed dose, mainly to evaluate the safety of irradiated foods. Such decision was carried out in agreement with the Food and Organization (FAO) and the International Atomic Energy Agency (IAEA) [5]-[7].

The IAEA defines doses of up to 56 kGy to Cobalt, or electrons with energies of up to 10 MeV for not having risk to be consumed nutritionally. The JECFI documented that any food irradiated with a dose of 10 kGy would not pose any toxicological problem and that it would not lead to nutritional or microbiological problems.

These recommendations were accepted by the Codex Alimentarius Commission and from that time on, the number of countries and facilities that adhered to the use of ionizing radiation in food have grown [8]. Today, irradiated food is accepted in many countries, including Brazil [9].

The irradiation process comprises the exposure of food, either prepacked or in bulk (without packaging), to a pre-established level of ionization radiation. It is very important to know the sources of ionizing radiation, i.e., how the energy is quantified, its limitations and advantages. Ionizing radiation interacts with the molecules of materials by allocating or displacing electrons. This way, by creating negative ions (Anions) or positive ions (Cations) respectively, energy is transferred to the irradiated body. The effects of radiation on biological materials can be direct or indirect. One of the direct effects occurs due to the chemical reactions, as a result of the bombardment of irradiated energy in the molecule. The indirect effects are due to the consequences of the reactive diffusion of free radicals formed by the radiolysis of the water, as for example, the hydroxide radical $OH^-$, the H atom and the hydrogen peroxide ($H_2O_2$).

In this context, several sources of radiation can be used. Among them, the gamma radiation, the radiation produced by the use of X-ray equipment and the radiation produced by an electron beam are more prominent. The use of the electron beam machines, and also the X-rays, has the advantage of being able to be switched on and off according to the need, which leads to better compliance with security protocols.

An electron-based accelerator machine uses electromagnetic fields to propel the charged particles to nearly light speed and to contain them in well-defined beams. However, such field of knowledge is still open to research, development, and innovation, i.e., in relation to the establishment of transducers and sensors that can provide conditions for an adequate evaluation of the beam for food quality control, as well as the doses the food is subject to.

This work presents the use of a crystal prepared with $PbZrO_3/PbTiO_3$ and $La_2O_3$, which has pyroelectric properties, for measuring the absorbed dose in the processes related to the use of electron beam for food disinfection in the agricultural industry.

After this introduction, this paper is organized as follows. Section 2 presents the main related theoretical background and modelling for both the pyroelectric crystal and the electron beam and its interaction with matter; Section 3 presents the materials and methods for the development of the sensor, and its validation when measuring the absorbed dose in the disinfection of food products by electron beam. The results and discussions are presented in Section 4, followed by the conclusion and future work in Section 5.

## II. RELATED THEORY AND MODELING

In pyroelectric crystals, a change in temperature alters the lattice spacing of a non-symmetrically located ion which varies the spontaneous polarization of the crystal [10][11].

This variation of spontaneous polarization produces a displacement current (*i*) parallel to the polar axis described by:

$$i = Ap(T)\frac{\partial T}{\partial t} \tag{1}$$

where p(T) is the pyroelectric coefficient evaluated at temperature (T) and (A) is the surface area normal to the polar axis. Since the field across the crystal is zero, the conduction current through the crystal is zero, and the measurement is not affected by the crystal resistance. Therefore, the energy deposited per second by the electron beam is obtained by the product of the current of the beam and the energy losses of the electron in the crystal. Despite the fact that some of this deposited energy will escape the crystal in different forms, such as electromagnetic radiation, mainly in the X-ray region, a considerable part of the energy will be transferred to the crystal as heat.

The equivalent circuit for measuring is shown in Figure 1, where it is possible to observe ($R_x$) and ($C_x$), which are the crystal resistance and capacitance, respectively. When exposed to a modulated radiation, the incident power of a beam which hits the crystal that presents pyroelectric properties can be given by [12]:

$$P_i = P_0 + Pe^{j\omega t} \tag{2}$$

where ($P_i$) is the incident energy, $\omega=2\pi f$, (f) is given in Hz, and it can be written as a discrete sum of trigonometric or exponential functions with specific frequencies.

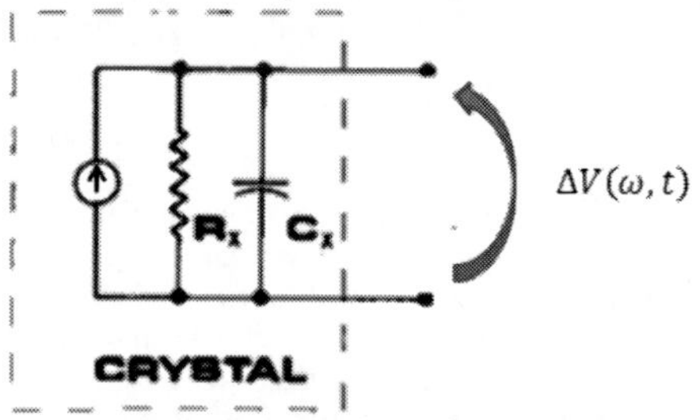


Figure 1. An equivalent circuit for the pyroelectric crystal, where $R_x$ and $C_x$ are the equivalent resistance and capacitance respectively.

In this context, the thermal properties for an ideal pyroelectric crystal can be described as follows:

$$H\frac{d\Delta T}{dt} + G_R\Delta T = \eta P_i \tag{3}$$

where (H) is the thermal capacitance of the crystal, which operates as a sensor to detect the amount of radiation from an electron beam, ($\Delta T$) is the temperature rise of the sensor, i.e., caused by an incident and modulated radiation, ($G_R$) is the radiative heat conductance, and ($\eta$) is the fraction of the incident radiation that is absorbed by the crystal and transformed into heat [13]. Equation (3) is used to determine the variation in temperature. Therefore, by solving (3) in the steady state, it is possible to obtain:

$$\Delta T(\omega,t) = \frac{\eta P_i}{G_R + j\omega H} e^{j\omega t} \tag{4}$$

Due to the pyroelectric effect, the variation in temperature $\Delta T(\omega,t)$ leads to the generation of surface charge $\Delta Q(\omega,t)$ on the sensor's electrodes, i.e., when connected to an electric load. Then, the amount of charge can be determined by:

$$\Delta Q(\omega,t) = A\Delta P(\omega,t) = Ap(T)\Delta T(\omega,t) \tag{5}$$

Besides, the surface charges produce a voltage in the equivalent open circuit board of the crystal, and can be given by:

$$\Delta V(\omega,t) = \frac{A\Delta Q(\omega,t)}{C_d} \tag{6}$$

where ($C_d$) is the capacitance of the pyroelectric sensor.

By combining (8) and (9), it is possible to verify that, for an open circuit, the voltage becomes equal to:

$$\Delta V(\omega, t) = \frac{p(T) d \Delta T(\omega,t) A}{k_{\varepsilon_0}} \tag{7}$$

where (k) is the dielectric constant and ($\varepsilon_0$) is the dielectric permittivity in the vacuum. The performance of the sensor is determined by the minimum radiation power it can measure. This minimum power is determined by the responsiveness and noise present in the detection process [14]. Among the noise to be considered, it can be: thermal or radiation noise [15], dielectric noise [16], amplifier noise [17], and Johnson noise [18].

Now, rewriting (7) in terms of the stopping power for electrons, it is possible to find the output voltage as a function of the incident energy flow, i.e., in terms of the absorbed dose. For this, it is important to observe the rate at which charged particles lose energy as they travel through a given material, i.e., called the stopping power of that material. The stopping power, it is made up of two parts, the electronic stopping power due to the interaction with the atomic electrons of the material and the nuclear stopping power. In relation of the interaction of radiation with matter, the electronic stopping power is, in general, much larger than the nuclear stopping power. However, it is important to observe that the nuclear stopping power is not zero and nuclear reactions do take place even in few processes.

Besides, a minus signal is used together with the stopping power to make the association with the phenomena that occur when an ion is losing kinetic energy. When electrons bombard a target, their energy is given up in the two processes mentioned above, which are referred to as collision losses and radiation losses.

The collision losses process involves Coulomb-force interactions with the electrons of the atom, while the radiation losses process result from interactions with the nuclei.

A high-speed electron will lose its energy in a target by many interactions of both physical phenomena types. Besides, each interaction will usually give rise to a change in the direction of the electron, i.e., resulting in tortuous paths in a thick target. On the other hand, if one is using a thin target, through which the electron pass with little energy loss, or even by changing direction, the deposited energy will escape the crystal mainly in the form of X-rays.

The same situation can be faced, when using higher accelerating potentials, i.e., may occur above 10 MeV. In addition, there are some target materials that allow the change of incident energy into heat, i.e., for such cases one can use them to detect radiation, they can be recognized as potential material for the development of sensors, as thermal detectors. Then, the minimum impact parameters will correspond to those collisions in which the maximum amount of kinetic energy is transferred to target. Furthermore, the maximum impact parameter also has to be estimated from different considerations. The basis of this process is that the ion rapidly moves past the electrons in the material and delivers a sharp impulse to them. In the material the electrons are bound in atoms and are orbiting with their own characteristic frequencies or time scales. Thus, in order to have an adiabatic collision, the time for the ion to cross the atom should be less than the average time for an electron orbit [19]. Then, the total stopping power for a mixture with density (ρ) can be found based on the Bohr`s classical formula and using the expression presented by Bethe and Bloch [20]-[22]. Such concept is based on momentum transfer in a quantum mechanical correct formalism, i.e., with the expanded form of the electron number density, that means:

$$\left(-\frac{1}{\rho}\frac{dE}{dx}\right)_{tt} = 4\pi N_A r_e^2 m_e c^2 \frac{Z_{eff} q^2}{A_{tt}^m \beta^2}\left[\ln\left(\frac{\eta P_i}{I}\right) - \beta^2\right] \tag{8}$$

where ($N_A$) is the Avogadro's number, ($r_e$) is the classical radius of the electron, ($m_e$) is the mass of the electron, ($c$) is the speed of light, ($Z_{eff}$) is the effective atomic number of the crystals 'mixture, ($q$) is the charge of the ion, ($A_{tt}^m$) is the total mass number of the crystals 'mixture, (β) is the relation given by the speed of the ion over the speed of light, ($I$) is the ionization potential, and the normalized total stopping power for the crystal is represented by ($-1/\rho(dE/dx)_{tt}$).

From the expression (4), it is now possible to find ($\eta P_i$) as a function of the total stopping power for the crystals 'mixture, i. e., given by:

$$\eta P_i = e^{\left\{\left(-\frac{1}{\rho}\frac{dE}{dx}\right)_{tt}\left(\frac{A_{tt}^m \beta^2}{4\pi N_A r_e^2 m_e c^2 Z_{eff} q^2} + \ln(I) + \beta^2\right)\right\}} \tag{9}$$

By combining (7), (8) and (9) it is possible to find the sensor`s output voltage as a function of the total stopping power, which can be given as follows:

$$\Delta V(\omega, t) = \left(\frac{p(T) dA\{[G_R \cos(\omega t) + \omega H \sin(\omega t)] - j[\omega H \cos(\omega t) - G_R \sin(\omega t)]\}}{k_{\varepsilon_0}(G_R^2 + \omega^2 H^2)}\right) \cdot \left(e^{\left\{\left(-\frac{1}{\rho}\frac{dE}{dx}\right)_{tt}\left(\frac{A_{tt}^m \beta^2}{4\pi N_A r_e^2 m_e c^2 Z_{eff} q^2} + \ln(I) + \beta^2\right)\right\}}\right) \tag{10}$$

Since the pyroelectric crystal is obtained from a mixture of elements ($Z_{eff}$) is taken as a function of the elemental composition [23] present in the sensor´s material. In other words, it is considered the fraction of the total number of electrons associated with each element, and its atomic number. Therefore, by using (10) it is possible to evaluate $\Delta V(\omega,t)$ as a function of the absorbed radiation dose.

## III. MATERIAL AND METHODS

The sensor is based on the use of a multi-component ceramic system consisting of Lead, Zirconium, Titanate, and Lanthanum oxide with a thickness of 2.2 mm, radius of 8.3 mm, and (ρ) equal to 7.47 g/m$^3$. It is assembled in a cylindrical aluminum chamber. Figure 2 shows the electronic circuit for signal processing. To insulate the detector from external noise a carbon black window was used over the circular flat top surface of the crystal, i.e., to decrease the environmental light radiation noise. The ceramic used is a crystal having a 54/46 mol% of a $PbZrO_3/PbTiO_3$ mixture, where 1% by weight of $La_2O_3$ was added. Such arrangement allows properties that are quite desirable for sensors application, i.e., it yields a higher Curie temperature, of about 339°C, and substantially increases the dielectric constant. Table I shows the weight composition of the crystal, which is used as the basis for the sensor of radiation dose from electron beam, as well as the percent number of atoms/molecule.

The electron beam doses and all the measuring were performed using an industrial linear electron accelerator with selective voltage in the range of 200 kV to 10,000 kV. This linear electron accelerator covers the useful energy range of 0.3 MeV to 10 MeV, i.e., a Linac® type, which is suitable for application in the sterilization of food products. Besides, the measurements were obtained with a chopper device, which enabled the modulation of the electron beam in a suitable range of frequencies, i.e., from units to hundreds of Hertz.

TABLE I. WEIGHT COMPOSITION OF THE CRYSTAL, AS WELL AS THE NUMBER OF ATOMS/MOLECULE.

| Element | Atomic Number | Mass Number | % Weight Composition | % Number of Atoms/Molecule |
|---|---|---|---|---|
| Oxygen | 8 | 16.00 | 14.7024 | 60.0 |
| Lanthanum | 57 | 139.91 | 0.8442 | 0.4 |
| Titanium | 22 | 47.90 | 6.6821 | 9.1 |
| Zirconium | 40 | 91.22 | 14.9384 | 10.7 |
| Lead | 82 | 207.19 | 62.8329 | 19.8 |

Based on the frequency used in the chopper, the input electron beam is controlled by periodic opening and closing of a switch used in its arrangement. Then, the electron beam can be controlled, i.e., the incident radiation flux. Therefore, the instruments that have been used with the signal processing and conditioning circuit were a variable frequency chopper, and an accurate voltmeter.

The signal conditioning circuitry was implemented to allow adequate voltage level and a good signal/noise ratio. Figure 2 shows the circuit based on the use of the LF347, having four JFET operational amplifiers (OpAmp). This integrated circuit presents broad bandwidth (4MHz), high slew-rate (13V/µs), high impedance in their input (1TΩ), and fast settling time (2 µs). In addition, it has a well matched high voltage JFET input which provides very low input bias and offset [24]. Besides, a buffer circuit was also implemented using a CA3140 BiMOS OpAmp with a gate protected MOSFET (PMOS) transistors to provide input impedance equal to 1.5 TΩ, i.e., useful to allow a better impedance matching with a voltage meter [25]. For the implemantation of the signal processing circuit, due to the ability to shield from outside interferences, we used BNC`s connectors and coaxial cable.

The beam chopper can be shielded with a 2.0 mm thick copper disk. The electron beam can be collimated to an area slightly larger than the area (A) of the crystal. The output signal from the crystal´s sensor can be connected to the input of the low noise amplifier, and the resulting averaged signal, which correspond the irradiated dose can be measured.

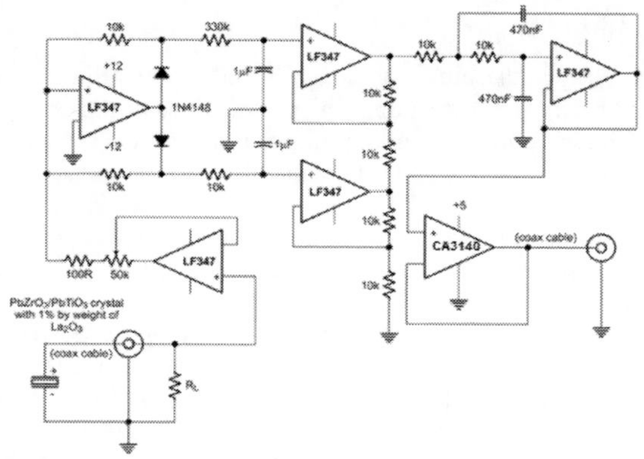


Figure 2. Electronic circuit for signal processing (resistors are in Ω units).

During the measuring process, we also used an industrial dosimeter for the cross-calibration procedure [26], i.e., in order to obtain information from both the crystal`s sensor and the calibrated parallel-plate ion chamber [27], which is recommended to be used up to 10 MeV.

## IV. RESULTS AND DISCUSSIONS

Figure 3 shows a photograph of the sensor`s prototype and the electronic circuit used for signal processing. The output voltage intensity from the sensor based on the $PbZrO_3/PbTiO_3$ with $La_2O_3$ was found to be inversely proportional to the chopping frequency, as expected for a pyroelectric response [28], i.e, because such kind of crystal has a longer time for relaxation at lower frequencies.

Equation (10) was evaluated by taking into account all the values of the parameters as presented in the literature, including the stopping power values for such mixture of elements. The simulation was performed by using a broad range of ion beam energies and a computer code [29].

The theoretical results obtained from equation (10), at different energy values, for an incident radiation flux of 3.5 µW are shown in Figure 4. It is possible to observe in this result the dependence of the output voltage in relation of the stopping power values, which are function of the incident energy and the material of the crystal. Therefore, to operate as a sensor for absorbed dose measurements, the crystal must be enable to fully stop the electron beam. This factor is also dependent of the crystal thickness.

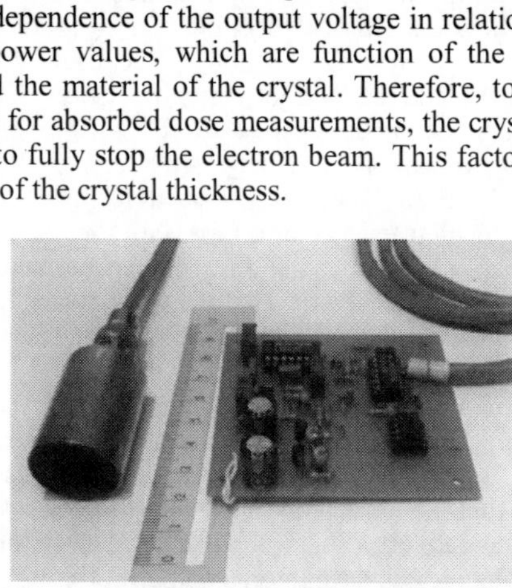

Figure 3. Photograph of the sensor`s prototype with the electronic circuit used for signal processing.

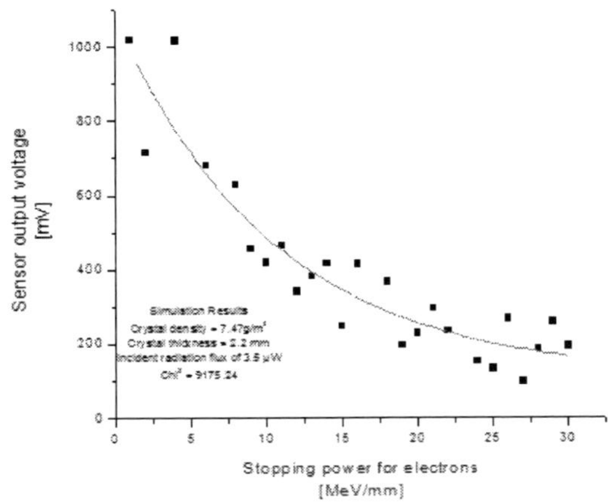


Figure 4. Theoretical results for the pyroelectric voltage at different incident electron energy values.

Based on such results, one can assume that if using both an adequate beam energy and thickness of the crystal, the slope of the response, as well as the efficiency for measuring absorbed dose, become energy independent. Besides, the calibration in radiation dose can be obtained by taking into account the output pyroelectric voltage of the sensor versus the electron beam dose measured. Therefore, the beam dose was obtained with the use of an industrial dosimeter based on the use of parallel-plate chamber. Figure 5 shows the calibration curve obtained when considering an electron beam having an energy of 5MeV, the amplified $\Delta V(\omega,t)$ in mV, and the absorbed dose in kGy.

The absorbed dose is a physical quantity representing the mean energy imparted to matter per unit mass by the ionizing radiation. In the International System of Units (SI), the unit of measure for the absorbed dose is J/kg, and its special name is Gray [Gy]. The calibration curve was obtained in the range of 0.5kGy to 10kGy, taking into account the variation in the exposure time.

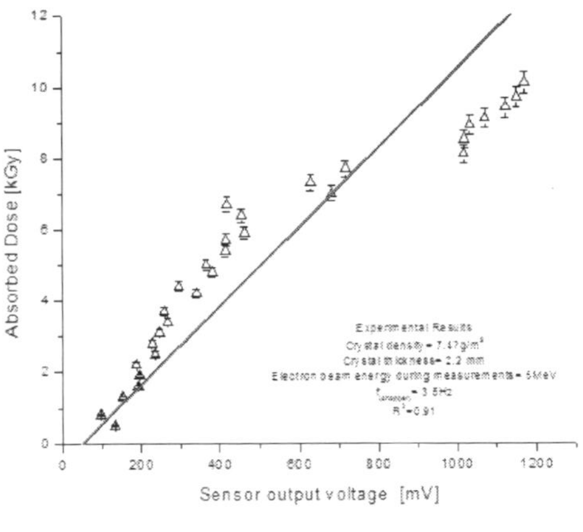


Figure 5. Calibration curve for the absorbed dose in the range of 0.5kGy to 10kGy, i.e., based on chopping frequency equal to 3.5 Hz and a 5MeV electron beam energy.

This result is suitable for the application of the developed sensor in the area of food irradiation, where the control, monitoring and calibration of irradiation devices based on the use of electron beam is continuously required.

## V. CONCLUSIONS AND FUTURE WORK

Due to the obtained results, it is possible to conclude that the developed sensor is suitable to measure the absorbed dose in the food disinfection processes of the agricultural industry based on the use of electron beam. Besides, the theoretical modeling of the sensor was presented, including the output voltage as a dependent variable of the total stopping power for electrons. Such model was analyzed taking into account the mixture of the elements of the crystal used, as well as its response over a wide range of energies. In such context, the sensor´s calibration was performed in relation to the absorbed dose, where the analysis took into account the amplified output voltage as a function of the incident 5 MeV electron beam, i.e., considering different time-windows for the exposures. For such evaluation, it was possible to observe a sensor output voltage in the range from 50 mV to 1.5 V, considering the use of a crystal having a thickness of 2.2 mm. This validation presented a linear correlation coefficient equal to 0.91 for doses in the range of 0.5 Gy to 10 kGy. Therefore, its response has been practically linear with respect to the absorbed dose. For such validation, we took into account the full stopping power for the electron and the crystal's thickness. This aspect must be observed to guarantee the correct operation of the sensor.

Additionally, as a pyroelectric sensor, when it was exposed to a radiation flux, the absorbed energy caused an increase in temperature. This increase in temperature was proportional to the magnitude of the energy absorbed and inversely proportional to the specific heat, i.e., as observed, the electrical output of the sensor was proportional to the amount of energy absorbed. Furthermore, in terms of future prospects, this sensor can be embedded with its electronic circuits for signal processing, as well as be prepared with the aggregation of smart characteristics and functionalities. In this context, it will be able to bring potential benefits not only for the calibration of the electron beam accelerators but also for the automation and application of a pre-selected dose for specific foods and related absorbed dose for disinfection.

## ACKNOWLEDGMENT

This research was partially supported by the Brazilian Corporation for Agricultural Research (Grant numbers: 03.10.05.011.00.00 and 01.14.09.0.01.05.05). The author also recognizes the motivation received from Sérgio Mascarenhas for the development of sensors based on ceramic materials.

## REFERENCES

[1] X. Fan, B. A. Niemira, and A. Prakash, "Irradiation of fresh fruits and vegetables," Food Technology, vol. 62, no.3, 2008, pp.36-43.

[2] E. S. Josephson, "An historical review of food irradiation," Journal of Food Safety, vol. 5, 1983, pp. 161-190.

[3] United States Food and Drug Administration (FDA): "Food Irradiation: What You Need to Know". [Online, retrieved: January, 2018]. Available from: https://www.fda.gov/downloads/ Food/IngredientsPackagingLabeling/UCM262295.pdf.

[4] United States Department of Agriculture (USDA): "Irradiation Resources". [Online, retrieved: January, 2018]. Available from: https://www.fsis.usda.gov/wps/portal/fsis/topics/food-safety-education/get-answers/food-safety-fact-sheets/production-and -inspection/irradiation-resources/.

[5] A. P. Almeida, "Evaluation of the influence of the irradiation process on spices using the X-ray diffraction technique," pp.102, (Master's Dissertation in Nuclear Engineering)-Federal University of Rio de Janeiro. Rio de Janeiro, Brazil, 2006.

[6] R. G. Crede, "Studies on the effects of gamma radiation and electron accelerators on the detection of genetically modified corn (Zea mays)," pp. 185, (Master's Dissertation in Nuclear Technology) – IPEN, University of São Paulo, São Paulo, Brazil, 2005.

[7] A. P. Urwaye, New Food Engineering Research Trends, 284pp., Nova Science Publishers Inc: New York, pp. 284, 2008.

[8] The Science of Food Standards The Road from Codex Alimentarius Commission, In: Food and Agriculture Organization of the United Nations and World Health Organization, Rome, pp. 51, ISBN 978-92-5-109823-3, 2017.

[9] M. Behnoush et al.,"World market development and consumer acceptance of irradiation technology," Foods, vol. 5, 2016, pp. 79-85.

[10] R. L. Byer and C. B. Roundy, "Pyroelectric coefficient direct measurement technique and application to a nsec response time detector," IEEE Transactions on Sonics & Ultrasonics, vol. 3, 1972, pp. 333-338.

[11] P. E. Cruvinel, S. Mascarenhas, J. Miranda, and R. G. Flocchini, "The use of a Perovskite crystal as a detector for proton beam current", IEEE Transactions on Nuclear Science, vol. 39,1992, pp. 25-28.

[12] A. A. de Carvalho and A. J. Alter, "Measurement of X-ray intensity in medical diagnostic range by a ferroelectric detector", IEEE Transactions on Ultrasoics, Ferroelectrics and Frequency Control, vol. 44, no. 6,1997, pp. 1198-1203.

[13] J. Cooper, "Minimum detectable power of a pyroelectric thermal received", Review of Scientific Instruments, vol. 33, 1962, pp. 92-101.

[14] S.T. Liu and D. Long, "Pyroelectric detectors and materials" Proceedings of the IEEE, vol 66, issue: 1, 1978, pp. 14-26.

[15] J. F. Nye, Physical Properties of Crystals, Oxford: University Press, pp. 78-189, 1957.

[16] M. Sayer et al., "Dielectric properties and electrical noise in ferroelectric devices," Integrated Ferroelectrics, vol. 5, issue 1,1994.

[17] R. Moghimi, "Low noise signal conditioning for sensor-based circuits," Applications Engineering Manager, Analog Devices Inc., MS-2066, pp. 1-16, 2010. [Online, retrieved: January, 2018]. Available from: http://www.analog.com/media/technical-documentation/technical-articles/MS-2066.pdf.

[18] D. V. Perepelitsa, "Johnson noise and shot noise," White Paper, MIT Department of Physics, pp. 4, November 27, 2006. [Online, retrieved: January, 2018]. Available from: http://web.mit.edu/dvp/Public/noise.pdf.

[19] A. Mozumder and Y. Hatano, Charged Particle and Photon Interactions with Matter: Chemical, Physicochemical, and Biological Consequences with Applications. New York: Marcel Dekker, pp. 870, 2004.

[20] G. F. Knoll, Radiation Detection and Measurement, 3rd ed.,New York: Wiley, pp. 830, 2000.

[21] S. Tanuma, C. J. Powell, and D. R. Penn, "Calculations of stopping powers of 100eV to 30keV electrons in 10 elemental solids," Surface and Interface Analysis, vol. 37, issue 11, 2005, pp. 978 - 988.

[22] Z. Tan and Y. Xia, "Stopping power and mean free path for low-energy electrons in ten scintillators over energy range of 20–20,000eV," Applied Radiation and Isotopes, vol. 70, issue 1, 2012, pp. 296-300.

[23] R. C. Murty, "Effective atomic numbers of heterogeneous materials," Nature, vol. 207, 1965, pp. 398-399.

[24] Texas Instrument, "LF147/LF347 wide bandwidth quad JFET input operational amplifiers", Snosbh1d, May 1999, Revised version on March, 2013. [Online, retrieved: January, 2018]. Available from: http://www.ti.com/lit/ds/symlink/lf347-n.pdf.

[25] Intersil, "CA 3140 - 4.5MHz, BiMOS operational amplifier with MOSFET input/bipolar output", Data Sheet, File Number 957.4, September, 1998. [Online, retrieved: January, 2018]. Available from: http://www.qsl.net/n9zia/spec/ca3140.pdf.

[26] K. A. Johansson, L. O. Mattsson, L. Lindborg, and H. Svensson, "Absorbed-dose determination with ionization chambers in electron and photon beams having energies between 1 and 50 MeV", Proc. Symp. National and International Standardization of Radiation Dosimetry, (IAEA-SM-222/35), Atlanta, vol. 2, IAEA, Vienna, 1978, pp. 222-235.

[27] L. O. Mattsson, K. A. Johansson, and H. Svensson, "Calibration and use of plane-parallel ionization chambers for the determination of absorbed dose in electron beams," Acta Radiologica. Oncology, vol. 20, 1981, pp. 385-399.

[28] J. Fraden, Handbook of Modern Sensors: Physics, Design, and Applications. 3rd ed., USA: SpringerVerlag, 2004.

[29] J. P. Biersack and L. Haggmark, "A Monte Carlo computer program for the transport of energetic ions in amorphous targets," Nuclear Instruments and Methods, vol. 174, 1980, pp. 257-269.

# Scattering Parameters Measurements with the Microwave Transmittance Technique Using a Microstrip Patch Antennas as Non-Invasive Tool for Determination of Soil Moisture

Paulo Sergio de Paula Herrmann
Embrapa Instrumentation
São Carlos (SP), Brazil
e-mail: paulo.herrmann@embrapa.br

Felipe Nieves Marques Porto
Maastricht University
Maastricht, Netherlands
e-mail: porto.felipe94@gmail.com

Viktor Sydoruk
Forschungszentrum Jülich / IBG-2: Plant Sciences
Jülich, Germany
e-mail: v.sydoruk@fz-juelich.de

*Abstract*— **Interactions of soil moisture with plant's root system are very important for plant growth. For non-invasive determination of volumetric soil moisture in a Rhizobox a microwave system based on transmittance of electromagnetic waves in the microwave frequency range was developed using microstrip patch antennas. A Vector Network Analyzer (VNA) was used to measure the S-parameters at frequency range close to 5 GHz. A transmission system with microstrip patch antennas was developed. The result of this attenuation is in the frequency domain. The antennae were designed resonant microstrip antennae. The antennas were placed on both sides of a rhizobox, which allows measuring non-invasively soil moisture in the box. The attenuation (S12(dB)) was used to measure the effect of temperature in different kinds of soils. Sensitivity, reproducibility and repeatability were evaluated as well. This works presents quantitative results of soil moisture in rhizobox. The microwave technique, using microstrip patch antennas, is a reliable and accurate system, and showed very promising potential applications for rhizobox-based investigations of root performance.**

***Keywords-*** *microwave technique;, transmittance; soil moisture; microstrip patch antennas; rhizobox.*

## I. INTRODUCTION

New tools or approaches are considered important to investigate and evaluate soil-water-plant interactions in the plant phenotyping investigations [1]. A central parameter determining root system response to water availability is that water is usually not homogeneously distributed in the soil and the heterogeneity significantly increases when drought stress occurs. Thus, the development of non-invasive instruments and sensors to measure soil moisture distribution would open up new approaches to investigate plant strategies to deal with low water content or, in particular, heterogeneities in water availability of soils during periods of drought cycles.

Electromagnetic soil water content sensors are now widely accepted for soil water content determination because these sensors allow continuous, fast, stable, and nondestructive sensing of the spatial-temporal dynamics of soil water content at the lab and field scale [2].

From the electromagnetic point of view, the soil-plant-water set is considered a mixture of four dielectric compositions consisting of air, soil volume, bound water, and free water and roots. A water molecule attached to the soil interacts with an incident electromagnetic wave different from the free water molecule, thereby exhibiting a dielectric dispersion spectrum which is very different from free water. The dielectric constants in the complex form of free and bound water are functions of the electromagnetic frequency (f), the physical temperature (T) and the salinity (S).

The dielectric properties of the wet soil are characterized by frequency dependence as a function of dielectric constant response.

In a soil-plant-water system, the $\varepsilon_r$ values for the soil are typically between 3 and 5. In water, the values are around 80 and, for the roots of a plant, they oscillate between 42 and 56. The volumetric water contents of the root samples vary linearly with the volume. The $\varepsilon_r$ of the air is equal to 1. In this way, relatively small amounts of free water in the soil will greatly affect its electromagnetic properties [3][ 4].

For non-invasive determination of volumetric soil moisture ($\theta_V$) a microwave system based on transmittance of electromagnetic waves in the frequency range close to 5.0 GHz was developed using microstrip patch antennas. The antennas were placed on both sides of a rhizobox. The evaluation is made using scattering parameters (known as S-parameters) describing dispersion and dielectric properties of a soil-water. In the figure 1(a) is showing the basic principle of the electromagnetic wave (EM) interactions with the matter. A block diagram of the system that was developed to conduct this experiment can be seen in the Figure 1(b).

Calibration curves for four porous media are presented for two soils, the Nullerde - Einheitserde Typ 0 - Einheitserde- und Humuswerke, and a peat-sand-pumice substrate - Dachstaudensubstrat SoMi 513 (Kaktus soil), and Cerrado soil (tropical soil); and one for glass beads. The results presented in this work show a potential of using microwave transmittance technique and microstrip patch antenna for development of a new non-invasive determination of volumetric soil moisture ($\theta_V$) which will be possible to be applied for better understanding of roots growth.

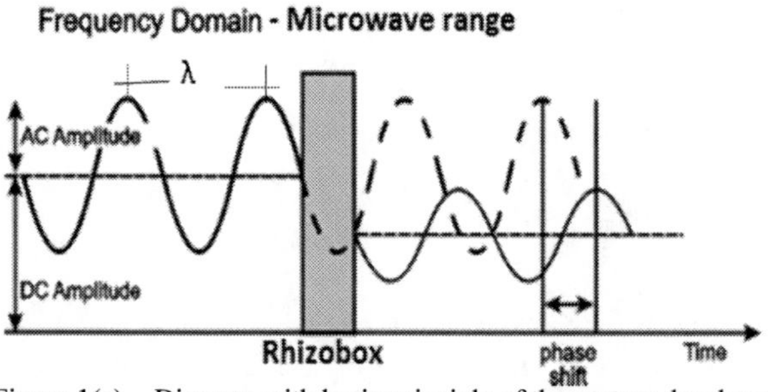


Figure 1(a). Diagram with basic principle of the system developed to this investigation. (Attenuation and phase shift) (Modified from [5]).

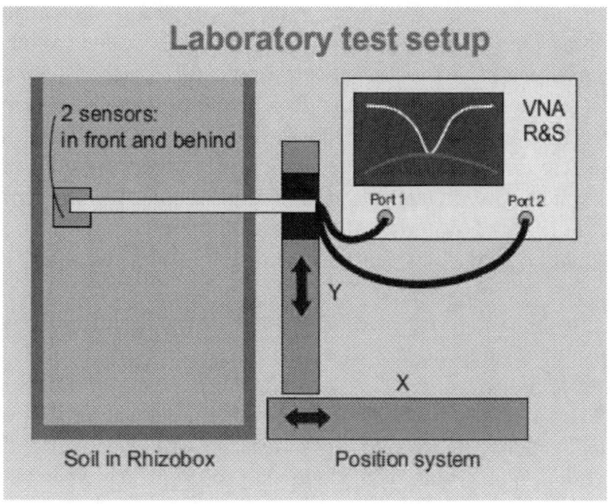


Figure 1(b). The block diagram of the system developed to measure S21 (dB) of the soil moisture in the rhizobox, using Vector Network Analyzer, in the microwave range (4.6 GHz to 5.0 GHz).

## II. MATERIALS AND METHODS

### A. *Vector Network Analyzer (VNA)*

The antennas are connected to Vector Network Analyzer (VNA) (ZNB 8, Rohde & Schwarz) which is generally used to generate and measure radio frequency/microwave signal. Some features about the equipment used: Frequency range from 9 kHz up to 40 GHz; Wide dynamic range of up to 140 dB and High temperature stability 0.01 dB/°C. Using VNA, we measured scattering parameters (S-parameters (S21 (dB)) in a frequency range from 4.6 GHz to 5.0 GHz to characterize transmission of microwaves through a soil with a resolution of 6 x $10^{-3}$ dB.

### B. *Design of Microstrip Patch Antenna*

The antennas were designed as $\lambda/2$-resonant microstrip antennas [6] and executed on a circuit board with a 1.5 mm thickness and a dielectric constant ($\varepsilon_{r,sub}$ of 4.4). Each antenna was 15.7 mm wide and 15.4 mm long. The total size is 25.0 x 25.0 x 1.5 $mm^3$. Such a design allows working at frequencies close to 4.8 GHz. Figure 2 is presents the picture of the microstrip antenna design to microwave range.

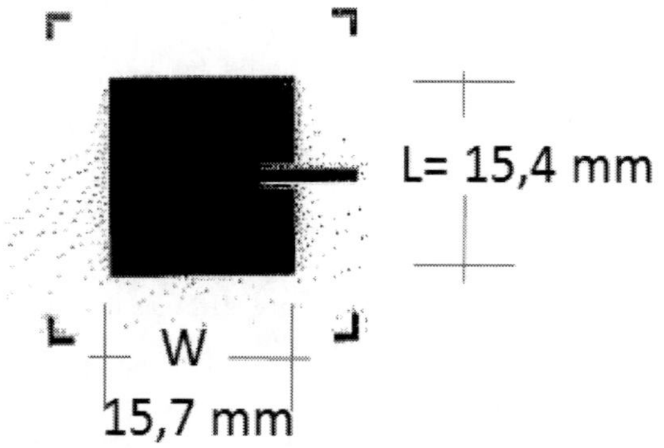


Figure 2. The mask used to develop the microstrip antenna on to circuit board

### C. *Rhizobox*

The rhizobox were made out of PVC and Plexiglas ($\varepsilon r \sim 2.6$) and PVC ($\varepsilon r \sim 2.9$) with walls of about 5.0 mm in thickness, a length of 315.0 mm and a width of 200.0 mm. The internal space for the porous media samples is 20.0 mm.

### D. *Measurement of reproducibility and repeatability (Dielectric Constant vs Attenuation)*

The two chemical solutions used were 1,4-Dioxane (C4H8O2) and 2-Isopropoxyethanol ((CH3)2CHOCH2CH2OH), abbreviated as i-C3E1. The objective was to make an "ideal solution" by combining water ($\varepsilon_w$= 79 (1.2 GHz)) and another liquid fully miscible in water. Dioxane is a strong solvent with a low flash point and a high volatility.

The mixtures, values and relative complex dielectric permittivity parameters are derived from [7]. The real and imaginary part of the complex dielectric permittivity of the reference liquids were described by the Cole-Cole model [8]. The model can be seen in the equation (1):

$$\varepsilon = \varepsilon_\infty + \frac{(\varepsilon_s - \varepsilon_\infty)}{1 + (j\omega\tau)^{1-\alpha}} - j\frac{\sigma}{\omega\varepsilon_0} \tag{1}$$

The $\varepsilon$ represents the complex dielectric permittivity, while $\varepsilon_s$ [-] and $\varepsilon_\infty$ [-] are the permittivity at frequencies $f$ much lower and much higher than the relaxation frequency $f_{rel}$ [Hz], respectively, $\alpha$ [-] is the dispersion factor for the relaxation time ($0<\alpha<1$), $\sigma$ [S $m^{-1}$] is the electrical conductivity and $\varepsilon_0$ is the free space permittivity.

The concentrations of the liquids were created as is shown in Table I.

TABLE 1: THE VOLUME FRACTION OF THE LIQUIDS, THE DIELECTRIC CONSTANT AND A RELATION WITH SOIL MOISTURE

| Reference Liquid | Medium | Volume Fraction | | $\varepsilon_s \approx \varepsilon_{ref}$ | $\theta_{eq}$ |
|---|---|---|---|---|---|
| | | Dioxane / i-$C_3E_1$ | Deionized Water | | |
| | | [-] | [-] | [-] | [$m^3$ $m^{-3}$] |
| M1 | Dioxane | 0.90 | 0.10 | 6.65 | 0.117 |
| M2 | i-$C_3E_1$ | 1.00 | 0.00 | 11.95 | 0.228 |
| M3 | i-$C_3E_1$ | 0.92 | 0.08 | 18.14 | 0.331 |
| M4 | i-$C_3E_1$ | 0.86 | 0.14 | 22.15 | 0.388 |
| M5 | i-$C_3E_1$ | 0.80 | 0.20 | 26.26 | 0.441 |
| M6 | i-$C_3E_1$ | 0.73 | 0.27 | 31.38 | 0.502 |
| M7 | i-$C_3E_1$ | 0.68 | 0.32 | 34.82 | 0.540 |

### *E. Calibration Curve*

Each sample was prepared to have the same bulk density (ρb) of a dry soil and its different volumetric soil moisture, θV(%). We used three different porous media (PM): Nullerde (Einheitserde Typ 0, Einheitserde- und Humuswerke Gebr. Patzer GmbH & Co. KG), peat-sand-pumice substrate (Dachstaudensubstrat SoMi 513, Hawita GmbH, Vechta, Germany) and glass beads (particles size ~ 0.5 mm). The soil used in these experiments was the dystrophic Red Latosol/Oxisol (Cerrado - Brazil ($\rho_b$ = 1.19 g/$cm^3$)). The ρb, during the experiments were about 0.28 g/$cm^3$, 0.59 g/$cm^3$ and 1.40 g/$cm^3$, respectively. The experiments were made under laboratory conditions at temperature of about 25.0 ± 0.5 °C and relative humidity of ~30.0%. Additionally, we measured influences of temperature for Nullerde soil under climate controlled environment at temperature range from 13.0 ± 0.5 °C to 39.0 ± 0.5 °C.

The equation 2 can be used to calculated the volumetric soil moisture (θV(%)):

$$\theta V(\%) = \left( \left( \frac{V_{H_2O}}{M_{ds}} \right) x \rho_{ss} \right) x\ 100 \quad (2)$$

where: $V_{H2O}$ is the volume of the water ($cm^3$); $M_{ds}$ is the weight of the dry soil (g); $\rho_{ss}$ is the dry soil density (g*$cm^{-3}$)

## III. RESULTS AND DISCUSSION

### *A. Evaluation of reproducibility and repeatability of the system developed*

The aim of this experiment was to correlate attenuation values received from the rhizobox with the concentration of chemical organic solution placed for analysis. This experiment aimed to correlated the dielectric permittivity constant of certain concentrations of organic chemical solutions (in this case mainly 2-isopropoxyalcohol) with the microwave attenuation values. The results clearly show a relation between the two variables – mainly which as the dielectric permittivity increases, so does the attenuation. The graph demonstrating the percentage of reliability of reproducibility and repeatability shows that this same experiment should theoretically be possible to perform in any circumstance, resulting in the same values.

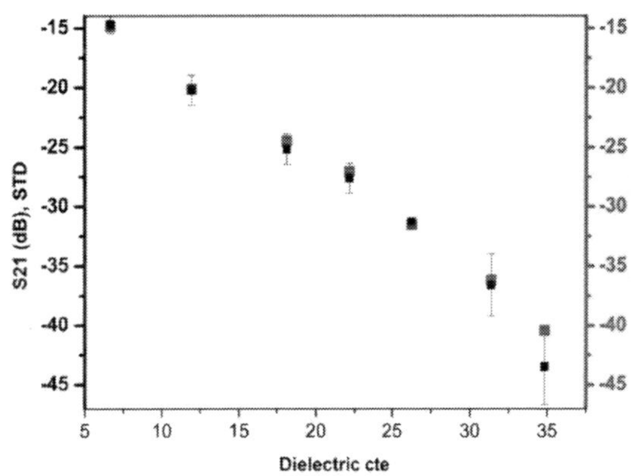


Figure 3. The repeatability and reproducibility of the system developed were calculated. The measurement was carrying out three times to each dot (n=3). The red dots represent the reproducibility (98.9%) averages and the black dots represent the repeatability (93.0%) averages.

### *B. The influence of temperature during the measurement of volumetric soil moisture (θV(%)).*

The influence of temperature (°C) is an important parameter in the measurement of soil moisture. In the figure 4 has been shown the influence of temperature during the measurement of volumetric soil moisture of the Null Erde sample. The situation is dramatically changed when PM has high amount of water. The ΔT (°C) was equal 26.0 ± 0.5 °C and the maximum variation of S21(dB) was 35.3% to θV (%) = 45.0%.

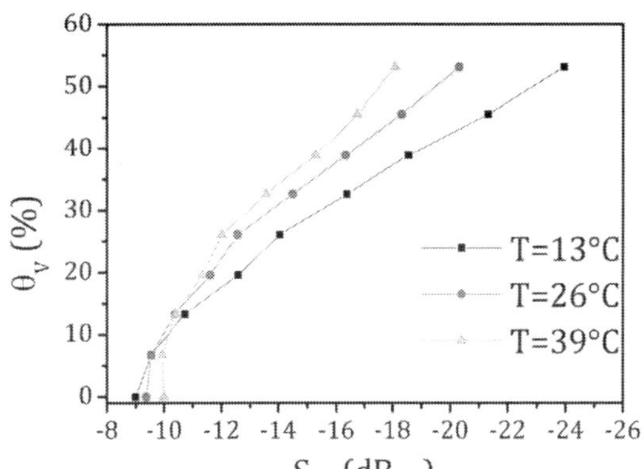


Figure 4.The influence of temperature in the measurement of θV (%) using the attenuation (S21 (dB)). The porous media used was Null Erde and the temperature set up to this experiment was between 13.0 ± 0.5 °C to 39.0 ± 0.5 °C.

### C *Influence of salty water in the measurement.*

Dissolving of salts leads to increasing of conductivity which has a major effect to the attenuation of the transmitted signal. To take into account and separate influence of water and salts/nutrients in a soil it is necessary to measure the resonance frequency shift of the antennas together with attenuation.

### D *The calibration curve and modeling of volumetric soil moisture (θV(%)) in function of S21(dB).*

Therefore, different calibration curves are needed for different PM. Calibration curves were obtained by measuring S21-parameter (dB), which reflects transmission of EM waves. Measuring the attenuation of transmitted signal we obtained clear dependence of θV (%) on S21 (dB). The dependence tends to be comparable for different PM when it is relatively dry, below 20.0 % of θV(%), and has a small dependence of bulk density, as well the soil physical and chemical properties of each PM, mainly the typical tropical soil (Cerrado soil).

The curve obtained to four (04) samples (Cerrado Soil, Null Erde, Kaktus Soil and Glass Beads) is shown in the figure 6 and the equation the table (2):

Figure 7 is shows the preliminary results of the measurement of S21(dB) attenuation of volumetric soil moisture in the rhizobox, during the time (16 days:21hr:17 min). The sample is a Katus soil with maize. The experiment was organized to obseve the attenuation of soil moisture during the time of the roots growth. The measurement was taken in the lab conditions (T=24,3 ± 1,1 C and RU=62,8 ± 5,0 %) during the morning, the afternoon and the night to measure the behaviour of the water.

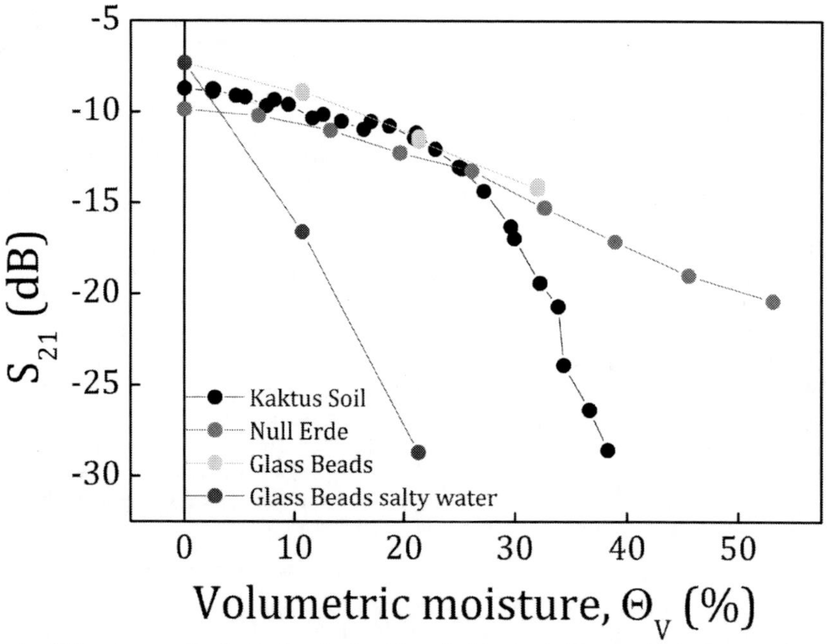


Figure 5. Calibration curves for different types of soil and glass beads with and without salt. The graphic is showing dependencies on salinity, moisture and properties (such as bulk density, dielectric constant etc.) of soil.

TABLE II: EQUATIONS USED TO MODEL THE CALIBRATION FOR EACH SAMPLE

| Samples | Equation | $R^2$ |
|---|---|---|
| Cerrado Soil $\rho_{ss}$=1,19 g*cm$^{-3}$ | $\Theta_v(\%) = -0,00258*S_{21}(dB)^3+0,07924*S_{21}(dB)^2+0,27515*S_{21}(dB)-4,72555$ | 0,9834 |
| Null Erde $\rho_{ss}$=0,28 g*cm$^{-3}$ | $\Theta_v(\%) = -0,18679*S_{21}(dB)^3-7,79899*S_{21}(dB)^2-112,0218*S_{21}(dB)-524,374$ | 0,9804 |
| Kaktus Soil $\rho_{ss}$=0,59 g*cm$^{-3}$ | $\Theta_v(\%) = 0,1555*S_{21}(dB)^3+4,16601*S_{21}(dB)^2+29,24777*S_{21}(dB)+42,96299$ | 0,9725 |
| Glass Beads $\rho_{ss}$=1,54 g*cm$^{-3}$ | $\Theta_v(\%) = -0,19723*S_{21}(dB)^2-8,78181*S_{21}(dB)-52,87515$ | 0,9923 |

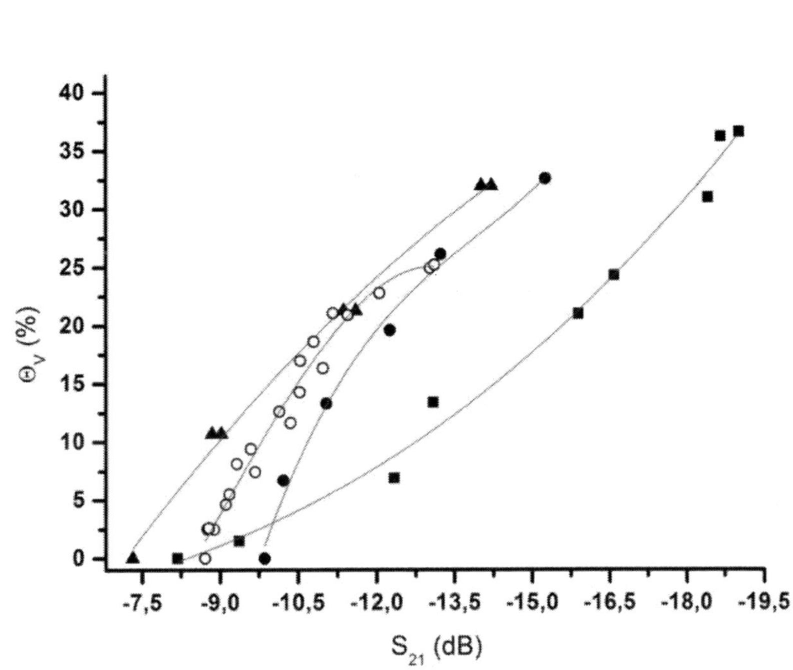


Figure 6. Relation between the S21 (dB) measured with the system developed and the volumetric soil moisture (θV(%)) determined and calculated by second and third order polynomial equation. The equations were presented in the table 2. The four (04) samples used are: Cerrado Soil (■), Null Erde (●), Kaktus Soil (○) and Glass Beads (▲).

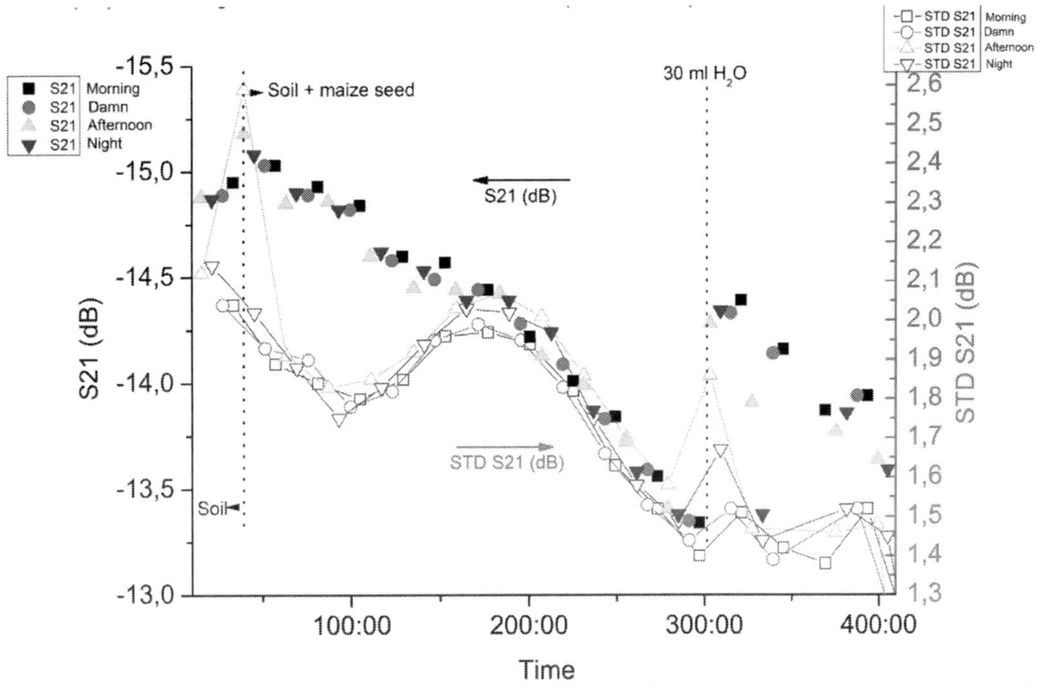


Figure 7. Results of the measurement of S21(dB) attenuation of volumetric soil moisture in the rhizobox, during the time (16 days:21hr:17 min) and a calculation of standard deviation (STD S21(dB)). The sample is a Katus soil with maize. The experiment was organized to measure the attenuation of soil moisture during the time of the roots growth. The measurement was taken in the lab conditions (T=24,3 ± 1,1 C and RU=62,8 ± 5,0 %) during the morning, the afternoon and the night.

## IV. CONCLUSION

From the measured results, it is possible to conclude that the developed non-invasive microwave method, using microstrip antennas, is an innovative sensing method to measure the water status in rhizobox filled with soil. This can be used to investigate the growth of plant roots together with soil physics properties. This kind of approach gives an opportunity to apply it to study and monitor non-invasive volumetric soil moisture θV (%) distribution, using rhizobox.

## ACKNOWLEDGMENTS

The Forschungszentrum Jülich (FZJ/Jülich) / IBG-2: Plant Science to the support and facilities, the Jülich Plant Phenotyping Center (JPPC), as well the Enabling Technologies group to good discussion and use of the laboratories. This research was financially supported by Embrapa Labex Europe Program, Agropolis, Montpellier, France, number DZ002947.

## REFERENCES

[1] F. Fiorani and U. Schurr,. "Future Scenarios for Plant Phenotyping," Annual Review of Plant Biology, vol.64, pp.267 – 291, 2013.

[2] W. Qu, H. R. Bogena, J. A. Huisman and H. Vereecken, "Calibration of a Novel Low-Cost Soil Water Content Sensor Based on a Ring Oscillator," Vadose Zone Journal, vol. 12, Iss.: 2, 2012

[3] T. J. Schmugge and T. J. Jackson, "Survey of methods for soil moisture determination," Water Resources Research, vol. 16, n. 6, pp. 961 – 979, 1980

[4] M. A. Mojid and H. Cho, "Evaluation of the time-domain reflectometry (TDR)-measured composite dielectric constant of root-mixed soils for estimating soil-water content and root density," Journal of Hydrology, vol. 295, pp. 263–275, 2004

[5] A. Pellicer and M. D. C. Bravo, "Near-infrared spectroscopy: a methodology-focused review," Seminars in fetal & neonatal medicine, vol. 16, Iss.: 1, pp. 42-49, 1744-165X, 2011

[6] A. Cataldo, G. Monti, E. De Benedetto, G. Cannazza and L. Tarricone, "A noninvasive resonance-based method for moisture content evaluation through microstrip antennas," IEEE Transactions on Instrumentation and Measurement, vol. 58, Iss.: 5, pp. 1420-1426, 2009,

[7] U. Rosenbaum, J. A. Huisman, J. Vrba, H. Vereecken and H. R. Bogena, "Correction of Temperature and Electrical Conductivity Effects on Dielectric Permittivity Measurements with ECH2O Sensors, " Vadose Zone Journal, vol. 10, Iss.: 2, pp. 582-593, 2011

[8] K. S. Cole, R. H. Cole, "Dispersion and Absorption in Dielectrics - I Alternating Current Characteristics", J. Chem. Phys., vol. 9, pp. 341–352, 1941.

# Soft-Sensor Approach Based on Principal Components Analysis to Improve the Quality of the Application of Pesticides in Agricultural Pest Control

Elmer A. G. Peñaloza[1,2], Vilma A. Oliveira[2], Paulo E. Cruvinel[1]

[1]Embrapa Instrumentation
Brazilian Agricultural Research Corporation, São Carlos, SP, Brazil
Email: paulo.cruvinel@embrapa.br

[2] Department of Electrical and Computer Engineering
University of São Paulo, São Carlos, SP, Brazil
Email: egamboa@usp.br, voliveira@usp.br

***Abstract*—Pesticide application has been an important activity for pest control in agricultural production and in sustaining food security. The quality of an application plays an important role to decrease human and environmental risks, as well as in relation to the costs for food production. To evaluate the quality of the application by sprayers, several quality descriptors are used. Such descriptors are related to the average diameter of drops and the distribution of drops in the application. This paper presents the construction of a soft-sensor, based on Principal Components Analysis (PCA), to infer the quality of application. The soft-sensor has as inputs the operating conditions of agricultural sprayers and offers as output the quality descriptors that serve as a base of information to estimate the level of quality that a pesticide application can meet at a certain time. Hence, the selection of historical data, the exploration and filtering of data, as well as the structure and the validation of the soft-sensor are presented. The results have shown the usefulness of the soft-sensor in the aggregation of value to the process of pesticide application and decision-making in agriculture.**

***Keywords–Soft-sensor; Inferential sensors; Quality of application; Principal component analysis; Agricultural sprayers.***

## I. Introduction

As the population has increased, the need to produce more food has caused the agricultural techniques to constantly evolve. The development of new technologies for the production of inputs, pesticides and agricultural machines such as tractors and sprayers, as well as genetic engineering, have made possible the increase of agricultural production and the reduction of the environmental impacts of agricultural activity. Among the activities of crop management, one of the most expensive is the spraying of pesticides. Spraying is the application of a liquid in the form of small particles on a surface. These particles are called drops or droplets.

An efficient spraying application is based on the following factors: applied chemical efficiency, quality of the product, climatic conditions and biological characteristics of the pest [1] [2]. Among the factors that determine the efficiency of the application, the quality is one of the most important, that is, precision agriculture based on the use of automation and control plays an important role. The knowledge of the size, the distribution and the process of formation of drops are essential factors for the success of the pulverization of pesticides [3]. These factors have an influence on the drift, evaporation of products, penetration capability inside the canopy of crops and deposition on phytosanitary treatment targets [4].

Since agricultural crops can vary in height as they grow and as the agricultural sprayer is used on different crops on the farm, the sprayer boom height must be accurate to ensure that crops receive the proper application of the liquid being dispensed. A set of sensors have been used to help the operators in such arrangements and also, for calibration of the temperature of the engine, flow and pressure of the pesticides hydraulic pump, among others variables, required in the spraying processes. Furthermore, today advanced sprayers generally include additional sets of sensors which are useful for precision spraying management. However, it is still a challenge to measure and control in the spraying processes all the variables required for spraying quality and a complete characterization of the spraying systems during operation in order to increase precision.

Therefore, regarding this subject and in order to improve the performance of such processes, the concept of soft-sensors can be used to estimate values of important variables that cannot be taken by traditional measurements.

Soft-sensors are computer programs established from models and used for estimating not measurable outputs from production processes. Specifically, they are based on estimation and prediction techniques which use a priori information collected from sensors and mathematical models to describe physical processes. The approach based on soft-sensors is used in cases where sensors (hardware) are not available or their implementation is difficult, have high cost or simply there are no instruments that can do the type of measurement required [5]. In the literature, there are several applications of soft-sensors in production processes and they have achieved good results. In 1995, Luo et al. [6] designed an inference estimator based on fuzzy logic to measure and control the purity of the resulting propylene from the distillation process of a high-purity distillation column. In 1998, Casali et al. [7] used soft-sensors to estimate the size of the particles in a grinding plant where sensors were not available. The authors used an Autoregressive Moving Average Model (ARMAX) as soft-sensor to estimate and test the model predictive capability. Then, in 2007, Lin et al. [8] designed a soft-sensor to detect nitrogen oxide emissions (NOx) produced by a cement kiln system. The authors used robust regression techniques to derive an inferential model, making possible a basis of estimation with dynamic least squares. Recently, in 2016, Liu et al. [9] used the soft-sensor approach to predict and monitor the indoor air quality in the Seoul metro systems. The authors used a technique of learning Just-In-Time (JIT) to model the nonlinear process based on two local models of prediction, and a linear Partial Least Squares (PLS) method and a nonlinear Least Squares Support Vector Regression (LSSVR) method for the prediction of the indoor air quality were used.

The conception and construction of a data-driven soft-sensor have five main pillars: collection and selection of historical data of the process, detection of outliers and data filtering, selection of the model structure, estimates of the model and validation of the model [5]. Therefore, these five pillars or steps must be executed sequentially to obtain a soft-sensor with a high degree of accuracy. The main focus of this work is the improvement in the quality of pesticide application. For this, a soft-sensor based on Principal Components (PC) was built in order to predict the quality descriptors of the application as a function of operating conditions of the agricultural sprayers.

The next sections of the paper are organized as follows. In Section II, the main concepts and the theoretical foundation of the analysis of principal components are given. In Section III, the electrohydraulic devices and the experimental configuration used for data collection are shown. Also, in this section the setup of the soft-sensor in the control loop of the pesticides spraying system is studied. Subsequently, in Section IV, the simulated results of the application of the soft-sensor in the control loop are shown. Finally, some concluding remarks and future works are presented in Section V.

## II. Principal Component Analysis

The main idea of PCA is to reduce the dimension of the data set by keeping the variation of the original data set as much as possible. To achieve this goal, this technique transforms the data set into a new set of principal components. The PCs are ordered so that the first components keep most of the variation present in the original data or variables [10]. To start with the formulation, the simplest one-dimensional space case ($M = 1$) is used, that is the projection of the data is in an one-dimensional space. The mean of the set of samples is calculated with the following expression:

$$\overline{x} = \frac{1}{N}\sum_{n=1}^{N} x_n \tag{1}$$

where $x_n$ is the sample vector, with $n = 1, \cdots, N$. The covariance matrix $\boldsymbol{S}$ is defined by the following expression:

$$\boldsymbol{S} = \frac{1}{N}\sum_{n=1}^{N} (x_n - \overline{x})(x_n - \overline{x})^T . \tag{2}$$

Define a D-dimensional vector $\boldsymbol{u_1}$ as the direction of this space which is chosen in such a way that $\boldsymbol{u_1^T u_1} = 1$. Each data point $x_n$ is then projected onto a scalar value $\boldsymbol{u_1^T x_n}$ and the idea is to maximize the variance of the projected data in relation to the vector $\boldsymbol{u_1}$. The variance of the projected data is given by:

$$\frac{1}{N}\sum_{n=1}^{N} \left\{\boldsymbol{u_1^T} x_n - \boldsymbol{u_1^T}\overline{x}\right\}^2 = \boldsymbol{u_1^T S u_1}. \tag{3}$$

To prevent that $\|\boldsymbol{u_1}\| \to \infty$, the maximization of the projected variance must have a constraint. Thus, the constraint comes from the normalization condition $\boldsymbol{u_1^T u_1} = 1$. To comply with the constraint, a Lagrange multiplier $\lambda_1$ is introduced [11]:

$$\boldsymbol{u_1^T S u_1} + \lambda_1\left(1 - \boldsymbol{u_1^T u_1}\right). \tag{4}$$

Thus, deriving (4) in function of $\boldsymbol{u_1}$ and equating to zero, the following expression is obtained:

$$\boldsymbol{u_1^T S u_1} = \lambda_1. \tag{5}$$

Therefore, $\boldsymbol{u_1}$ is an eigenvector of the covariance matrix $\boldsymbol{S}$ and the variance is maximized when the set $\boldsymbol{u_1}$ is equal to the eigenvector having the largest eigenvalue $\lambda_1$. This eigenvector is known as the first principal component [11]. Considering the case of a projection of M-dimensional space, the optimal linear projection for which the variance of the projected data is maximized is defined by the $m$ eigenvectors $\boldsymbol{u_1}, \cdots, \boldsymbol{u_m}$ of the covariance matrix $\boldsymbol{S}$ that corresponds to the largest $m$ eigenvalues $\lambda_1, \cdots, \lambda_m$. To establish the principal components as a basis for regression, first define an $\boldsymbol{X}$ $(n \times p)$ matrix which consists of $n$ observations of the $p$ predictor variables whose $(i,j)$th element is the value of the $j$th predictor (or regressor) variable for the $i$th observation. Accordingly, the corresponding standard regression model is defined as:

$$y = \boldsymbol{X}\beta + \epsilon. \tag{6}$$

where $y$ is the vector of $n$ observations of the dependent variable, measured about their mean, $\beta$ is a vector of $p$ regression coefficients and $\epsilon$ is a vector of error terms; the elements of $\epsilon$ are independent, each with the same variance $\sigma^2$. Also, in matrix form, one can define the PC values for each observation as $\boldsymbol{Z} = \boldsymbol{XA}$, where the $(i, k)$th element of $\boldsymbol{Z}$ is the value (score) of the $k$th PC for the $i$th observation, and $\boldsymbol{A}$ is a $(p \times p)$ matrix whose $k$th column is the $k$th eigenvector of $\boldsymbol{X'X}$. The idea is to use the PC to replace the original predictor variables. For this purpose, the orthogonality concept of the eigenvector matrix is used. Since matrix A is orthogonal, then $\boldsymbol{X}\beta$ can be rewritten as $\boldsymbol{Z}\gamma = \boldsymbol{XAA'}\beta$, in which $\gamma = \boldsymbol{A'}\beta$. Then, (6) can be rewritten as [10]:

$$y = \boldsymbol{Z}\gamma + \epsilon \tag{7}$$

Thus, in (6) the predictor variables were replaced by their PCs in the regression model. In addition to the PCA regression model in (1), the following reduced model is also used:

$$y = \boldsymbol{Z_m}\gamma_m + \epsilon_m \tag{8}$$

where $\gamma_m$ is a vector of $m$ elements that are a subset of elements of $\gamma$, $\boldsymbol{Z_m}$ is an $(n \times m)$ matrix whose columns are the corresponding subset of columns of $\boldsymbol{Z}$, and $\epsilon_m$ is the appropriate error term. An estimate of $\beta$ can be found using $\hat{\beta} = \boldsymbol{A}\hat{\gamma}$. The vector $\hat{\gamma}$ can be calculated as $\hat{\gamma} = (\boldsymbol{Z'Z})^{-1}\boldsymbol{Z'}y$.

## III. Experimental Arrangement

To validate the developed soft-sensor, the platform that was developed at the Brazilian Agricultural Research Corporation (Embrapa Instrumentation) in partnership with the School of Engineering of São Carlos University of So Paulo (EESC-USP), both from Brazil, was used. This platform for sprayers development and analyzes operates as an Agricultural Sprayer Development System (ASDS) and uses a National

Instruments® embedded controller, known as NI-cRIO.

### A. Main Electronics and Mechanics used in the ASDS

The ASDS was designed and developed taking into account the concept of an advanced platform based on the use of sensors and actuators, controllers circuits, and intelligent electronics to enable the project and development of sprayer systems [12]–[14].

This laboratory infrastructure has an advanced development system that enables the design of architectures involving the connections of hydraulic components and devices, mechanical pumps, electronic and computer algorithms, as illustrated by Figure 1. On the other hand, the system also has the hydraulic devices that are used to make any configuration of commercial agricultural sprays and new prototypes of sprayers, the user interface for system monitoring and control, as well as an electromechanical structure which emulates the movement of the agricultural sprayer in the field, as shown in Figure 2.

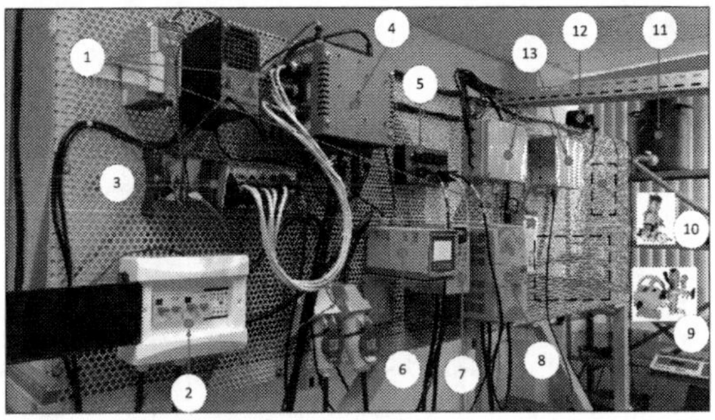

Figure 1. Front view of ASDS electro-hydraulic devices: (1) power supplies, (2) electrical protection circuits, (3) modules for automation and control of the inputs and outputs variables, (4) box with electronic circuits for signal conditioning, (5) CAN network bus, (6) transmitter for analog sensors, (7) frequency inverter for control of the spray pump, (8) frequency inverter for control of the Industrial belt that simulates the tractor movement in relation to the sprayers, (9) spray pump, (10) two piston pumps for injection of pesticides, (11) pesticide reservoir tank, (12) proportional valve for pressure and flow control, (13) valve actuation circuits via CAN network.

Figure 2. Development system for projects dedicated to the application of liquid agricultural inputs: (1) spray nozzle, (2) system that emulates the movement of the sprayer, (3) pesticide disposal tank, (4) user interface of the development system, (5) spray booms.

### B. Data Collection

Water-sensitive papers were used to collect the drop size distribution pattern. This type of paper collects the watermarks produced by the drops which can be analyzed by a pattern recognition program to obtain the average diameters. A detailed diagram of the experimental setup is shown in Figure 3. The water-sensitive papers were displayed in an aluminum bar, with an impermeable paint coating, positioned transversely to the movement of the application and spaced so as to collect all the information from the drop distribution of all the nozzles. The spraying was performed at a height of 51 cm. The distance between each nozzle was 50 cm (Figure 3) [15].

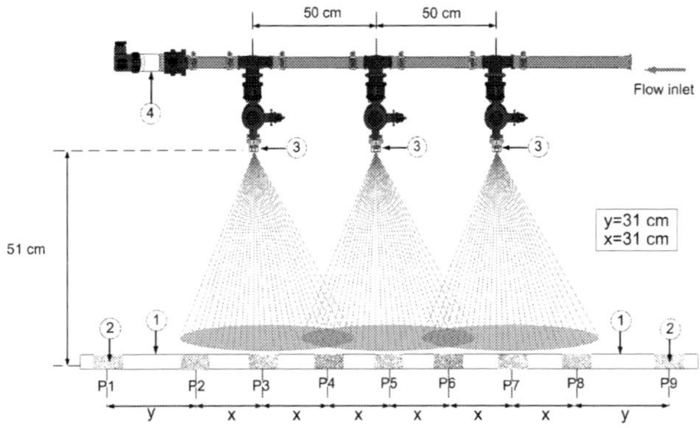


Figure 3. A zoom of the spray boom with the nozzles used for data collection containing: 1) aluminum bar with an impermeable paint coating; 2) water-sensitive papers; 3) set of nozzles; 4) pressure sensor.

The position of the water-sensitive papers, in the aluminum bar, obeys the critical points which are to be considered in the distribution of mean diameters, that is, the papers placed outside of the aluminum bar (P1 and P9 in Figure 3) in order to collect the data of the drops with potential of drifting. Two other papers were placed at the external nozzles to collect the application pattern without overlapping (P2 and P8 in Figure 3). A pair of papers was placed in the center of the overlapping of the nozzle cones (P4 and P6 in Figure 3) and three more papers were placed in the center of the cones, perpendicular to the nozzle (P3, P5 and P7 in Figure 3).

Table I shows the operating conditions used to collect data for each tested nozzle where $Q_p$ [$m^3$/s] is the nozzle flow, $D_p$ [ℓ/ha] is the application rate, $V_p$ [m/s] is the speed of application and $d_0$ [mm] is the discharge orifice of the nozzle. Four conditions were tested, one per nozzle with different discharge orifice diameters of the models CH0.5, CH 1, CH 3 and CH 6 of the Magnojtet® company. These four types of nozzles were selected with the help of a specialist in the area of agricultural application in order to have a wide range of drop sizes within the database.

TABLE I. OPERATING CONDITIONS FOR THE ASDS USING FULL CONE NOZZLES (magnojet®).

| | Nozzle | P [bar] | $Q_p$ $[L/min]$ | $D_p$ $[L/ha]$ | Temp [°C] | Humid [%] | $V_p$ [km/h] | $d_0$ [mm] |
|---|---|---|---|---|---|---|---|---|
| $1^{st}$ | CH0.5 | 3.4 | 0.53 | 67 | 23.6 | 51 | 10 | 0.5 |
| $2^{nd}$ | CH1 | 3.4 | 1.02 | 85 | 23.4 | 61 | 14 | 1.0 |
| $3^{rd}$ | CH3 | 3.4 | 1.46 | 100 | 24.0 | 49 | 18 | 1.5 |
| $4^{th}$ | CH6 | 2.4 | 1.90 | 120 | 23.7 | 58 | 20 | 2.0 |

Four conditions named full cone nozzles CH05, CH1, CH3 and CH6 were considered. For each condition, there were 5 replicates of which the first 3 had the same operating conditions (S in Table III). The fourth repetition was performed by lowering the sprayer boom pressure by 10% and the fifth repetition was done by increasing the sprayer boom pressure by 10%. For each paper positioned in the metal bar there are two samples and thus, the total of the samples per repetition are 18, so the total samples for each condition, which is composed of 5 repetitions, are 90 samples. Accounting for all four conditions, 360 samples were collected. The information collected experimentally, from each water-sensitive paper, was for the following quality descriptors: $D_{0.1}$, SMD, VMD, $D_{0.9}$, as well as the relative amplitude (RA) and the application rate (AR).

TABLE II. ARRANGEMENT OF SAMPLES, FOR EACH CONDITION, WHICH MAKE UP THE DATABASE.

| | Nozzle | N° repetition | | | Total | N° papers | N° samples | Total samples |
|---|---|---|---|---|---|---|---|---|
| | | S | -10% | +10% | | | | |
| $1^{st}$ | CH0.5 | 3 | 1 | 1 | 5 | 9 | 18 | 90 |
| $2^{nd}$ | CH1 | 3 | 1 | 1 | 5 | 9 | 18 | 90 |
| $3^{rd}$ | CH3 | 3 | 1 | 1 | 5 | 9 | 18 | 90 |
| $4^{th}$ | CH6 | 3 | 1 | 1 | 5 | 9 | 18 | 90 |
| | | | | | | Total collected samples | | 360 |

To obtain the average diameters in the papers sensitive to the water, the tool DropScope® of the Ablevision® company was used. The data exploration, the analysis of results and the construction of the soft-sensors were performed with the MATLAB® and Simulink® software.

## C. *Soft-sensor*

The applications of the soft-sensors can be divided into three large items: monitoring of processes, process control and off-line assistance of operations [16]. In this work, the soft-sensors were used in the monitoring of the spraying process, specifically as a predictor of the quality of the variables (PPQV), as well as in control to plan the operations (OPP). The soft-sensor used as PPQV applied to the agricultural spraying process is shown in Figure 4.

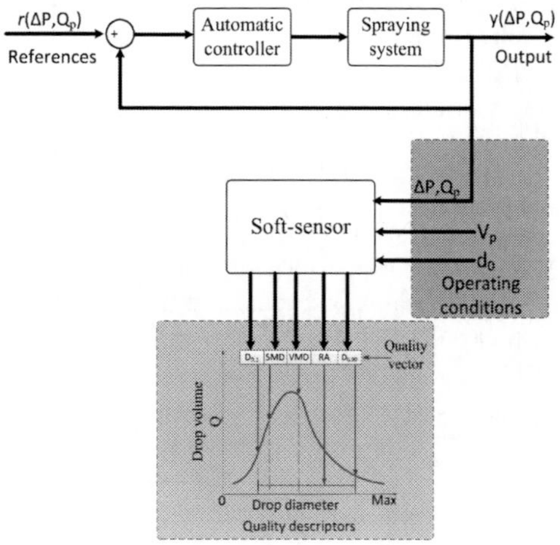


Figure 4. Block diagram of the soft-sensor used as predictor of process quality variables (PPQV) in the agricultural spraying process.

In the block diagram, the control loop of the spraying system is shown. In this loop, the inputs are the pressure and flow references $r(\Delta P_{ref}, Q_{pref})$. The outputs of this loop are the pressure $\Delta P$ and flow measured in the system by the sensors $Q_p$, which are the actual value that the spraying system has at a given time. In the case of the soft-sensor as PPQV (Figure 4), the operating conditions (red square with dotted lines) are the inputs to the soft-sensor. The operating conditions are the pressure and flow, which come directly from the spraying system, the speed of application $V_p$ and the diameter of the discharge orifice of the nozzle $d_0$. In the configuration as a predictor of quality variables, the soft-sensor offers as output the prediction of the quality descriptors, that is, the mean diameters: $D_{0.1}$, SMD, VMD, $D_{0.9}$.

On the other hand, the application of the soft-sensor, in process control, as an operations planner in the process, is shown in Fig 5. For this configuration, the soft-sensor receives as input the quality descriptors of the spraying and delivers as output the required operating conditions in the spraying system to obtain the given quality values.

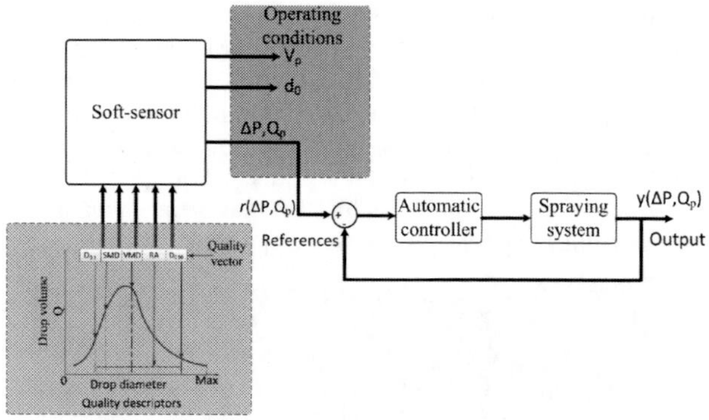


Figure 5. Block diagram of the soft-sensor used as an operations planner in the process (OPP) in the agricultural spraying process.

In the block diagram of Fig. 5, it is shown that the soft-sensor delivers the pressure and flow reference values for the control loop. The soft-sensor also delivers the model of the nozzle represented by the diameter $d_0$ and the speed $V_p$ that the sprayer must have at the time of making the application.

# IV. Results and Discussion

First, an exploration of the data was made. To apply techniques that work with maximization of variances, such as PCA, or reduction of errors, it is important that the data of the random observations fit a normal curve. Thus, a quantile-quantile graph (Q-Q plot) was used to determine the adjustment that the data can have to a normal distribution. Then, a Grubbs test to all the collected observations in order to detect possible outliers was carried out. The Q-Q plots and the Grubbs test are explained in more detail in [15].

The model chosen to build the soft-sensors was the PCA regression. The steps for the construction of the model are presented in Algorithm 1. The algorithm is divided into two procedures, the first procedure (REGRESSION) is the construction of the principal component regression model. This procedure has as entries the data matrix $\boldsymbol{X}$, the matrix of eigenvectors $\boldsymbol{A}$, the matrix of scores of the PC's $\boldsymbol{Z}$ and the vector of data required for the model $\boldsymbol{y}$. Also, this procedure returns the value of the regression coefficients $\hat{\gamma}$ and the prediction value $\hat{y}$. Therefore, the regression model is delivered based on the principal components. The second procedure in the Algorithm 1, has as its main function to estimate output values for new observed data (NEWOBSERV). Then, the procedure receives a vector containing new observations $x_{new}$, as well as receives the regression coefficients based on the PCs $\hat{\gamma}$ and the eigenvalue matrix $A$. In the procedure, a new score matrix $Z_{new}$, a new vector of values $\hat{x}_{new}$ and a new observed data $\hat{y}_{new}$ are estimated.

**Algorithm 1** PCA regression

**Require:** $\boldsymbol{X}$ consists of $n$ observations of $p$ predictor variables;
$\boldsymbol{A}$ Matrix of eigenvectors;
$\boldsymbol{Z}$ Matrix of scores of the PC's;
$y$ Vector of data required for the model;
**procedure** REGRESSION($\boldsymbol{X}, \boldsymbol{A}, \boldsymbol{Z}, y$)
$\boldsymbol{Z} = \boldsymbol{X}\boldsymbol{A}$ ▷ Calculate the matrix $\boldsymbol{Z}$ of the scores PC
$\hat{\gamma} = (\boldsymbol{Z}'\boldsymbol{Z})^{-1}\boldsymbol{Z}'y$ ▷ Returns the $\hat{\gamma}$ value
$\hat{y} = Z\hat{\gamma}$ ▷ Returns the prediction $\hat{y}$ value
**end procedure**
**procedure** NEWOBSERV($x_{new}, A, \hat{\gamma}$)
$z'_{new} = x'_{new}A$ ▷ Calculate the $x_{new}$ scores value
$\hat{x}'_{new} = z'_{new}A'$ ▷ Find the predicted value
$\hat{y}'_{new} = z'_{new}\hat{\gamma}$ ▷ Returns the predicted value
**end procedure**

Figure 6. Model construction algorithm.

To validate the model, four new repetitions were made, one for each operating condition (Table I), each repetition had 14 samples of water sensitive paper totalizing 56 new observations. Figures 7b, 8d, 9f, 10h show the xbar charts and error bars which describe the behavior of the PCA-based models in the presence of new observations. It is important to emphasize that the spraying process is highly random and therefore there are several values which are above the maximum (UCL) and minimum (LCL) values allowed. For the first three conditions (samples: 1-14 (first condition CH05), 15-28 (second condition CH1), 29-42 (second condition CH3)), the estimation errors are low, which showed that the models provide adequate estimates for the spraying quality descriptors. Observing the responses of the models, Figures 7a, 8c, 9e, 10g, one can consider that the best regression responses are for the descriptors SMD, VMD and $D_{0.9}$.

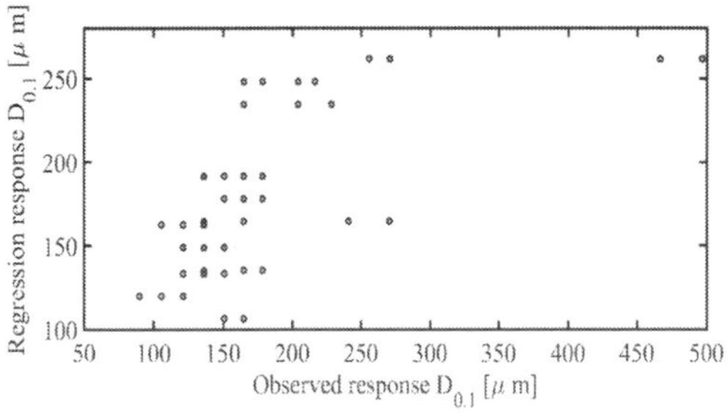


(a) $D_{0.1}$ scatter response

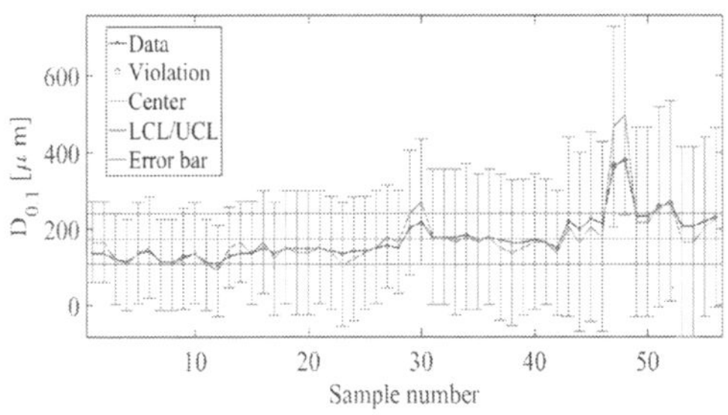


(b) $D_{0.1}$ xbar chart and error bars

Figure 7. Results of the soft-sensor for the $D_{0.1}$ descriptor.

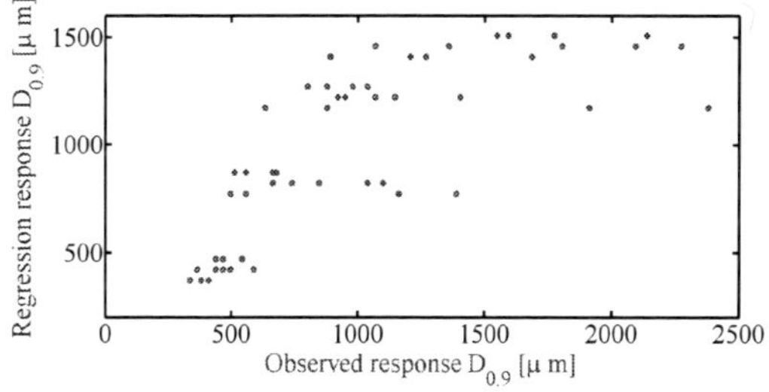


(a) $D_{0.9}$ scatter response

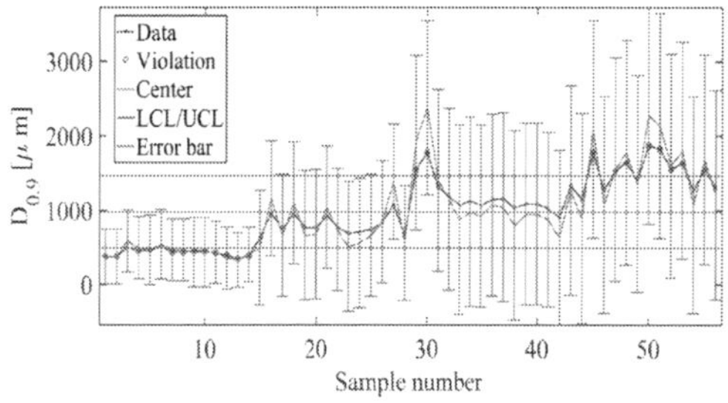


(b) $D_{0.9}$ xbar chart and error bars

Figure 8. Results of the soft-sensor for the $D_{0.9}$ descriptor.

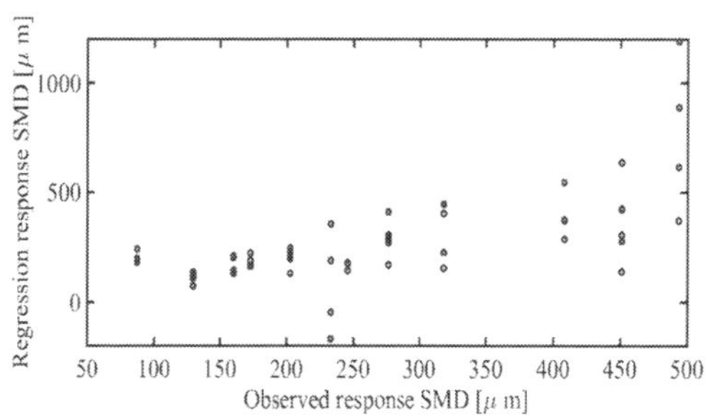


(a) SMD scatter response

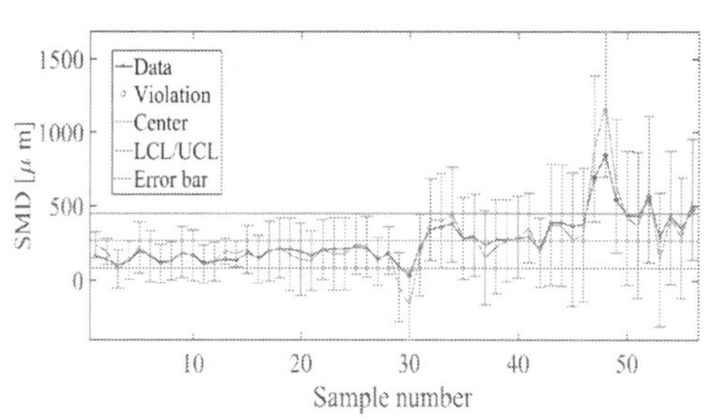


(b) SMD xbar chart and error bars

Figure 9. Results of the soft-sensor for the SMD descriptor.

The regression coefficients estimated with the scores of the principal components are shown in Table III. The coefficients $\beta$ relate the quality descriptors with the operating conditions.

TABLE III. ESTIMATED REGRESSION COEFFICIENTS $\hat{\beta}$.

| | $D_{0.1}$ | SMD | VMD | $D_{0.9}$ |
|---|---|---|---|---|
| $P$ | 0.41 | 0.36 | 0.50 | 0.45 |
| $V_p$ | 0.14 | 0.16 | 0.14 | 0.07 |
| $d_0$ | 0.00 | -0.03 | 0.21 | 0.33 |

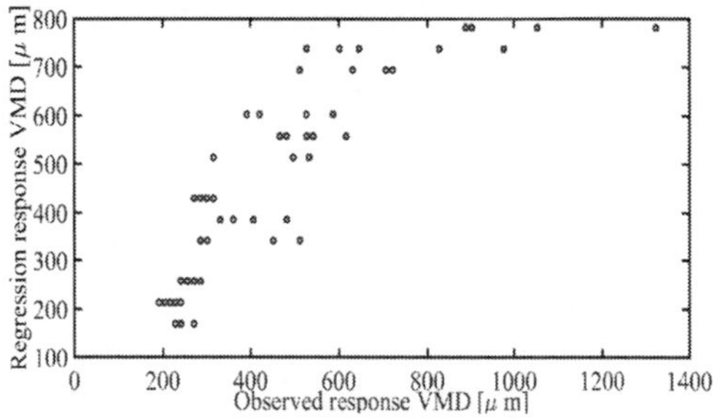


(a) VMD scatter response

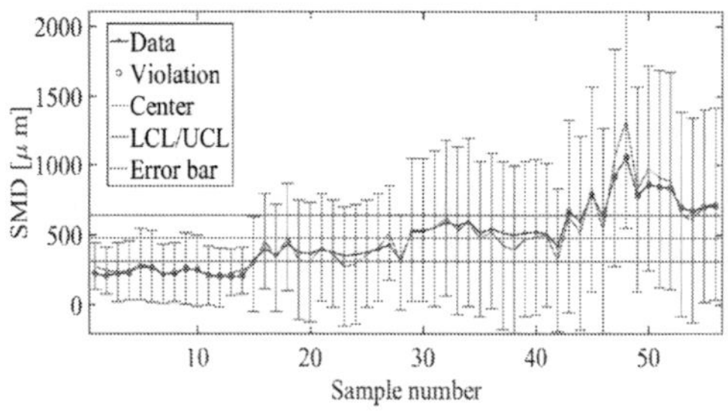


(b) VMD xbar chart and error bars

Figure 10. Results of the soft-sensor for the VMD descriptor.

## V. CONCLUSION AND FUTURE WORK

This work presented the development of customized soft-sensors for agriculture. The soft-sensors have shown the possibility to aggregate value in the processes, that is, improve the quality in the agricultural pesticide application. In addition, they serve as versatile tools to help agricultural producers to improve the application based on knowledge and the systems control, providing support for decision making in agricultural spraying for pest control. Furthermore, the models based on PCA regression proved to be useful and have allowed finding good estimators for spraying quality descriptors, as well as the adjustment of the operating conditions and calibration of the agricultural machinery. In future works, the soft-sensor will be embedded in a circuit, and prepared to operate with a CAN network, making it possible the actual sprayer operate in agricultural field conditions.

## ACKNOWLEDGMENT

This work was supported by Embrapa Instrumentation and partnership with the SINDAG (under grants: MP2 No. 02.11.07.025.00.00; MP1 No. 01.14.09.0.01.05.05), and the National Counsel of Technological and Scientific Development (CNPq, under grant 306.477/2013-0). The authors thank the Brazilian companies, Ablevision and Magnojet, for facilitating the use of the DropScope technology and for providing the nozzles for the practical experiments, respectively. The authors also acknowledge the relevant discussions with Heitor V. Mercaldi.

## REFERENCES

[1] Y. Suzumura and P. E. Cruvinel, "Analysis of the quality of the efficiency of agricultural spraying with image processing and neural networks," Sinergia, vol. 6, no. 2, 2005, pp. 129–137.

[2] Y. Ozeki and R. Kunz, Aerial application manual, São Paulo, SP, 1997.

[3] S. Mitra and X. Li, "A comprehensive model on spray formation process and probability distribution of subsequently formed spray droplets," in Energy Conversion Engineering Conference. IECEC-97., Proceedings of the 32nd Intersociety, vol. 2. Honolulu, HI: IEEE, Jul 1997, pp. 904–909.

[4] W. Boller and C. G. Raetano, "Spray nozzles of hydraulic power, adjustments and calibration of sprayers whit bars," in Application technology for Annual Crops, U. R. Antuniassi and W. Boller, Eds. Passo Fundo: Aldeia Norte, 2011.

[5] L. Fortuna, S. Graziani, A. Rizzo, and M. G. Xibilia, Soft Sensors for Monitoring and Control of Industrial Processes, ser. Advances in Industrial Control, M. J. Grimble and M. A. Johnson, Eds. Springer London, 2007.

[6] R. Luo, H. Shao, and Z. Zhang, "Fuzzy-neural-net-based inferential control for a high-purity distillation column," Control Engineering Practice, vol. 3, no. 1, 1995, pp. 31–40.

[7] A. Casali et al., "Particle size distribution soft-sensor for a grinding circuit," Powder Technology, vol. 99, no. 1, 1998, pp. 15 – 21.

[8] B. Lin, B. Recke, J. K. Knudsen, and S. B. Jorgensen, "A systematic approach for soft sensor development," Computers & Chemical Engineering, vol. 31, no. 56, 2007, pp. 419–425, 15th European Symposium on Computer Aided Process Engineering held in Barcelona, Spain, May 29-June 1, 2005.

[9] H. Liu and C. Yoo, "A robust localized soft sensor for particulate matter modeling in seoul metro systems," Journal of Hazardous Materials, vol. 305, 2016, pp. 209–218.

[10] I. Jolliffe, Principal component analysis. New York: Springer Verlag, 2002.

[11] C. M. Bishop, Pattern Recognition and Machine Learning (Information Science and Statistics). Secaucus, NJ, USA: Springer Verlag New York, Inc., 2006.

[12] P. E. Cruvinel, V. A. Oliveira, H. V. Mercaldi, E. A. G. Peñaloza, and K. R. Felizardo, An Advanced Sensors-based Platform for the Development of Agricultural Sprayers, ser. Advances in Sensors: Reviews. International Frequency Sensor Association (IFSA) Publishing, 2016, vol. 4, ch. 10, pp. 181–204.

[13] K. R. Felizardo, "Modeling and predictive control of a direct injection spray system," Doutorado: Programa de PósGraduação em Engenharia Elétrica e Àrea de Concentração em Sistemas Dinâmicos, Escola de Engenharia de São Carlos, Universidade de São Paulo, São Carlos, 2013.

[14] P. E. Cruvinel, V. A. Oliveira, K. R. Felizardo, and H. V. Mercaldi, "Automated workbench for testing and sprayer development of pesticides," in Agricultura de Precisão: um Novo Olhar, vol. 1. São Carlos, SP: Embrapa Instrumentação, 2011, pp. 96–100.

[15] E. A. G. Peñaloza, P. E. Cruvinel, V. A. Oliveira, and A. G. F. Costa, "A model approach to infer the quality in agricultural sprayers supported by knowledge bases and experimental measurements," International Journal of Semantic Computing, vol. 11, no. 03, 2017, pp. 279–292.

[16] S. Khatibisepehr, B. Huang, and S. Khare, "Design of inferential sensors in the process industry: A review of bayesian methods," Journal of Process Control, vol. 23, no. 10, 2013, pp. 1575 – 1596.

# Design and Fabrication of a Solid-State pH Sensor Module

Considering Its Possible Applications

Lan Zhang, Jian Lu, Ryutaro Maeda
Research Center for Ubiquitous MEMS and Micro Engineering (UMEMSME)
National Institute of Advanced Industrial Science and Technology (AIST)
Tsukuba, Japan
email: {chou-ran@aist.go.jp, jian-lu@aist.go.jp, maeda-ryutaro}@aist.go.jp

Hirofumi Nogami
Department of Mechanical Engineering
Kyushu University
Fukuoka, Japan
email: nogami.hirofumi.406@m.kyushu-u.ac.jp

***Abstract*— We developed a solid pH sensor, which can implement a real-time monitoring of pH value with low power consumption and high accuracy. The prototype of the pH sensor was fabricated and packaged well and can keep a linear output proportional to the changes in the pH value and has a high-sensitivity of >14 μA/pH. The developed pH sensor is believed to be significantly important for both the industrial and the civilian sectors for improving the efficiency of environment monitoring.**

***Keywords- pH value test; solid state; MEMS sensor; Indium Tin Oxide***

## I. Introduction

Measurements of pH are important in many fields [1][2], such as chemical engineering, agriculture, medicine, environmental science, water treatment and purification, and many other applications. However, conventionally, the pH sensor has a reference electrode with a large size because of high concentration of electrolyte solution in it. The shortcoming of big size and large power consumption seriously restrict the application of traditional pH sensors, especially in the coming "Internet of Things" age where maintenance-free and wireless communications are essential for arbitrary distributing of the sensor node.

State-of-the-art microelectromechanical systems (MEMS) and complementary MOS (CMOS) techniques have undergone many advances [3]. As MEMS researchers, we need to contribute to the industrial revolution and improve the pH measurement technology. We have engaged in developing a solid-type pH sensor for real-time pH measurement recently. Figure 1 shows a typical pH sensor prototype including the package, measurement electrodes, and testing and transmission boards. MEMS fabrication technology was used in this work to realize the sensing electrode with high dimensional and performance homogeneity. The developed pH sensor offers the advantages of field effect transistor (FET) and indium tin oxide (ITO) sensing techniques. The sensor system can be fabricated with a compact size by eliminating the reference solution. The solid-state sensor structure is fit for long-term pH measurement, and the separate ITO sensing electrode can be patterned with a suitable capture structure for various test environments. In Sections 2 and 3, sensor system setup and preliminary results will be presented.

## II. Electrode Fabrication and Sensor System Setup

### A. Sensor electrodes fabrication

The fabrication procedure of the pH sensor electrodes has been introduced comprehensively in our previous works [4] [5]. By the MEMS technique, 47 die chip sensor electrodes can be fabricated on a 4-inch silicon wafer. The flat area of every single electrode can be controlled at <120 mm$^2$. The die chip of sensor electrodes was fabricated with a compact size can induce the packaged sensor system enjoying a high flexible application potential in feature works.

### B. Sensor system setup

The given typical pH sensor prototype combines the functional components of sensor electrodes, testing and transmission boards, see upper left insert of Figure 1. An ITO-sensing electrode connects the gate terminal of a MOSFET, the specific FET was loaded on the testing board was used to measure the pH value of target solutions. Transmission board has a CPU, a wireless module, a chip temperature unit and an IR temperature sensor to coding and transmitting the tested date, recording the environment and board temperature, respectively.

## III. Preliminary Measurement Results

### A. Sensor sensitivity and output linearity

The output function of given solid pH was evaluated first. The lower right insert of Figure 1 shows the coded data of the output current versus pH characteristics, considering that the pH sensor is immersed in a solution with varying pH values. The coded data of the output current decreased as the pH value increased from 5 to 7, accordingly. Moreover, the output data was linearly proportional to the changes in the pH value, i.e., the output data can be represented by a first-

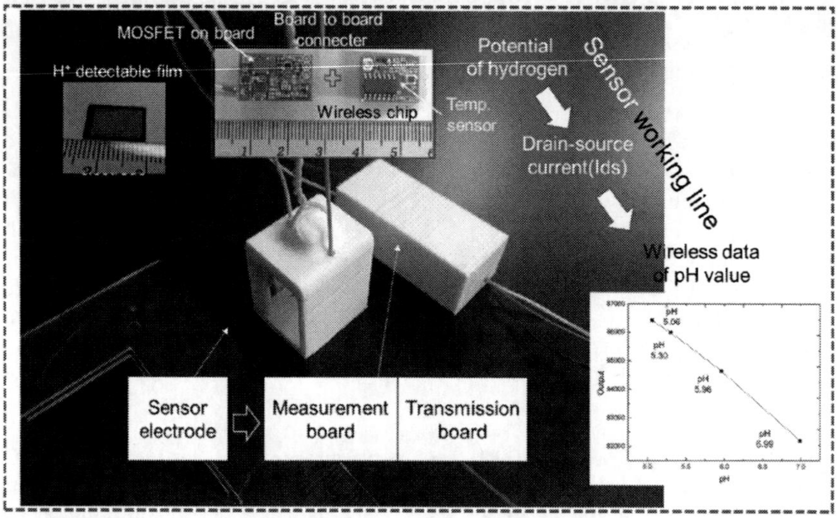


Figure 1. pH sensor system

degree polynomial equation. Thus, the pH sensor can be easily used to measure the pH of target solutions by fitting the output current to the pH value.

### *B. Temperature calibration for long-term measurement*

Normally, in a commercial pH sensor, several temperature sensors are placed into the sensor system to calibrate the output from the effect of temperature. As previously mentioned, for our sensor, two types of temperature sensors (chip sensor and IR temperature device unit) were loaded on the transmission board to calibrate the given pH sensor. Figure 2 shows the results of pH sensor output versus on-board temperature at the same time. A pH=7.3@25 solution was simultaneously tested by the given pH sensor and temperature sensor. The comparison results can be used to eliminate the temperature effect of the given pH sensor system for the next long-term field measurement.

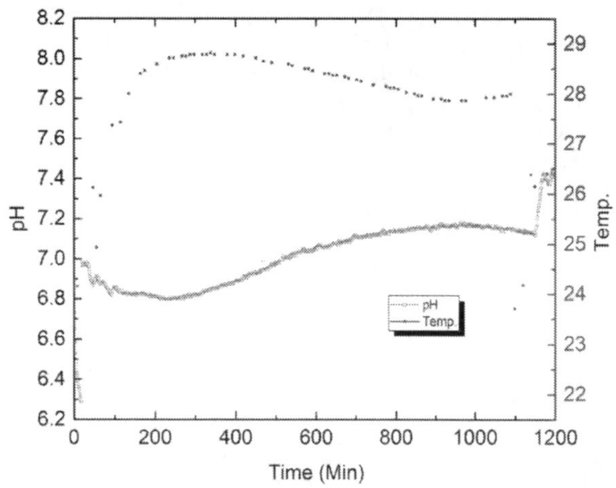


Figure 2. Temperature and pH test feature of the given sensor.

## IV. CONCLUSION

We developed a solid-state pH sensor for real time pH monitoring. The given sensor was packaged and preliminary tested. As the results show, the developed pH sensor has a good stability and linear output performance. After the temperature calibration process, a long-term field measurement for industrial application is going on, and the tested data can provide very important database information for the management system to realize of smart manufactory. Moreover, in order to realize a commercial pH sensor with a long time stable performance, the fabrication method of sensor electrodes, cost of testing and transmission boards and package approach are also considered to be improved.

## REFERENCES


[1] P. Batista, "An embedded measurement system for the electrical characterization of EGFET as a pH sensor," Sci. Technol, vol. 25, pp. 027001-1-6, 2014.

[2] J. Bausells, J. Carrabina, A. Errachid, and A. Merlos, "Ion-sensitive field-effect transistors fabricated in a commercial CMOS technology," Sens. Actuators B, vol. 57, pp. 56-62, 1999.

[3] A. Richter et al. "Review on hydrogel-based pH sensors and microsensors," Sensors, vol. 8, pp. 561-581, 2008.

[4] L. Zhang, J. Lu, H. Okada, H. Nogami, and T. Itoh, "Development of ITO- and FET-based cow rumen sensor for long-term pH value monitoring," Symposium on Design, Test, Integration and Packaging of MEMS/MOEMS (DTIP), vol. 2016, pp.92-96, May 2016.

[5] L. Zhang et al. "Low-Power Highly Sensitive pH sensor with μ-dots protective structures for monitoring rumen in cows in real-time," IEEE Sens. J. vol. 17, pp. 7281 - 7289, 2017.

# Reduced Graphene Oxide-ZnO Nanotubes Based Binary Hybrid Structure as Room Temperature Ethanol Sensor

Partha Bhattacharyya, Debanjan Acharyya
Nano thin films and solid state gas sensor devices laboratory,
Department of ETCE, Indian Institute of Engineering
Science and Technology (IIEST), Shibpur, India
e-mail:pb_etc_besu@yahoo.com,
iammdebanjan@gmail.com

Indranil Maity
School of VLSI Technolog, Indian Institute of Engineering
Science and Technology (IIEST), Shibpur, India
e-mail: indrnilmaity026@gmail.com

*Abstract*— **In this paper, we report a highly sensitive and fast responsive room temperature ethanol sensor based on rGO-ZnO nanotubes (NTs) hybrid structure. ZnO NTs were grown on Indium doped Tin Oxide (ITO) substrate using a two-step process, consisting of electro-deposition (for ZnO nanorods deposition) and electrochemical etching (for etching of ZnO nanorods to form nanotubes). After that, rGO layer was deposited on top of the ZnO NTs employing a programmed dip coating technique. Subsequently, detailed structural and morphological characterizations were carried out using FESEM (Field Emission Scanning Electron Microscopy), Raman spectroscopy and XPS (X-Ray photo electron Spectroscopy) techniques to confirm the formation of hybrid structure. After that, alcohol (i.e. ethanol, methanol, 2-propanol) sensing properties of the device were investigated in the concentration range of 1-700 ppm at different temperatures (27–175°C). ~70% response magnitude, (towards ethanol) was observed at room temperature. Moreover, fast response time and recovery time were also noticed (response time: ~56 s and recovery time: ~202 s at 100 ppm concentration of ethanol). Such sensing performance is attributed to the synergistic hybridization of ZnO NTs and rGO, which offer an extremely large number of gas adsorption/desorption sites and high carrier mobility.**

***Keywords- rGO-ZnO nanotubes; hybrid structure; room temperature ethanol sensor; fast response time/recovery time.***

## I. INTRODUCTION

Metal oxide based nanostructures have widely been used in the development of solid-state gas sensors in different application arena, such as environmental gas/volatile organic compound monitoring, food processing, detection of toxic, flammable and explosive gases etc. [1]. However, the high operating temperature of such sensors inevitably increases the power consumption, cost and hampers the long-term stability [2]. Therefore, in recent years, the development of room temperature gas sensors has attracted serious attention around the globe. The room temperature sensing performance can be achieved by (i) decreasing the activation energy of sensing surface and (ii) enhancing the carrier transport kinetics of the sensor [1]-[4]. In this context, nanotube structure having high surface to volume ratio (which decrease the activation energy of the sensing layer) proved its promising candidature as a room temperature sensing layer [4]. On the other hand, the high mobility and intrinsic defects of rGO, make it as an essential material to improve the transport kinetics of the sensor [1]. Now, hybridization of nanotube and rGO facilitates room temperature sensing performance as well as fast transport kinetics. Several metal oxide based (i.e. $TiO_2$, $SnO_2$, $WO_3$ etc.) nanotubes structure have already been reported for room temperature volatile organic compound sensor [1], [3]. However, these sensors exhibited sluggish response time and recovery time (in minutes) towards ethanol. Therefore, to obtain room temperature fast responsive ethanol sensor, ZnO NTs and rGO layer were hybridized in this work.

The sensing performance of the rGO-ZnO NTs structure was carried out in the concentration range of 1-700 ppm, targeting ethanol, methanol and 2-propanol. Alcohol (i.e. ethanol, methanol, 2-propanol) sensing properties of the device were investigated in the concentration range of 1-700 ppm at different temperatures (27–175°C). ~70% response magnitude, (towards ethanol) was observed at room temperature. Moreover, fast response time and recovery time were also noticed (response time: ~56 s and recovery time: ~202 s at 100 ppm concentration of ethanol). Such sensing performance is attributed to the synergistic hybridization ZnO NTs and rGO, which offers extremely large amount gas adsorption/desorption sites and high carrier mobility. The formation of hybrid junction between rGO and ZnO NTs possibly enhance the sensitivity as well as response kinetics towards ethanol.

The rest of the paper is structured as follows. In Section 2, device fabrication and measurement procedure are discussed. In Section 3, the morphological and surface characterization outcomes, sensing performance of the rGO-ZnO NTs based hybrid device are discussed and correlated with the possible physical phenomenon. Finally, we conclude the work in Section 4.

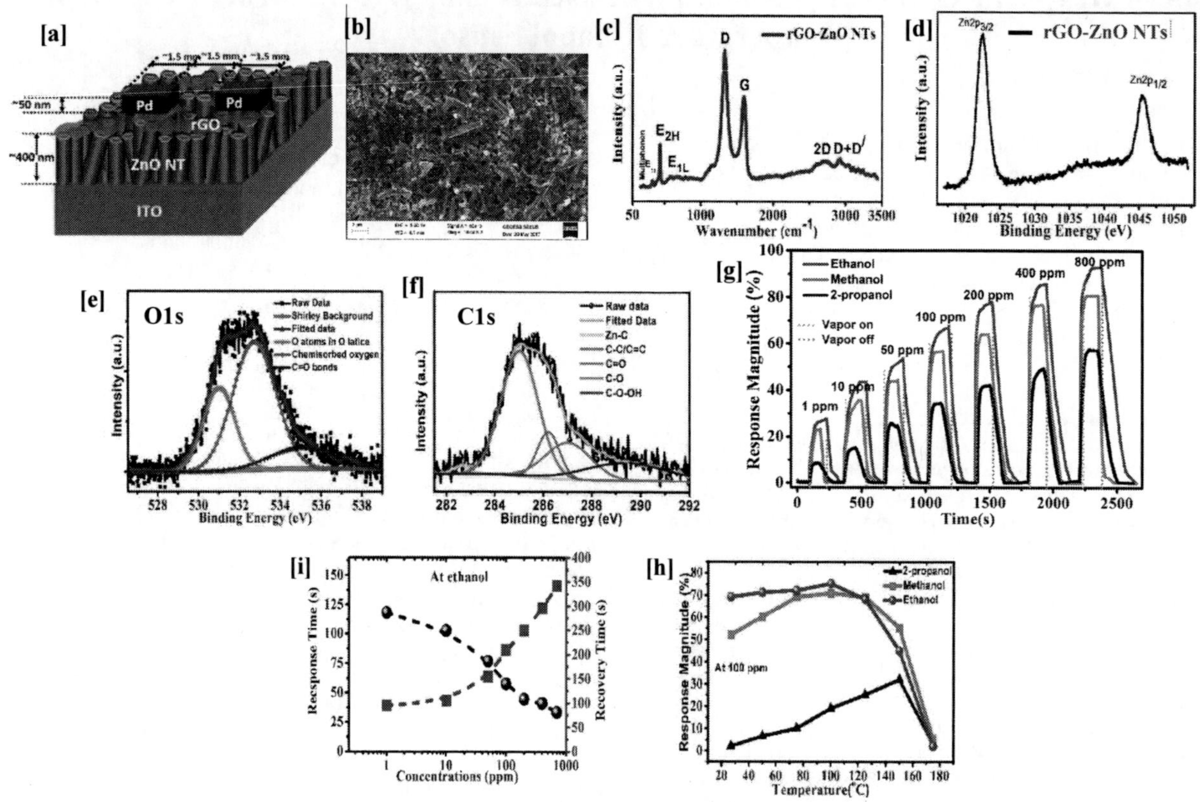


Figure 1. (a) A schematic representation of rGO-ZnO NTs binary hybrid sensor device with requisite dimensions (b) FESEM image of rGO-ZnO NTs (c) Raman spectra of rGO-ZnO NTs (d-f) XPS spectra of rGO-ZnO NTs; (d) Zn ($2p_{3/2}$ and $2p_{1/2}$) and (e) O (1s) peak (f) C1s spectra of rGO-ZnO NFs. (g) Transient response characteristics towards ethanol, methanol, 2-propanol, of rGO-ZnO NTs (green line and red line indicate vapor on and off, respectively), (h) Response time (in black) and recovery time (in blue) as a function of different vapors concentrations (1–700 ppm) for the rGO-ZnO NTs (i) The response magnitude as a function of temperature for rGO-ZnO NTs at 100 ppm concentration of ethanol, methanol, and 2-propanol.

## II. EXPERIMENT

In an experiment, ZnO nanotubes were fabricated on an Indium doped Tin-Oxide (ITO) coated glass substrate (from Sigma Aldrich, thickness: 0.9 mm, surface resistivity: ~10 Ω/sq), by a two-step process, consists of (i) electro-deposition of ZnO nanorods, followed by (ii) selective electrochemical etching of those nanorods to form nanotubes [2]. In first step, ITO was connected to the negative polarity, while during etching of ZnO nanorods, positive voltage was applied to ITO. In the first step, aqueous solution of equi-molar (5 mM each) Zinc Nitratehexahydrate ($(Zn(NO_3)_2$, $6H_2O$, 99%, MERCK) and Hexamethylenetetramine (HMT) ($(CH_2)_6N_4$, 99%, MERCK) was used to deposit ZnO nanorods. After that, the electro-deposition was carried out for 40 minutes at 78°C with a bias voltage of -1.8 V [2]. In the second step, electrochemical etching of grown ZnO nanorods was carried out for 1 hours at 65°C, using an aqueous solution of 0.01M Ethylenediamine (EDA) ($C_2H_4(NH_2)_2$, 99.5%, MERCK) with an applied potential of -0.06V. After that, the grown ZnO NTs were annealed in a horizontal tube furnace (heating and cooling rate of 5°C/min) at 350°C for 3 hours. Further, on top of the ZnO NTs layer, rGO layer was deposited employing a programmed dip coating technique. After that, rGO-ZnO NTs hybrid device was again annealed at 300°C for 2 hrs. Subsequently, a planar device structure was fabricated employing rGO-ZnO NTs as the sensing layer and palladium (Pd) as contact electrodes. Sensor device schematic is shown in Figure 1(a).

## III. RESULTS AND DISCUSSIONS

FESEM image (top surface) of rGO-ZnO NTs is shown in Figure 1(b). Raman spectroscopy of rGO-ZnO NTs is depicted in Figure 1(c), where the presence of D band (centred at 1334.22 cm$^{-1}$), G band (centred at 1601.15 cm$^{-1}$), 2D band (centred at 2705.25 cm$^{-1}$) and D+D/ (centred at 2921.95 cm$^{-1}$) validate the existence of rGO [1]. D band attribute to $sp^3$ defects at the graphene edges and G band signifies $E_{2g}$ phonon [1]. Moreover, the existence of non-polar optical phonon of ZnO, i.e. E(high) band (centred at 432.03 cm$^{-1}$) and E(low) band (centred at 532.53 cm$^{-1}$) represents the wurtzite crystal phase of ZnO [2] which further confirms that the wurtzite phase of ZnO unaltered even after deposition of rGO. Further, to observe morphological properties of rGO-ZnO NTs surface, XPS characterization was carried out. As revealed from Zn (2p) peak (Figure 1(d)) that the doublet spectral line of Zn $2p_{3/2}$ and Zn $2p_{1/2}$ were observed at 1022.35 eV and 1045.24 eV, respectively [1]. Gaussian fitting of O1s spectra for rGO-ZnO NTs (depicted in Figure 1(e)) revealed that the amount of chemisorbed oxygen vacancies dominates the lattice oxygen content of rGO-ZnO NT surface. Moreover, the presence of C-C/C=C, C-O, C=O and C-O-OH peaks in C1s spectra (Figure 1 (f)) confirms the existence of rGO on ZnO NTs surface [5][6]. The sensing performance of rGO-ZnO NTs hybrid structure was investigated in the resistive mode with three different alcohol vapors (ethanol, methanol and 2-propanol) in the concentration range of 1–700 ppm at different temperatures (27–175°C). For each ppm, the gas/vapor was exposed for ~380 sec. The developed sensor offered higher response magnitude towards ethanol followed by methanol and 2-propanol. However, the optimum operating temperature of the device towards ethanol and methanol was found to be ~100°C and ~150°C for 2-propanol (Figure. 1(i)). Moreover, stable transient response characteristics towards ethanol was observed and depicted in Figure 1(g). The operating temperature for Figure 1(g) was ~27°C (i.e. room temperature). It is evident from Figure 1(g), that the sensor showed appreciably high response magnitude towards ethanol (e.g. 17.37 % at 1 ppm, 70.19 % at 100 ppm and 97.82 % at 700 ppm) at room temperature (RT). The response times and recovery times for rGO-ZnO NTs sensor towards ethanol are depicted in Figure 1(h) (in a concentration range of 1–700 ppm). For example, rGO-ZnO NTs sensor offered ~56 s response time and ~202 s recovery time at 100 ppm concentration of ethanol. Such high response magnitude and fast response and recovery kinetics at room temperature are far better than our previous report on pristine ZnO nanotube based ethanol sensor [7]. Such enhancement in sensing results is attributed to the incorporation of rGO on top of the ZnO NTs layer. ZnO NTs radially offers higher amount of gas adsorption/desorption sites (as target gas can adsorbed on the both inner and outer walls). On the other hand, high carrier mobility of rGO increase the carrier transport from the gas-interaction sites to the collecting electrode(s), which improves the response and recovery kinetics of the sensor [5]. To the exposure of air, oxygen molecules are adsorbed on the inner and outer wall of ZnO NTs and oxygen vacant sites of rGO layer, which inevitably increase the adsorb oxygen ions (which are active sites for gas interaction). Moreover, exchange of electrons and holes between ZnO NTs and rGO space charge regions are formed on hybrid surface which also penetrate towards the core from the outer surface of the NT wall. This phenomenon increases the barrier potential of the hybrid structure [4]. On the other hand, with the exposure of ethanol vapour, adsorbed oxygen species on the hybrid surface, oxidize the ethanol, which eventually reduces barrier potential at the surface. Therefore, the sensor resistance decreased dramatically [7].

## IV. CONCLUSION

Room temperature ethanol sensing performance of the rGO-ZnO NTs binary hybrid structure is reported in this paper. Hexagonal ZnO NTs were fabricated on the ITO substrate employing two-step process; (i) electro-deposition for ZnO hexagonal nanorods growth, followed by (ii) electro-chemical etching of ZnO nanorods to form nanotubes. The existence of rGO layer was authenticated by FESEM, Raman and XPS characterizations. The sensing characteristics of the sensor was experimented in the concentration range of 1-700 ppm towards ethanol, metanol and 2-propanol. The sensor showed promising sensing characteristics towards ethanol with a response magnitude of 70.19 % at 100 ppm and 97.82 % at 700 ppm at room temperature. However, optimum temperature of this sensor was found to be ~100°C towards ethanol. Moreover, the response time and recovery time were also found to be faster than that of earlier reported room temperature ethanol sensor. Large amount of gas-interaction sites of ZnO NTs along with high carrier mobility of rGO layer possibly offered such improved response characteristics.

## ACKNOWLEDGMENT

This work was supported by Visvesvaraya young faculty research fellowship (DeitY) and DST-NM, India. D. Acharyya thankfully acknowledges the CSIR, Govt. of India, for his Fellowship for pursuing Ph.D. Authors thankfully acknowledge Prof. Mon Shu Ho, Department of Physics, National Chung Hsing University, Taiwan for providing material characterization facility.

## REFERENCES

[1] S. Basu, and P. Bhattacharyya, "Recent developments on graphene and graphene oxide based solid state gas sensors," Sens. Actuators, B, vol. 173, pp. 1–21, 2012.

[2] D. Acharyya, and P. Bhattacharyya, Alcohol Sensing Performance of ZnO Hexagonal Nanotubes at Low Temperatures: A Qualitative Understanding, Sens. Actuators, B, vol. 228, pp. 373–386, 2016..

[3] F. L. Meng, Z. Guo, and X. J. Huang, "Graphene-based hybrids for chemiresistive gas sensors," Trends Anal. Chem., vol. 68, pp. 37–47, 2015.

[4] A. Hazra, K. Dutta, B. Bhowmik, P. P. Chattopadhyay, and P. Bhattacharyya, "Room temperature alcohol sensing by oxygen vacancy controlled $TiO_2$ nanotube array," Appl. Phys. Lett., vol. 105, pp. 081604 Aug. 2014.

[5] Q. Wan, Q.H. Li, Y.J. Chen, and T.H. Wang., "Fabrication and ethanol sensing characteristics of ZnO nanowire gas sensors", Appl. Phys. Lett., vol. 84, no. 18, pp. 3654-3656, 2004.

[6] Y. Xia et. al.., "Confined Formation of Ultrathin ZnO Nanorods/Reduced Graphene Oxide Mesoporous Nanocomposites for High-Performance RoomTemperature $NO_2$ Sensors", ACS Appl. Mater. Interfaces, vol. 8, pp. 35454 –35463, 2016.

[7] W. Li, J. Liu, and C. Yan, "Reduced graphene oxide with tunable C/O ratio and its activity towards vanadium redox pairs for an all vanadium redox flow battery", CARBON, vol. 55, pp. 313–320, Jan. 2013.

# Electromagnetic Metamaterial Based Sensor Design for Chemical Discrimination

Debasis Mitra
Dept. of Electronics and Telecommunication Engineering,
Indian Institute of Engineering Science and Technology,
Shibpur, Howrah-711103, India
e-mail: debasisiit@gmail.com

Tarakeswar Shaw
Dept. of Electronics and Telecommunication Engineering,
Indian Institute of Engineering Science and Technology,
Shibpur, Howrah-711103, India
e-mail: tarakeswar.shaw@gmail.com

***Abstract*— In this paper, a simple and efficient approach is presented for the design of a metamaterial based high sensitive chemical sensor. The sensor is designed by incorporating metamaterial Split Ring Resonator (SRR) unit cell within a small square loop. A high Quality-factor of 419 is obtained for the proposed design which is highly desirable in the field of sensing applications. Here, the proposed configuration is applied for chemical discrimination. The experimental results for various liquid samples, such as distilled water, alcohol and acetone are discussed. Also, the measurement of these three liquid mixtures is performed. The proposed metamaterial based sensor is small in size and compact in its shape.**

***Keywords—metamaterial; split ring resonator; high-Q; chemical sensing.***

## I. INTRODUCTION

Nowadays, liquid chemicals are widely used in different industrial and clinical applications. Therefore, rapid detection and categorization of chemical samples have gained tremendous attention in clinical settings, drug discovery, security, safety and industrial applications.

Microwave sensors are usually preferred for many of biomedical, electronic and industrial applications [1]. These sensors provide different advantages such as robustness, high sensitivity, low fabrication costs and easy measurement procedure [2]. Due to these advantages, the microwave sensors become superior choices for biosensing and microfluidic applications. In [3], the microwave resonator method has been used for the measurement of complex permittivity of the biological liquids. To determine the complex permittivity of the samples, the transmission characteristics at resonance and the resonance frequency changes have been used. Also, the concentration measurement of liquid solutions with the help of microwave resonator has been presented and validated in [4]. However, for integrated system design, the sensors reported in [3] [4] are not suitable due to their large size. In [5], a compact microwave and microfluidic sensor has been demonstrated with complicated mathematical post-processing, dedicated to bioengineering application.

Recently, the design of metamaterial (MTM) based sensor has gained a tremendous attention in the field of microwave sensor design [6]. The metamaterials are artificially engineered metallic structures designed to obtain unusual material properties not available in nature. The resonance frequency of the MTM structures greatly depends upon the inductive and capacitive property of the resonator structure [7]. This property suggests that the MTM based structures are suitable for sensing applications. Also, these structures provide improved compactness and a high Quality-factor which is highly sensitive to change in environment [8]. Different types of sensors have been presented in the literature based on metamaterial for various sensing applications, such as thin-film sensing [9], rotation [10] and strain sensing [11]. Most recently, the metamaterial based microfluidic sensors have also been reported in [12] [13]. A microstrip coupled complementary split-ring resonator has been used for microfluidic dielectric characterization [12]. Also in [13], a dual gap meta-atom split-ring resonator has been used to determine the dielectric properties of the liquid. The microfluidic channels have been designed to provide the fluid sample to the resonators producing a significant variation of the resonance frequency elaborated in [12] [13]. However, these configurations need a large volume of liquid sample for characterization.

This paper presents a simple, compact and highly sensitive chemical sensor design by using MTM unit cell. The sensor is designed by incorporating metamaterial SRR within a small square loop. Here, the loop is used for the excitation of SRR. The overall size of the metamaterial based sensor is $0.14\lambda_0 \times 0.14\lambda_0 \times 0.02\lambda_0$, where $\lambda_0$ is the free space wavelength. A high Q-factor of 419 is obtained for the proposed sensor. The proposed configuration is designed and measurements are performed. The experimental result shows a shift in resonance frequency and return loss during the measurement of distilled water, alcohol and acetone.

The rest of the paper is organized as follows. The next section describes the characterization of metamaterial unit cell. In Section III, the configuration of the proposed liquid sensor using metamaterial unit cell is presented. The measurement setup and measured results for different liquid samples are discussed in Section IV. Finally, the conclusion is furnished in Section V.

## II. DESIGN AND CHARACTERIZATION OF METAMATERIAL UNIT CELL

The schematic configuration of the metamaterial SRR unit cell used for the design of chemical sensor is shown in Figure 1. Also, the simplified circuit model is shown on the right side of the figure. The circuit is denoted by an LC tank where the resonant frequency is given by, $f_r = 1/(2\pi\sqrt{L_S C_S})$. The copper pattern which introduces self-inductances is represented by $L_s$ and due to the cut in SRR results in capacitances denoted by $C_S$. The dimensions of the configuration are given in Table 1.

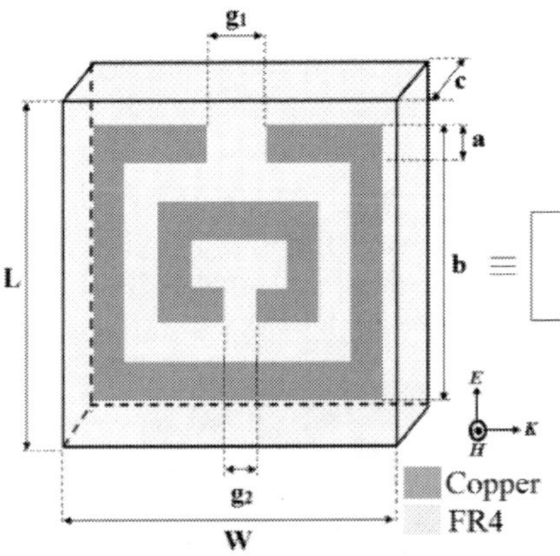


Figure 1. Configuration of metamaterial SRR unit cell and its simplified equivalent circuit model as an LC tank.

Here, the dimensions are optimized by the numerical simulation. The FR4 dielectric substrate is used to design the MTM unit cell has a dielectric constant of 4.4, the substrate thickness of 1.6 mm, and loss tangent of 0.02 with the copper pattern thickness of 0.017 mm. A parallel incident plane wave having a polarized electric field in the direction of $x$ is considered for the calculation of the scattering parameters of the MTM structure. By using periodic boundary conditions, the reflection and transmission coefficients are obtained from a single metamaterial unit cell structure.

TABLE I. DIMENSIONS OF METAMATERIAL SRR UNIT CELL

| L (mm) | W (mm) | b (mm) | $g_1$ (mm) | $g_2$ (mm) | c (mm) | a (mm) |
|---|---|---|---|---|---|---|
| 6.7 | 6.7 | 5.8 | 2.4 | 1.2 | 1.6 | 0.6 |

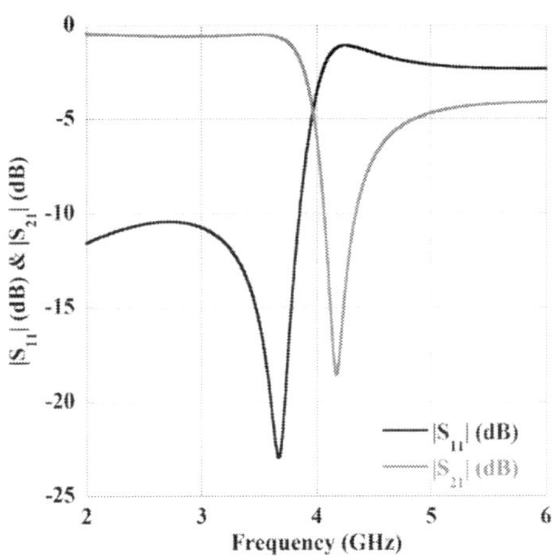


Figure 2. The simulated $S_{11}$ and $S_{21}$ characteristics of the SRR unit cell.

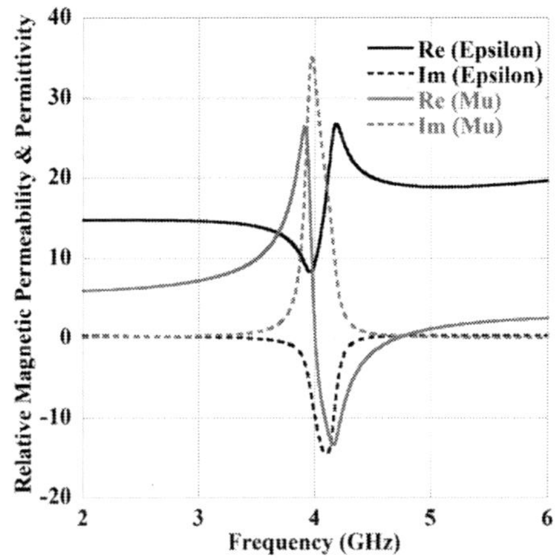


Figure 3. Retrieved relative magnetic permeability and relative permittivity of the SRR unit cell.

The simulated S-parameter plot of the unit cell is shown in Figure 2. The extracted relative magnetic permeability and relative permittivity characteristics of the SRR unit cell are also shown in Figure 3. The magnetic behavior is obtained from the SRR structure observed from Figure 3. The retrieval method has been used for the parameter extraction is described in [14]. All the simulations have been performed using the high-frequency structure simulator (HFSS-15).

## III. SENSOR DESIGN USING METAMATERIAL UNIT CELL

In this section, the design of a compact metamaterial based chemical sensor is presented. The schematic configuration of the proposed metamaterial based sensor is shown in Figure 4. Here, the SRR unit cell discussed in the previous section is incorporated within a small square loop. The combined structure acts as a sensor. The different dimensions of the proposed configuration are given in Figure 4.

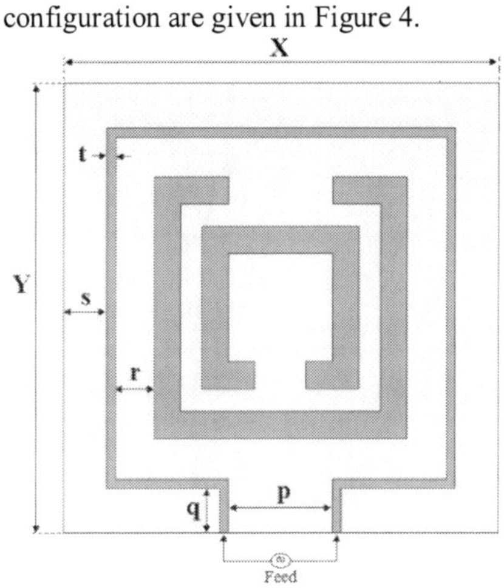


Figure 4. Schematic configuration of MTM based sensor and dimensions are in mm: X=10, Y=10, p=2.4, q=1, r=0.9, s=1, t=0.2.

A simulation has been performed using 50Ω characteristics impedance line coupled to the square loop as shown in Figure 4. The gap (r) between SRR and loop is optimized by numerical simulation to obtain a better matching in resonance frequency. As a consequence, a high Q-factor is obtained which is essential for sensing applications.

## IV. RESULTS AND DISCUSSION

To verify the design concept, a prototype of the proposed sensor was fabricated and measurements have been performed for different chemical samples. The simulated electric field distribution of the proposed sensor at the resonant frequency is shown in Figure 5. From the figure, it is observed that the field density near the cut gap of SRR is much higher compared to other metallic parts. Hence, the disturbance of electric field by the liquid sample is highly sensed by these particular part. For this reason, during measurement of chemical response, only the SRR part is inserted into the sample to obtain the change in resonance frequency.

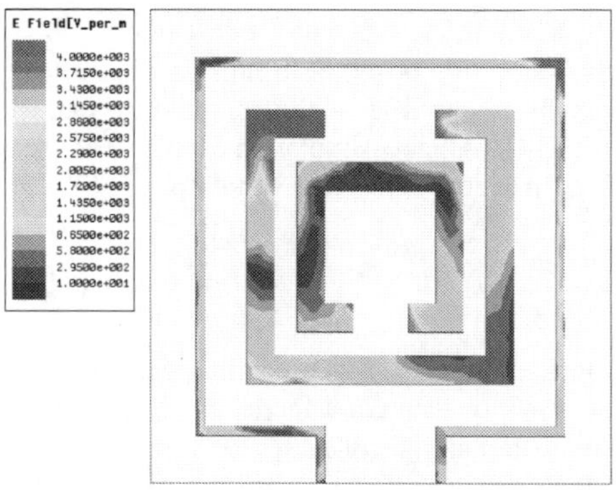


Figure 5. Simulated electric field distributions for the proposed sensor configuration.

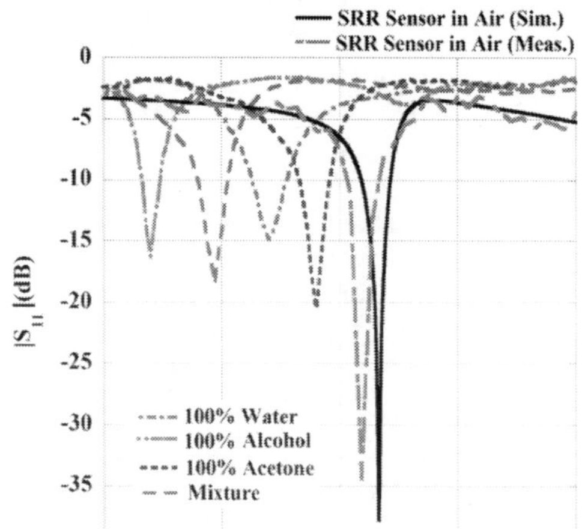


Figure 6. Simulated and measured return loss characteristics of the proposed sensor and different liquids.

The simulated and measured return loss characteristics of the SRR based sensor are shown in Figure 6. It can be pointed out from the figure that the measured resonant frequency of the sensor in the air is 4.19 GHz, whereas the simulated frequency is 4.32 GHz. The high Q-factor is obtained for the proposed sensor which is 432 for the simulated result, and 419 for measured result. The Q factor is defined as $f_r / \Delta f$, where $f_r$ is the resonance frequency and $\Delta f$ is the bandwidth at +3 dB with respect to the minimal reflection. The discrepancy occurred in between the measured and simulated results are due to measurement and fabrication tolerances.

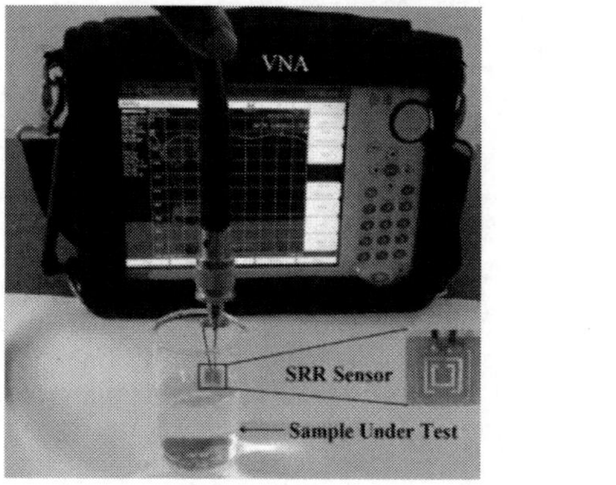


Figure 7. Measurement setup for the liquid sensor using vector network analyzer (VNA), in inset the fabricated prototype is shown.

The measured response of different liquids such as distilled water, alcohol and acetone is also shown in Figure 6. It can be observed from the figure that during the measurement of different liquid samples a huge shift in resonance frequency is observed. In case of 100% water, alcohol and acetone, the resonance frequencies are obtained at 3.4 GHz, 2.4 GHz, and 3.84 GHz, respectively with the return loss of -14.9 dB, -16.3 dB and -20.2 dB. Also, a measurement is performed with the mixture of water, alcohol, and acetone. It can be seen from Figure 6 that the resonance frequency of the liquid mixture is 2.94 GHz with the return loss of -18.64 dB. The measurement setup is shown in Figure 7.

## V. CONCLUSION

In this paper, a metamaterial based high sensitive chemical sensor is proposed and designed. The sensor is designed by incorporating magnetic metamaterial SRR within a small square loop. The overall size of the metamaterial based sensor is $0.14\lambda_0 \times 0.14\lambda_0 \times 0.02\lambda_0$. A high Quality-factor of 419 is obtained for the proposed sensor configuration. The experimental results for the shifts in resonance frequency and return loss of distilled water, alcohol and acetone are studied. The sensor proposed here is simple in design and easily fabricated on the commercially available FR4 dielectric substrate by using metal etching procedure. The proposed metamaterial based sensor is small in size and compact in its shape.

ACKNOWLEDGMENT

For research support, T. Shaw acknowledges the Visvesvaraya PhD scheme for Electronics & IT research fellowship award and D. Mitra acknowledges the Visvesvaraya Young Faculty research fellowship award, under MeitY, Govt. of India.

REFERENCES

[1] A. Gregory and R. Clarke, "A review of RF and microwave techniques for dielectric measurements on polar liquids," IEEE Trans. Dielectr. Electr. Insul., vol. 13, no. 4, pp. 727–743, 2006.

[2] C. Mandel, B. Kubina, M. Schubler, and R. Jakoby, "Passive chipless wireless sensor for two-dimensional displacement measurement," in Proc. 41st Eur. Microw. Conf., pp. 79–82, 2011.

[3] K. Yu, S. G. Ogourtsov, V. G. Belenky, A. B. Maslenikov, and A. Omar, "Accurate microwave resonant method for complex permittivity measurements of liquids [biological]," IEEE Trans. Microw. Theory Tech., vol. 48, no. 11, pp. 2159–2164, 2000.

[4] G. Gennarelli, S. Romeo, M. Scarfi, and F. Soldovieri, "A microwave resonant sensor for concentration measurements of liquid solutions," IEEE Sensors J., vol. 13, no. 5, pp. 1857–1864, 2013.

[5] K.. Grenier et al., "Integrated broadband microwave and microfluidic sensor dedicated to bioengineering," IEEE Trans. Microw. Theory Tech., vol. 57, no. 12, pp. 3246–3253, 2009.

[6] M. Huang and J. Yang, "Microwave Sensor Using Metamaterials," In Wave Propagation, In Tech, pp. 13–36, Vienna, Austria, 2011.

[7] W. Withayachumnankul, C. Fumeaux, and D. Abbott, "Compact electric-LC resonators for metamaterials," Optics express, vol. 18, no. 25, pp. 25912–25921, 2010.

[8] T. Chen, S. Li, and H. Sun, "Metamaterials application in sensing," Sensors, vol. 12, no. 3, pp. 2742–2765, 2012.

[9] W. Withayachumnankul, K. Jaruwongrungsee, C. Fumeaux, and D. Abbott, "Metamaterial-inspired multichannel thin-film sensor," IEEE Sensors J., vol. 12, no. 5, pp. 1455–1458, 2012.

[10] A. Horestani, D. Abbott, and C. Fumeaux, "Rotation sensor based on horn-shaped split ring resonator," IEEE Sensors J., vol. 13, no. 8, pp. 3014–3015, 2013.

[11] R. Melik, E. Unal, N. K. Perkgoz, C. Puttlitz, and H. V. Demir, "Metamaterial-based wireless strain sensors," Appl. Phys. Lett., vol. 95, no. 1, pp. 011106:1–3, 2009.

[12] A. Ebrahimi, W. Withayachumnankul, S. A. Sarawi, and D. Abbott, "High-sensitivity metamaterial-inspired sensor for microfluidic dielectric characterization," IEEE Sensors Journal, vol. 14, no. 5, pp.1345-1351, 2014.

[13] R. A. Awang, F.J.T. Lopez, T. Baum, S. Sriram, and W. S. Rowe, "Meta-atom microfluidic sensor for measurement of dielectric properties of liquids," Journal of Applied Physics, vol.121, no. 9, pp.094506:1–8, 2017.

[14] X. Chen, T. M. Grzegorczyk, B. I. Wu, J. Pacheco, Jr., and J. A. Kong, "Robust method to retrieve the constitutive effective parameters of metamaterials," Phys. Rev. E, vol. 70, pp. 016608:1–7, 2004.

# Scale-down and Package of Wireless Sensor Nodes for Biotelemetry

Jian Lu, Lan Zhang, Sohei Matsumoto, Hiroshi Hiroshima, Ryutaro Maeda
Research Center for Ubiquitous MEMS and Micro Engineering (UMEMSME)
National Institute of Advanced Industrial Science and Technology (AIST)
Namiki 1-2-1, Tsukuba, Ibaraki, 305-8564, Japan
e-mail: {jian-lu, chou-ran, sohei.matsumoto, hiroshima-hiroshi, maeda-ryutaro}@aist.go.jp

***Abstract*—Biotelemetry and its applications have seen an explosive growth in recent years. This paper presents our recent research work on ultra-compact wireless sensor nodes from both system scale-down and packaging point-of-view for biotelemetry and MedTech innovation. In addition to the results of our work, we also present state-of-the-art technologies and challenges to better understand the market needs and the essential technologies for the coming new era of biotelemetry.**

***Keywords- biotelemetry; wireless sensor node; scale-down; package; MedTech innovation.***

## I. INTRODUCTION

Decades before Internet of Things (IoT) and Wireless Sensor Network (WSN) came to our field of knowledge, biotelemetry systems have been developed for remote monitoring and gathering of various vital signs from animals and ambulatory patients [1]. However, the explosive growth in practical applications has happened in recent years because of the advances in wireless sensing technology, artificial intelligence, smart portable electronics devices, as well as medical diagnostic techniques. The so-called new era of biotelemetry aims at not only sick people, but also keeping people healthy, especially in the population aging societies [2]. Therefore, it requires more accurate and reliable data in real time, as well as acceptable production cost. In addition, a bio-compatible package and a user-friendly interface are essential requirements as well for ubiquitous applications.

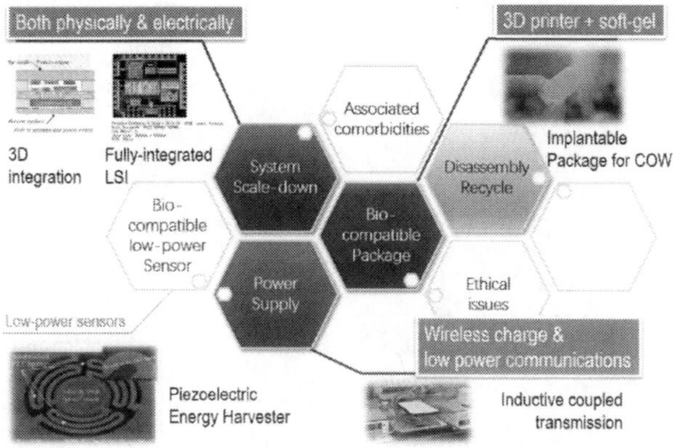


Figure 1. Challenges and some of our related works to scale-down wireless sensor nodes applicable to biotelemetry.

As shown in Figure 1, besides ethical and privacy matters, it is believed that the significant and major challenges associated with the devices for biotelemetry are scale-down of the device both physically and electrically, assembly of the device in a flexible and reliable way, and package of the device with sufficient compatibilities.

In this paper, we present our recent research works on ultra-compact wireless sensor nodes and their applications for biological information monitoring and MedTech innovation. The state-of-the-art technologies and challenges are discussed as well, along with the results of our works, for better understanding the market-needs and the key technologies for the new era of biotelemetry.

In Section II of this paper, the sensor node design and fabrication will be presented. Then, the experimental results will be discussed in Section III. Finally, this paper will be summarized with conclusions in Section IV.

## II. SCALE-DOWN OF WIRELESS SENSOR NODES

System scale-down is extraordinary important to biotelemetry because most of the devices are designed as implantable to secure the data accuracy, as well as to avoid any influence from surrounding environments. Different from electronic system, scale-down in telemetry includes not only reducing module size and components counts, but also using the lowest possible power, or even energy harvesting devices, to power the system for a sufficient lifespan.

A highly integrated circuit chip, which has universal interfaces to various sensors, power management, and radio frequency communication functions, may contribute to reduce the components count. However, the development cost may exceed most of the acceptable market requests due to the small quantity. Therefore, in our work, a commercially available radio frequency integrated circuit (RFIC) transmitter (Si4010, Silicon Laboratories) with embedded microcontroller unit (MCU), clock, memory, and general input/output (I/O) interface was selected; by using this sensor, the size of a wireless temperature sensor node can be as small as 7 mm, with total component count of less than 10. The 3D assembly of integrated circuit (IC) chips and passive components is strongly expected to reduce the system volume [3], while it is clearly shown in Figure 2(a) that it may not be effective if the component count is small enough.

The carrier frequency was set as 920 MHz for the pursuit of lowest return-loss from the skin [4]. Then, an 8.3cm-long wire antenna was twisted round the sensor node to avoid package difficulties of the chip antenna which requires relatively large ground pattern. The detailed system blocks and diagrams have been published in a previous work [3].

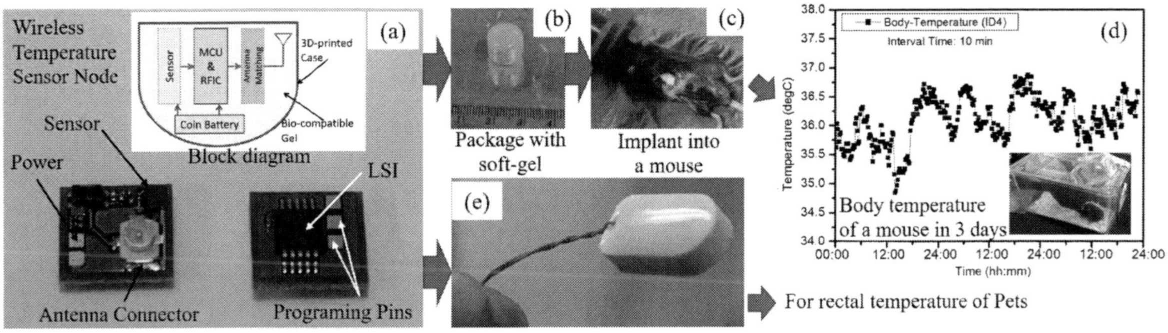


Figure 2. Photo of developed ultra-compact wireless temperature sensor nodes (a) and their packages (b)(e) for implantation (c) and rectal temperature monitoring, respectively. The recorded body temperature of a mouse for the duration of 3 days indicating excellent repeatibility and accuracy (d).

By using RFIC transmitter instead of RFIC transceiver, it may compress standby current from a few mA to a few uA. Thus, the power consumption of the sensor node in Figure 2 (a) was measured as low as 50-100 uW depending on duty time. To change the measurement mode and switch the power ON/OFF especially after the implantation, a hybrid radio frequency identification (RFID) chip (LXMS2HACNF-165, Murata Manufacturing Co., Ltd.) was introduced in our 2nd prototype to communicate with MCU by shared memories, at the cost of 2 more components and 5x10 mm antenna ground pattern.

Besides saving the energy, inductive links between power source and sensor node may supply continuous power even after package and implantation. In our work, besides using battery CR1025, a wireless module was developed too for remote power delivery, in which super capacitors were used to quickly store electricity [5].

## III. PACKAGE AND EVALUATION

The sensor node, battery, and antenna were finally assembled into a 3D printed case, and then packaged by bio-compatible soft-gel, i.e., silicon as shown in Figure 2 (b). Experimental results clearly demonstrate that temperature accuracy and communication distance were not affected by the package. The size of the sensor node was ϕ12mmX10mm, and the weight was around 1.6 gram. Figure 2(c) shows that the sensor can be successfully implanted into a mouse. Besides, as shown in Figure 2 (e), diffident package geometries were designed in our work too for various other applications, i.e., rectal temperature monitoring for pets.

The results in Figure (d) suggested that variation of the body temperature in a single day was surprisingly in between 34.5 °C and 38.5 °C (sensor accuracy: 0.05°C). Body temperature is closely related to heart-rate, thus inter-activities of multiple mice in one cage can be recorded simply by the developed sensor nodes.

The sensor node with RFID and wireless power module was implanted into a cow to investigate its performance. The results indicate that the measurement mode can be changed by using a RFID writer at the distance of ~6 cm after implantation. Wireless power transmission module enables 1-2 weeks lifespan extension by a few minutes charge. However, the inductive receiver coil and the super capacitor still need improvements for the above applications, particularly the size, from a system scale-down point-of-view.

## IV. CONCLUSIONS

This works summarized our recent efforts on wireless sensor nodes for biotelemetry and MedTech innovation. The preliminary results demonstrated its feasibilities and future necessary improvement to meet the market needs for the coming new era of biotelemetry.

## ACKNOWLEDGMENT

The authors would like to thank Prof. Toyoda of Ibaraki University for his valuable discussion and support on implantation using mice. The authors would like to thank Prof. Gotoh of Kagoshima University for his valuable discussion and support on implantation using cow.

The animals used in this study were treated according to the Guidelines for Animal Experiments in the Faculty of Agriculture of Kyushu University (Fukuoka, Japan), Ibaraki University (Ami, Japan), AIST (Tsukuba, Japan) and to the laws of the Japanese Government (Law No. 105 with notification No.6). Clearances from the ethical review board of Kyushu University, Ibaraki University and AIST were received before animal experiments.

## REFERENCES

[1] A. Inmann and D. Hodgins, "Implantable sensor systems for medical applicaitons",Woodhead Publishing, 2013 (1st edition).

[2] M. Cousin, T. Castillo-Hi, and G. H. Snyder, "Devices and diseases: how the IoT is transforming medtech: the internet of things in the medical devices industry", Deloitte University Press, 2015.

[3] J. Lu, H. Okada, T. Itoh, T. Harada, and R. Maeda, "Toward the world smallest wireless sensor nodes with ultralow power comsumption", IEEE Sensors Journal, vol.14, no.6, pp.2035-2041, 2014.

[4] M. S. Islam, K. P. Esselle, D. Bull, and P. M. Pilowsky, "Converting a wireless biotelemetry system to an implantable system through antenna redesign", IEEE Transactions on Microwave and Techniques, vol.62, pp.1890-1897, Sept. 2014.

[5] J. Lu, L. Zhang, M. Arakawa, and T. Harada, "Wireless power supply for all-in-one LTCC packaged sensor nodes applicable to infrastructure monitoring", IEEJ Transactions of Sensors and Micromachines, vol.137, no.9, pp.267-271, 2017.

**International Academy, Research, and Industry Association (IARIA)**
412 Derby Way
Wilmington, DE 19810

CURRAN ASSOCIATES INC.
proceedings.com

ISBN 978-1-5108-6176-3
9 781510 861763

# International Workshop on Flavour Changing and Conserving Processes (FCCP 2017)

EPJ Web of Conferences Volume 179 (2018)

Anacapri, Italy
7 - 9 September 2017

edp sciences